D1172170

THE FILMS OF
JAMES
MASON

THE FILMS OF
JAMES MASON

BY
CLIVE HIRSCHHORN

WITH SOME SECOND THOUGHTS BY JAMES MASON

RESEARCH BY CORIN MOORE

THE CITADEL PRESS   SECAUCUS, N.J.

ACKNOWLEDGEMENTS

Mr. James Mason
The British Film Institute
Mr. P. Nicholson
Lady Gardner
Mr. Allen Greenberg
Metro-Goldwyn-Mayer
Twentieth Century-Fox
The Rank Organisation
British Lion
Columbia-Warner
The Cinema Bookshop
CinemaTV Today
Mr. Ivan Foxwell
Mr. Peter Noble
Mr. Peter Seward
and
The John Kobal Collection

Library of Congress Cataloging in Publication Data

Hirschhorn, Clive.
    The films of James Mason.

    1. Mason, James, 1909-   I. Mason, James,
1909-   II. Moore, Corin. III. Title.
PN2598.M34H5 1977   791.43'028'0924 [B]   77-4172
ISBN 0-8065-0584-2

First American edition, 1977
Copyright © 1975 by LSP Books Limited
Published by Citadel Press
A division of Lyle Stuart, Inc.
120 Enterprise Ave., Secaucus, N.J. 07094
By arrangement with LSP Books Limited, London, England
Manufactured in the United States of America by
Halliday Lithograph Corp., West Hanover, Mass.
Edited by Tom Hutchinson
Designed by Jeff Tarry

CONTENTS

INTRODUCTION

James Mason, who was born in Huddersfield, England, on May 5, 1909, first received a film actor's pay cheque in the summer of 1934. Alexander Korda had visited the Old Vic several times during the season of 1933–34, attracted by the presence of his friend Charles Laughton. James had made an impression in several of the parts he had played there, and Korda had seen fit to offer him a good rôle in the film *The Return of Don Juan* with Douglas Fairbanks Snr. But, after four days' work, a Korda minion named David Cunningham drew Mason aside and told him that it had been decided that he was unsuitably cast in the rôle; but not to worry, they would find another part for him. In other words, Mason would be paid for the ten days guaranteed in his contract. However, the disappointed actor forewent his financial consolation because he knew there were no worthwhile small parts that remained un-

James: aged three.

cast. In fact he spent a season (1934–35) at the Gate Theatre in Dublin, where, to much critical acclaim, he played Brutus in *Julius Caesar*.

Shortly after his return he was 'discovered' at a cocktail party by Al Parker, an American film director who was lending his talents to the manufacture of 'Quota' products for Fox Films at Wembley Studio. The first of the films that James worked in for Al Parker is thus quite properly referred to as the occasion of his screen début. Al Parker had been an actor in New York, friend and contemporary of Doug Fairbanks Snr. and John Barrymore, and had, as was the fashion, 'gone west' to California in the early twenties, where he prospered as a film director (best-known opus: *The Black Pirate* with Fairbanks). 1935 found him in England, making bargain-price films. In 1938 he became an agent, and James was one of his first clients.

James's first film for Al Parker was *Late Extra*, a newspaper drama. Virginia Cherrill, Charlie Chaplin's leading lady in *City Lights*, was the principal star, but more scintillating was Alastair Sim in the rôle of the editor. James served Parker in three such productions at Wembley, and in the intervals found employment in an even more reasonably priced line of merchandise turned out by George Smith Enterprises at Walton-on-Thames.

Late Extra was quickly followed by *Troubled Waters* in which he played a secret-service agent (with Virginia Cherrill, and directed by Albert Parker), *Twice Branded*, as the son of a man who has been wrongly imprisoned, and *Prison Breaker* as a discredited secret agent.

When James first saw himself on film he was 'quietly disappointed and displeased', and it took a great deal of flattery and encouragement to make him feel he was not a complete flop. He was comforted only by the fact that he was getting the parts rather than by what he saw on the screen.

'You can learn your trade by watching yourself work, but only to a certain extent,' he said. 'The right way is to feel easy and confident while you're doing the thing. Whenever I was good, I learned it was because I was behaving in an absolutely natural manner. And this was very difficult to achieve because I was very shy and tense. The ease that I instinctively knew was essential to good film acting was, initially, quite beyond my reach.'

During the time these 'quickies' were being churned out, James had signed a seven-year contract with Fox-British—the only strictly long-term contract he has ever had in his career.

This contract could have been pre-empted by the parent company in Hollywood. George Sanders, who had an identical contract, and Patrick Knowles likewise were wafted to Hollywood, but James was left to Al Parker's and his own devices. After two and a half years, the company allowed his contract to lapse,

James: aged five.

partly perhaps because of a falling out between himself and Parker. For, while the latter was assembling what would have been the fourth Parker-Mason vehicle, James asked the company to allow him to accept an outside offer (*The Mill on the Floss*) which promised to be a 'big picture' and one which was more likely to advance his career.

In 1936, however, Parker and Mason were still working happily together in *Blind Man's Bluff* which starred Basil Sydney and Enid Stamp-Taylor. It concerned a doctor (Sydney) thought to be blind who kept to himself the knowledge that he was recovering his sight and could thus sneakily keep track of his wife's carryings-on.

The stars of *The Mill on the Floss*, made in 1936 but released in 1937, were Frank Lawton and Victoria Hopper. Featured were James (as Tom Tulliver), Fay Compton, Geraldine Fitzgerald, Griffith Jones and a bunch of excellent established stage actors, which included J. H. Roberts and Sam Livesey. Director's credit went to Tim Whelan, but he quit when the somewhat erratic producer (Johnny Clein) fell behind with the weekly payments.

1936 also took Mason to Istanbul for *The Eunuch of Stamboul*, a spy drama based on a novel by Dennis Wheatley. The distributors could be forgiven at that time for altering this title to *The Secret of Stamboul*. James played an ex-guards officer sent to Stamboul to investigate the curious happenings at a tobacco factory. Frank Vosper was cast as the villain of the piece, a left-over Imperial eunuch, and between James and a youthful Valerie Hobson, Vosper was successfully thwarted in a plot which involved the overthrow of the Turkish government. It was nonsensical stuff, with very little to recommend it, as, indeed, had been the case with all of his films. Nothing he had done for the screen so far had stretched him as an actor and, for James, film acting was little more than 'hitting the right mark' for the camera.

His next appearance (still 1936) was in a classier affair, entitled *Fire Over England*, but his own part was much smaller. It was made by Mayflower Productions, one of Alexander Korda's companies.

This was a period drama about Elizabeth I and the events leading up to the defeat of the Spanish Armada. As James remembers it, his part was that of a bearded young English spy in the pay of Philip II of Spain. He was killed in the first reel of the film, at which point the Earl of Leicester, played by Leslie Banks, thought it would be a smart idea to cause a thoroughly loyal young man (Laurence Olivier) to grow a beard and masquerade as the dead spy, penetrate Philip's court and come back with some good secrets—thus launching the action-packed drama which followed. This included much romantic play involving Olivier and Vivien Leigh and a redoubtable portrayal of Elizabeth by Flora Robson.

James, however, did not go entirely unnoticed. The celebrated Chinese-American cameraman James Wong Howe, who photographed *Fire Over England*, was interviewed by a writer on the *Daily Express* and, when asked if he had spotted any promising talent during his stay in England, he unexpectedly picked on James for a shower of praise. It seemed that he had spotted this alleged talent not so much during the shooting of James's actual scenes in the picture, but when he had helped in the making of a test of one of the supporting actresses. For this purpose they had enacted one of the Olivier/Leigh romantic passages.

James ended 1936 by playing Heverell in *The High*

James in his middle twenties.

Command, a melodrama set in Africa about an affair between an officer (Heverell) and a trader's wife. The director was Thorold Dickinson. It was James's ninth film and, with the possible exception of *Fire Over England*, was as undistinguished as the rest.

In March 1937, James wrote a letter to *Picture Show*, concerning the future of the British film industry—a subject about which he was frequently to wax vehement over the years, and which by no means enhanced his popularity. On this occasion, he confirmed his faith in the industry and pledged his devotion to it.

'But,' he said, 'if we are to compete seriously with Hollywood, we shall do so only by improving the standards of our cheap unpretentious films, and forgetting our extravagant endeavours to capture the world market with super productions. The cheap film,' he went on, 'should have as much chance of a world release as any colossal masterpiece, provided that sufficient attention is paid to the story and the writing of the dialogue and to the casting of the small supporting parts.'

In 1937, no giant steps were being taken, either by the British film industry in general or by James in particular. He appeared in a number of largely unsuccessful theatrical productions. Even the hitherto enormously successful Dodie Smith play, *Bonnet Over the Windmill*, in which he appeared, lasted no more than three months.

The only film James made that year was *Catch as Catch Can* (also known as *Atlantic Episode*)—the last under his old Fox contract. It was a melodrama set on board an ocean liner and in it he played an American customs officer who breaks up an attempt to smuggle jewels into the United States. It was written by Richard Llewelyn (author of *How Green Was My Valley*), directed by Roy Kellino and featured Finlay Currie and Margaret Rutherford.

Although James next appeared as Tallien in *The Return of the Scarlet Pimpernel*, directed by Hans Schwartz, only two or three British films were being made at the beginning of 1938. Both in front of and behind the camera jobs were scarce. It was a situation, in fact, not unlike the present. 'The only way to work', James said, 'was to write, direct and act in something of one's own. So Pamela and Roy Kellino and I formed a company called Gamma Productions, pooled our limited resources which amounted to about four and a half thousand pounds and decided to go it alone. Pamela conceived a story called *I Met a Murderer*, about a farmer who murders his nagging wife and who is helped in his flight from the law by a young authoress, and Roy and I developed this into a screenplay. We wrote the story in such a way that it could be shot on location with the minimum of dialogue—for the minute we entered a studio, we would have to lay out more money than we had. The most we could afford for studio work was one day's post-synchronising. As it was, we were penny-snatching wherever we could. All the smaller parts were played by our friends who stayed over at the country house we were living in, and who agreed to appear in the film by way of repayment for a week in the country. We couldn't even afford a regular continuity girl, but we persuaded the efficient Jo Harcourt to visit us at the weekends and tidy up what we had done. Roy Kellino was the director as well as the cameraman, which took care of those two major items of expense, and his assistant was Ossie Morris who, of course, went on to become one of Britain's finest cinematographers.'

Since the industry was practially at a stand-still, it was not too difficult to borrow a camera. Kellino had good contacts and negotiated the acquisition of 'short ends' (leftovers at the end of 1,000-foot reels) with notable success. A major expense was the purchase of a second-hand station wagon, which was considered essential for general transportation purposes and for tracking shots.

With daughter Portland.

The love, enthusiasm and initiative that went into *I Met a Murderer* paid off. The film received splendid reviews when it opened at the Marble Arch Pavilion, scooping M.G.M.'s prestigious *Marie Antoinette* as the film of the week in *The Times* newspaper. Unfortunately, it was scheduled for general release the week war was declared and, as the cinemas in Britain closed for the first three months of the war, it was denied a wider showing and was 'dead' as far as recouping its costs in the United Kingdom were concerned. The distributors of *I Met a Murderer*, National, left for America with the film. The negative was lost in the Atlantic after a submarine attack on the ship carrying it. But clearly the distributors were not empty-handed when they arrived in New York, for *I Met a Murderer* was shown and well reviewed there and enjoyed considerable success, eliciting from columnist Walter Winchell an accolade in which he extravagantly claimed: 'This is the best picture I have ever seen.' In 1939 Pamela and Roy Kellino were divorced.

In December of 1939, Gabriel Pascal, who had recently directed Vivien Leigh and Claude Rains in the costly *Caesar and Cleopatra*, told James he very much wanted him to appear in a production of Shaw's *Major Barbara* which he was preparing. Pascal took some 'stills' in which James was encouraged to 'act' as if he were making a film test—a most embarrassing experience. James was not at all surprised when the part was given to Andrew Osborne. He had to find his own level again in a modest little thriller made at Welwyn Studio, entitled *This Man Is Dangerous*, presumably in order to cash in on the success of the recent and successful *This Man Is News*. A few years later after James had become celebrated internationally the film was disinterred and given a showing in New York, but under the title *The Patient Vanishes*, to attract the public that had been thrilled by Hitchcock's *The Lady Vanishes*. In it the heroine was Margaret Vyner; Michael Rennie made his movie début, and Lawrence Huntington directed.

At this point, February 1941, James married Pamela Kellino. And there was a follow-up to the *Major Barbara* incident. Gabriel Pascal summoned him to Denham Studios where he was making the film. A gloomy and despondent Gabby greeted James with the words: 'Jimmy, we have made a great mistake!' James resented the 'we', since he had always been convinced that he was the right man for the rôle of 'Dolly'. Gabby gave James a copy of the script and told him to go home and study it, with the implication that the rôle would be wrenched from Andy Osborne and given to him instead. So James went home and waited for confirmation in the form of a

James and Clarissa.

James with Huddersfield painter Peter Brook. James and Clarissa have 16 of his paintings.

James and Silvie Narizzano at a Player's lecture at the Film Institute.

Off set with the Finneys and Michael Medwin during the shooting of *Spring and Port Wine*.

contract. Four days later he read in the paper that Rex Harrison was to play the part.

James had to settle for the rôle of the shy young doctor in *Hatter's Castle*, which starred Robert Newton most effectively.

Thereafter, once more to Welwyn for *The Night Has Eyes*, a very popular melodrama and his first encounter with director Leslie Arliss. It was shown later in the United States under the title of *Terror House*. *Alibi* (1942) was directed by Brian Desmond Hurst. James and his implacable agent Al Parker thought that his name should go above the title, but it seemed that the names of the other two leading players were more firmly established than James's and the producers thought it inappropriate to star a third name. They promised to print the name in the same-sized type as the other two immediately below the title. The Parker-Mason team was not satisfied, however, until the producers further undertook that there be no 'and' or 'with' before his name, since this they construed as demeaning. So the final billing was:

MARGARET LOCKWOOD AND HUGH SINCLAIR

IN

ALIBI

JAMES MASON

This gave Mason/Parker the illusion that honour had been satisfied. Meanwhile most of the acting in the film was contributed by Raymond Lovell, whose billing was even less obtrusive.

After *Alibi* came an equally forgettable spy drama called *Secret Mission*, directed by Harold French, in which James again played a French secret agent—this time in Occupied France. The other protagonists were Hugh Williams, Michael Wilding and Roland Culver. Stewart Granger, Herbert Lom and Beatrice Varley were in support. The producer was Marcel Hellman and it was made at Denham Studios.

Thunder Rock with Michael Redgrave, Lilli Palmer and Barbara Mullen came next. It was directed by Roy Boulting and enjoyed the distinction of being chosen by the National Board of Review as one of the best films shown in America for that year. The film was about a journalist who, despairing of the future of the world, decides to spend the duration of the War in a lighthouse on Lake Michigan. It was based on a play by Robert Ardrey, was written for the screen by Jeffrey Dell and Bernard Miles, and in it James played an American friend of the journalist.

Thunder Rock was followed by an undistinguished war-time comedy-drama called *The Bells Go Down*,

Practising ice-skating with Claire Bloom (for *The Man Between*).

about an East End auxiliary fire service unit during the 1940 blitz. It was directed by Basil Dearden and the comedy was supplied by Tommy Trinder. James played a fireman.

After *The Bells Go Down*, James went to Gainsborough Films for *The Man in Grey*—a period melodrama by Lady Eleanor Smith about infidelity. He appeared as the arrogant Marquis of Rohan, and his co-stars were Margaret Lockwood and Phyllis Calvert. It was directed by Leslie Arliss. Although James's popularity was increasing with each new picture, *The Man in Grey* made him into a star. (Originally Eric Portman was to play the Marquis and James was cast as Rokeby. Portman withdrew, the part was offered to James, and Stewart Granger finally played Rokeby.)

The infamous Lord Rohan and his cavalier treatment of Hesther Shaw made a tremendous impact on British audiences and provided James with a characterisation which, for many years, was to be his trademark: mean and moody. The scene in which he takes a horsewhip to Margaret Lockwood is already part of the mythology of the British cinema. For his memorable portrayal as Rohan, James was voted actor of the year by the readers of *Picturegoer* magazine; and in America, *Time* magazine's film critic had this to say: 'Swaggering through the title rôle, sneering like Laughton, barking like Gable, and frowning like Laurence Olivier on a dark night, he is likely to pick up many a feminine fan.'

Indeed he was, and after his appearance in *The Man in Grey* which he did not enjoy making, women found him irresistible. He was the man they loved to hate, and the fascination he wielded over them was soon translated into currency at the box-office.

The offer of the part of Lord Rohan was conditional on James's acceptance of a contract requiring him to work in two films a year for three years. 'My willingness to sign a multiple contract—which is highly distasteful to me,' he wrote in an article for the London *Sunday Times*, 'was earnest of my own faith in the commercial potential of Lady Eleanor Smith's novel. There was nothing about it I could actually bring myself to like, and I had no clue how I could do anything with a part so monstrously nasty as that of Lord Rohan. To make matters worse, I had worked with the director, Leslie Arliss, on a previous film, and had failed to establish a happy relationship. We just could not get along with each other. Angered by my own inability to cope, I wallowed in a mood much blacker than could be justified by my disdain of the quality of the work that was being perpetrated around me. Since my own imagination had contributed nothing to the Lord Rohan who appeared on the screen, I have to conclude that my sheer bad temper gave the character

As Pierre Laval in *Woman of France*, which was never made.

colour, and made it some sort of memorable thing. The extraordinary success of the film made me even more cross, since I could claim none of the credit myself.

'During this period,' he went on, 'I was making a bad name for myself, partly because I was a compulsive tease, and partly because my experiences with producers had made me regard them as natural enemies . . . and I acted with uncalled-for hostility towards all the top brass at Gainsborough. To me, producers were men who polluted the artistic aspirations of writers, directors and actors; who responded only to the promptings of vulgar men in Wardour Street; who were bad sports and bad losers.'

His relationship with his next producer, Marcel Hellman, for whom he starred in *They Met in the Dark*, a spy drama, was anything but friendly. Hellman's constant interference on the set became a bitter source of resentment to James, who, in order to ensure the completion of the film, decided the best way to treat Hellman was to pretend he was not there.

His second film for Gainsborough – or so he was led

to believe—was to be *Woman of France*, in which he was to play Pierre Laval. But the idea was shelved in favour of a sure-fire Victorian melodrama called *Fanny by Gaslight* (U.S. title: *Man of Evil*). Its director was Anthony Asquith, and again James found himself co-starring with Phyllis Calvert and playing another aristocratic villain—Lord Manderstoke. It was in this guise that the public seemed most to respond to James's screen persona, and Gainsborough, dedicated to giving the public what it wanted, was naturally cashing in on the vogue.

He then made a modest but successful thriller called *Candlelight in Algeria*, a spy story set, as its title proclaims, in Algeria, with Carla Lehmann and Raymond Lovell. Because of its topicality, it was rushed out and released before *Fanny by Gaslight*. The last film that James made in 1943 was *Hotel Reserve*. This had nothing to recommend it save the name of the author, Eric Ambler, of the novel from which it was adapted, *Epitaph for a Spy*. James was cast as an Austrian refugee doctor who finds himself involved in espionage. Herbert Lom, Valentine Dyall and Patricia Medina were in it, and it was directed in committee by Victor Hanbury, Lance Comfort and Max Greene.

After *Hotel Reserve*, James let it be known at Gainsborough that he would like to play the part of the 70-year-old Mr. Smedhurst in their forthcoming production of Osbert Sitwell's ghost story *A Place of One's Own*. His request was coolly received. Would the public, queried Maurice Ostrer (who was in charge of production), accept James as an elderly gent who buys a haunted house?

After several other actors unsuccessfully tested for the rôle, James was, with great reluctance, finally given his way. The film co-starred Margaret Lockwood and Dennis Price, and although it turned out to be thoroughly delightful was not a success at the box-office.

During the filming of *A Place of One's Own*, the magazine *Picturegoer* in its issue of July 3, 1944, announced that James had won its Gold Medal Award for 1943 for his performance in *The Man in Grey*. He had polled 16 per cent of the votes against

14.2 per cent for Ronald Colman in *Random Harvest*. If the failure of *A Place of One's Own* indicated anything, it was the incontrovertible fact that a 'personality' actor, of the kind James had become since *The Man in Grey*, could not afford to confuse his public by changing character in mid-career; and for his next Gainsborough film, *They Were Sisters*, he was given the rôle of a sadistic husband who drives poor Dulcie Gray to suicide. Also in the film was Pamela Kellino playing James's 17-year-old daughter.

Although most critics complained that the picture, at one hour and 55 minutes, was too long, James was adamant that it should not be cut for its release in America. In an open letter to Earl St. John, of the J. Arthur Rank Organisation, he aired his views on the subject in his typically outspoken way: 'My feeling about the film,' he said, 'is that it is a poor film and that it is true that the Americans cannot be expected to put up with 115 minutes of tedium. But to cut it about will not only make it a very much worse film, but an utterly incomprehensible one. The

Sir Charles Chaplin, Sir Noel Coward and James at Knie Bros. Circus in Vevey, 1970.

matter,' he went on to say, 'affects me vitally. For I suppose that, in due course, efforts will be made to market *Odd Man Out* and *The Upturned Glass* (two films he was scheduled to make in the near future) in the States. I am expecting that both of these will be of a very different class from *They Were Sisters*, and should have a fair chance for success over there. This chance will be seriously compromised if, in the meantime, my own prestige and that of British films in general have been injured by the showing of a mutilated *They Were Sisters*.'

James won his battle and the film opened at the Winter Garden Theatre in New York with a couple of small censorship cuts, but nothing more. It was fairly successful, though most of the reviewers agreed it was needlessly overlong.

As soon as James completed *They Were Sisters*, he began discussions with director Michael Powell on *I Know Where I'm Going*, which was to co-star Wendy Hiller.

At first James and Powell could not agree on salaries, which prompted James to write a letter to his agent, Al Parker, pointing out that the money taken in the cinema is 'vastly different from that taken by a play running six months'; and that it is 'common sense' that, in films, all concerned should be paid proportionately larger salaries.

The point was obvious, and James won it. But his battles were not yet over. Next came the problem of billing. Once again, he felt he should top the bill in Britain, and that Miss Hiller should top it in America, where, he conceded, she was better known than he was.

Michael Powell disagreed, arguing with some justification that James had never appeared in a 'quality picture' before, and that Miss Hiller, therefore, should receive top billing on both sides of the Atlantic. He also pointed out that 'when your names are side by side, the name of the lady precedes yours, as is usual in society.' James promptly wrote back and asked him in what society a man and a woman were referred to either in conversation or in print as Mrs. and Mr.

Finally Roger Livesey was given the part, and James's differences of opinion with Powell turned out to be a godsend to his career, for had he accepted Powell's conditions and made the film, he would have missed the opportunity of appearing in *The Seventh Veil*, the film responsible for launching him on an international career. He was cast as Nicholas, a martinet guardian who falls in love with Francesca, his 'ward'—a talented concert pianist (played by Ann Todd).

James's rôle was originally intended for Francis L. Sullivan, but Sullivan had committed himself to Pascal for *Caesar and Cleopatra* at the time, and

James with son Morgan.

was unavailable. In the original screenplay (written by Sydney and Muriel Box) the film ended with Peter (Hugh McDermott), the orchestra leader, going off with Francesca. But when James agreed to replace Sullivan, the ending was re-written so that nobody got Francesca. The film was to finish as Francesca slowly walks down the stairs, and is confronted by her three suitors (the third being Herbert Lom). It would be left to the audience to guess who, if anyone, finally 'got the girl'.

On the last day of shooting, however, Box saw to it that a couple of extra shots were added in order to satisfy the public's curiosity. So, in the finished version, we see Nicholas leaving the room, and Francesca following him.

The Seventh Veil, directed by Compton Bennett, was a smash hit wherever it was shown. Again James was cast as a sadist (who brings down a rod upon Ann Todd's precious hands) and audiences adored him.

In New York, though, it opened to practically no advance publicity and for four weeks did poor business at the Winter Garden Theatre. Then word of mouth took over, and in the last few weeks of its run it played to capacity.

Although James had spoken out against producers, what he remembers most vividly about *The Seventh Veil* are the enthusiasm, the vitality and the creativity of Sydney Box. 'Through sheer skill, and a few grains of good luck,' James said, 'Sydney managed to contrive a fascinating construction for the telling of that story, and the whole thing worked. The total film was much greater than its parts, which is a very happy event when it takes place.'

As in Britain, James's personality became a runaway success with American audiences, and wherever *The Seventh Veil* was shown after its initial New York engagement, long queues formed outside the cinemas. James's fan mail began to arrive now by the sackful, fan clubs sprang up throughout the country, and in no time at all he became one of the 'hottest' properties around. His earlier (and less successful) films were re-screened, and feature articles about 'this great new British star' proliferated in the nation's press.

Predictably, James himself had very fixed views about the sudden, overwhelming international success *The Seventh Veil* was bringing him. 'If,' he said at the time, 'I find that, as a result of being a star I can no longer enjoy my private life, then I shall start to play only small character parts. If this is not the answer, I shall give up acting entirely and become a producer, a director, or a writer.'

His next film, *The Wicked Lady*, in which he played Captain Jerry Jackson, the lover of a country lady who, to assuage the boredom of her life, takes to highway robbery, was equally successful. (The part was first offered to Stewart Granger, who turned it down.) *The Wicked Lady*, which also consolidated Margaret Lockwood's ever-increasing popularity, was produced by Gainsborough and released by Eagle Lion.

But at this time James was no longer bound by the six-picture contract which he had signed prior to appearing in *The Man in Grey*. The 'Polish Corridor' in the studio at Shepherds Bush was traditionally the scene of executive power struggle. One of the protagonists in the current struggle, Ted Black, who was friendly to James, deliberately 'forgot' to pick up the option for the last two pictures which the contract had called for, thus restoring to him his freelance status.

'If ever I see *The Wicked Lady* advertised on TV,' he said, 'I make a point of watching it. The part I played in it was rather small, and for this reason

With Salvador Dali and Melina Mercouri during shooting of *Les Pianos Mécaniques*.

there was a clause in it which prevented the producer (R. J. Minney) from cutting anything out of my scenes without my approval. Thus, when during the editing process, Minney found himself wanting to snip a fragment from one such scene, he was obliged to run the film for me and point to the proposed excision. At the end I was surprised to hear myself saying: "Oh, I don't think you should cut anything from *my* scenes." It was the long stretches between my appearances that seemed to drag. I am sure that Minney was not surprised since my anti-producer attitude had doubtless persuaded him that I was a terrible bounder.'

The Wicked Lady was the third film on which James and the director Leslie Arliss 'co-operated'. But Mason comforted himself with the knowledge that his part was so confined that it could not take more than two weeks to put it on film; and that the resultant hunk of entertainment could not fail to be a box-office winner.

Because of the generous supply of cleavage exhibited by Margaret Lockwood and Patricia Roc in *The Wicked Lady*, the film acquired a notorious international reputation. In America, the puritanical production code, which controlled the morals of the nation, felt that the amount of flesh on view in the film was somewhat indecorous, and that unless something were done about it, it would not allow the film to be screened.

'Mr. Rank's public relations officer took advantage of the situation,' James said, 'and it was widely publicised that the film was to be re-cut for American distribution, and that, where it was not possible to substitute shots taken from an angle which showed less cleavage, scenes were to be enlarged by optical printer, so that the offensive anatomy was no longer visible within the frame.'

Among the occasional magazine articles which James wrote during this period was an innocuous contribution to *Summer Pie* on the subject of glamour. In this he made the not very startling point that glamour becomes devalued the closer you approach its source. 'It should follow', he wrote, 'that the movies can no longer do to me the things they used to. It is true that I find precious little glamour in British pictures. There might be more than one reason for this, but the reason which fits with my argument is that I know when I see such a film, what has happened to that strip of celluloid every inch of the way.'

He concluded the article by saying that Hollywood still retained its glamour simply because it was, to him, unfamiliar territory, as he had never worked there.

This article had surprising repercussions which caught up with the Masons while they were presenting a play of their own at the Wiesbaden Opera

House, for the entertainment of American Military personnel who were stationed in that town. It seemed that the article had caused offence in certain quarters, so much so that the Association of Cine Technicians wrote a letter signed by its president, Anthony Asquith, condemning James's remarks as unfair, and a copy of the letter was sent to the Trade Press, the Ministry of Information and the Board of Trade. The British Film Producers Association then wrote James a letter stating they would take definite action against him should he write any more derogatory articles about the British film industry.

At once, James contacted his agent with instructions to stop all negotiations for future films 'until further notice', and, in a letter to J. Arthur Rank, the president of the Producers Association and the A.C.T., told him of his decision to discontinue negotiations for future engagements in British pictures. 'No association or union', he wrote, 'has any right to intimidate me should they feel my remarks are unflattering. Such action is at variance with the liberal principles which form the basis of life and work among free people.' He then suggested to Mr. Rank that he read the offending article for himself. 'Anyone', he wrote, 'who reads into my words an attack on the industry is, I am afraid, a careless reader.' As a postscript he added: 'My decision to give up appearing in British films for the present was in no way influenced by negotiations with American film companies. The recent rumours in the press to the effect that I had signed a contract with such a company is entirely false. I have been consistently approached by American companies for the last ten years, but since 1939, I have not so much as discussed terms with them. This is a fact which you can easily check. I had always hoped that an amicable basis for co-operation between artists, producers and technicians could be achieved in my own country, where, naturally, I would most like to work. Infantile displays such as those which prompted this letter, may force me to adjust my attitude.'

J. Arthur Rank, who claimed he had no knowledge of the letter which was sent to James by the Producers Association (as he was in America at the time), wrote back saying he was sympathetic to James's point of view, and would discuss the matter further with him when he, James, returned from Germany.

Inevitably, the storm in the teacup subsided, and a couple of months later 'the Mason incident', as it was known, was over, and at the end of 1945, James found himself, ironically, heading the top of the Motion Picture Popularity Poll. (Later in 1946, he was also the recipient of the *Daily Mail's* English equivalent of the 'Oscar'—and he and Margaret Lockwood were voted the country's most popular stars.)

James had been genuinely shocked by the misinterpretation of his article as expressed in the letter from the A.C.T. and had derived some pleasure from writing his pompous letter to J. Arthur Rank, whose background and performance did not encourage belief that he would become a triumphant leader of the film industry which he now largely controlled.

But James had proved that he was then, as now, incapable of effective communication with the press, who harassed him with questions about his so-called feud with Rank. To make matters worse, they often misquoted him and then commented on the effect created by their own or their colleagues' misquotations, and this in turn aggravated those with whom he had hitherto enjoyed perfectly amicable relations. He says now that he may have been a bit paranoid at the time and that he was unfit to cope with the shock brought on by sudden, if belated, success.

Although in 1946 his popularity within the British film industry and the press was tainted, his stature as an actor and his popularity as a film star was increasing with each new film, and after his next assignment, that of the fugitive Johnny McQueen in Carol Reed's superb drama of the Irish rebellion, *Odd Man Out*, James finally managed, for a time at any rate, to crash out of the malevolent mould into which he had so frequently been poured, and reveal himself as the fine actor he is.

'Odd Man Out,' said James, 'caught a brilliant gifted director at the top of his form. The screenplay (by F. L. Green and R. C. Sherriff) was outstanding too, and contributed immeasurably to the success of the film, as a good screenplay usually does. Also, the film happened at the right moment in the history of the British film industry. Due to the enthusiasm of men like Alexander Korda, Carol Reed, Michael Powell and Emeric Pressburgher, David Lean, Noel Coward, Launder and Gilliatt—all vital personalities —there was an upsurge in the quality of what the British studios were making. The industry was also blessed with a crop of new and exciting actors who were not at all accustomed to film production, and whose approach, therefore, was different and more refreshing than the tried-and-tested approach of the older film actors. As far as *Odd Man Out* was concerned, we had a collection of marvellously real Irish characters which, at the time, was something of a breakthrough in the cinema, for until then, films with Irish backgrounds tended to be corny and full of caricatures.'

The last time he saw *Odd Man Out*, the tempo, he felt, had slackened slightly—but he still thought it 'pretty damn good' and his own performance 'fine'. 'I think it was the pre-recorded death-march music in the second half of the film, played throughout the

James at leisure with a pint of beer in an English pub.

"silent action", which helped to create the right mood and atmosphere,' he said.

After *Odd Man Out*, and the enormous success of *The Seventh Veil*, James and Sydney Box began work on *The Upturned Glass*—a story about the Brontë family which James and Pamela had always wanted to do. Unfortunately, Warner Brothers released a film on the same subject called *Devotion* with Ida Lupino and Olivia de Havilland, and, as was later to happen with *Jane Eyre*—another subject James had always wanted to do—the idea was jettisoned. The title, however, was retained, and Pamela set about devising a new story line. She eventually came up with an idea for a thriller in which a brilliant Harley Street surgeon (to be played by James) is slowly driven to murder and insanity after the woman he loves is purposefully pushed out of a window by her sister, and killed. James collaborated with Pamela on the screenplay and the film was directed by Lawrence Huntington. It was well reviewed and made a slight profit at the box-office, but was in no way comparable to *Odd Man Out* or *The Seventh Veil* on any level.

In November 1946, James and Pamela accompanied by a number of cats sailed in the Queen Elizabeth to the U.S., where he was to remain unemployed in motion pictures for a year and a half.

In the early months of 1946, James was talking about forming an independent production company with an experienced American executive. As the months passed it became clear that the two were unlikely to achieve a perfect meeting of minds in relation to movie-making aims and methods. But, unfortunately for James, he had at one time written a letter to his intended partner which testified to his willingness to go ahead with the project. His 'partner', whose name was David E. Rose, claimed that this letter could be regarded as a contract.

Thus there was a 'cloud on his title'. Had he been experienced in the Hollywood way of life he would have found a reasonably painless means of settling the dispute. But James, feeling that right was entirely on his side, applied to the courts of New York for a 'declaratory judgement'. It was 18 months before the judge finally handed down his decision: no contract existed, James was free to make whatever arrangements he wished for the furtherance of his movie career. His lawyer's fee was enormous and he had squandered his golden moment. However, his clumsiness enabled him to get to know the Eastern Seaboard of the U.S. better than he would otherwise have done. He and his wife made their Broadway début in *Bathsheba*, a failure.

James's new-found friend and 'Eastern Seaboard' representative, Wm. McCaffrey, found work for him in many radio shows including, to his great delight, a number of guest spots on the 'Fred Allen Show'. He also busied himself writing articles for magazines, some of which (characteristically) did not add to his popularity on the West Coast.

On the advice of McCaffrey and other New York friends, he signed up with the Morris Office for movie representation, largely on the grounds that the big man in that office, Abe Lastvogel, was universally liked and trusted. According to the dictates of common sense and Mr. Lastvogel, James should have had himself signed up promptly on a seven-year contract with one of the major studios, who alone could 'build up' a coming star in a way that would ensure acceptance by the big American public. But James, as we have already seen, shied at such a threat to his independence. Although through most of his Hollywood career he was 'free' to choose in what film he would next appear, the area of selection was minimal.

His first Hollywood film was *Caught*. On the credit side this film introduced him to Max Ophüls, whom he came to love and admire and whose 'irrepressible spirit and enthusiasm' greatly impressed him.

'Ophüls,' James said, 'was something of a fish out of water in Hollywood, and his career there was not what it should have been. He taught me one thing though: that when it came to handling executives, it never did any good to be pugnacious, which I tended to be. I remember watching some rushes with Max,' he said, 'when a group of people, from the producer (Wolfgang Reinhardt) downwards, insisted on a scene being reshot. If I had been Max, I'd have lost my temper for sure. But Max's attitude was one of an experienced, brave, resilient man who persuaded people to go along with him by being the soul of courtesy and consideration regardless of the circumstances. Hot-headedness, he preached, got one absolutely nowhere, and, of course, he was right.'

The screenplay for *Caught* was written by Arthur Laurents, and tells the story of an unhappy young woman (Barbara Bel Geddes) married to a ruthless millionaire (Robert Ryan) but in love with a poor doctor (Mason). The character of the millionaire was largely based on Howard Hughes, which presented problems in itself and was constantly being toned down to avoid easy identification. Furthermore, the whole subject of divorce, which the film raised, was a taboo issue at the time, and by skirting around it, the storyline suffered. Divorce was something which only 'bad' people indulged in, and as it was the heroine who was seeking a divorce, this was strictly forbidden. To ensure a happy ending, therefore, a situation had to be contrived in which the millionaire had a convenient heart attack. A similar situation presented itself in *The Upturned Glass* when the doctor, in order to be allowed to commit suicide, had first to be established as being mad, as suicide, like divorce, was not allowed to be depicted on the screen in a human or sympathetic light.

Caught was released in 1949, and was a total disaster. It was considered a mistake for James to have played the 'good guy', for Hollywood's idea of him was of a 'glamorous meanie'.

'Obviously,' he said, 'Ryan's part was the more gutsy and the more interesting. But I desperately wanted to get away from the bad guy image, not realising at the time that if an actor is lucky enough to have a recognisable persona, he should stick to it—and so I agreed to play the good doctor. I made the same alleged mistake in a film called *Cry Terror* and took the nice guy rôle in preference to the part played by Rod Steiger. To be a successful film star, as distinct from a successful actor, you should settle for an image—just as people like Cary Grant, Clark Gable, Gary Cooper, Humphrey Bogart or James Stewart did—and polish it for all it is worth.'

His second Hollywood film was *Madame Bovary* for Vincente Minnelli at M.G.M. From the outset James was sceptical about the project, believing it to be untranslatable to the screen. But Robert Ardrey's screenplay seemed so good that he agreed to appear in it—not as Boulanger, which was the part originally offered to him (and which was played by Louis Jourdan), but as Flaubert himself. It was a 'cameo' rôle which called for him to appear only in the prologue and at the end, and to serve as the narrator throughout.

The finished film, however, did not please him, and his fears that the story was not fit for English language filming seemed to be justified.

The same year, 1949, James made a second film with Max Ophüls—a melodrama about a blackmailer in a small Californian town who falls in love with his victim. It was called *The Reckless Moment*, starred Joan Bennett and Geraldine Brooks, and was made for Columbia by Walter Wanger.

He returned to M.G.M. to appear in *East Side, West Side* as Brandon Bourne, an American playboy who

James visiting daughter Portland on the set of a St. Trinian's comedy.

neglects his wife (Barbara Stanwyck) in order to pursue an affair with Ava Gardner. Despite its interesting cast, which also included Van Heflin, the film was in no way memorable, and at best is a slickly made soap opera.

James did not particularly enjoy working for M.G.M. 'Not being under contract to the studio,' he said, 'I felt I was an outsider—as though I didn't belong there. The whole atmosphere of the place suggested a military junta. The central administration block, for example, was the colonels' headquarters—and you were never allowed to forget it. The main entrance to the studio was policed by tough-looking security men carrying revolvers. In fact, there was something about the place,' he said, 'that made one think of concentration camps. I never met anyone at M.G.M. who loved the studio. Anyway, the best films were no longer being made at M.G.M. at the end of the forties, musicals excepted, and the studio was hardly the formidable treasure trove of talent it once was. 20th Century-Fox, which was a much friendlier, homelier, place all round, was doing far better work.'

'The thing about the Hollywood studios in general,' he said, 'regardless of my personal preferences, was that their technical crews were far better than the ones we had in England at that time—where everything moved at a snail's pace; where there were too many delays caused by sheer inefficiency and too many retakes as a result of incompetent camera and sound operators. What struck me most about the Hollywood crews was their extreme efficiency, and the speed at which they worked.

'On the other hand, I noticed that the authority most directors had in the making and editing of their pictures was far less than in Britain. Directors had to contend with the unnamed "they" in the major studios—those unseen powers-that-be whose approval on every aspect of the production had to be sought before one could go ahead. To someone like Max Ophüls, for example, this was a set-back—for Max, being a European, was brought up on the "auteur" theory of film-making and with the notion that the director is the man in charge who must bend to the producer's authority only on a point of budget.'

In 1950, James went to Universal for a crime drama called *One Way Street* in which he played a dissolute doctor who, after double-crossing a gang-leader, tries to make a new life for himself, but finds he cannot run away from his past. It was another undistinguished film, which did nothing to enhance the reputation he had made for himself with some of his better British films, a reputation which was fast diminishing. He saw a chance to regain some of his lost glory in 1951 when Al Lewin offered him the part of Hendrick van der Zee in *Pandora and the Flying Dutchman*, a romantic drama based on the legend of the Flying Dutchman, about a man condemned to sail the seven seas until he found a woman who was prepared to sacrifice her life for him.

'The ideas involved were not original,' he said, 'and contained nothing that hadn't previously been attempted in literature or the visual arts. But it was new as far as films were concerned. The writer (Albert Lewin) synthesised various ideas that had come to him through his perusal of literature and surrealist art and he wrapped them all up in this attractive parcel. Unfortunately, Lewin wasn't a good director, and the experience not a particularly happy one. Part of the film was made on location in Spain, and part of it was shot in London where my welcome, after all the bad publicity I'd received in the press before I left for America, was decidedly hostile. In a sense I was a "marked man". The British public, who claimed they had made me, regarded it as a slap in the face when I upped and left for Hollywood.'

Although *Pandora and the Flying Dutchman* was probably the most interesting film James had made since his arrival in America, it was not a success. *Rommel—Desert Fox*, on the other hand, was. It was also his most controversial film to date: 'I say this film is dangerous!' shrieked the *Evening Standard*; and from the *Daily Mail* came the cry: 'This film is a Glib Travesty of the Truth!' All the complaints were directed against the sympathetic interpretation of Rommel (played by James) as a 'jolly good chap' rather than at James's actual performance, which was generally considered to be excellent—certainly the best piece of acting he had done in America. 'Had we made the film today,' James said, 'we'd have had more facts at our disposal, and we'd have been able to go much deeper into the whole subject. But for the time in which it was written Nunnally Johnson's screenplay was, I think, splendid. And Henry Hathaway, the director did about as good a job as he has ever done.'

In order to get the part of Rommel, James had to sign a two-year contract with 20th Century-Fox which, normally, would have been anathema to him. 'But after my disastrous start to my American career,' he said, 'things didn't look too promising and I had to take what I could get. Besides, the part of Rommel appealed to me.'

He followed *Rommel—Desert Fox* with yet another spy drama to add to his ever-increasing list—this time, the memorable *Five Fingers* in which he played Ulysses Diello, a German spy known as 'Cicero', working in the British Embassy at Ankara. The film, tautly directed by Joseph L. Mankiewicz and also starring Danielle Darrieux and Michael Rennie,

James with brother Colin, father and mother on the occasion of his parents' Diamond Wedding Anniversary in Huddersfield.

received the unstinted approval of the critics and James's performance was justifiably singled out as being one of his most impressive.

While in Europe in 1951, James and Pamela began to perpetrate one of their least sensible ventures. Having some blocked sterling in England, they decided to shoot certain sequences, including all the exteriors, of *Lady Possessed*, based on Pamela's novel, *Del Palma*. They thought, mistakenly, that they would have no difficulty raising the rest of the backing in Hollywood and complete the film there. This turned out to be practically impossible, so that in the end they felt obliged to make a crippling deal with Republic Studios. The film, about a woman who is forced to take the place of a musician's dead wife, was an all-round disaster.

As Rupert of Hentzau in *The Prisoner of Zenda*, he was once again back on form. It was directed by Richard Thorpe, a workmanlike director with little finesse, and also starred Stewart Granger in a dual rôle: as the king, and the king's impersonator. But in spite of the two Stewart Grangers for the price of one, it was James who, in the film's showiest part, made the biggest impact.

He next appeared in a 'freakish' movie for producer Huntington Hartford at R.K.O. called *Face to Face*. Hartford wanted to make films in the mould of the British productions of *Trio* and *Quartet*—i.e. feature films comprising several short stories. Before James agreed to appear in *Face to Face*, he insisted that an episode which had already been shot—William Saroyan's *Hello Out There* with Henry Morgan—be scrapped, and something else be found in its place. The 'something else' turned out to be a Stephen Crane story called *The Bride Comes to Yellow Sky*, with Robert Preston and Marjorie Steele.

Though Huntington Hartford advertised his film as 'Duo-drama'—A New Concept In Film Making (the first story, in which James was starred, was *The*

Secret Sharer based on a story by Joseph Conrad and directed by John Brahm), it was given a poor release and is little more than an interesting curiosity —as indeed is James's own compendium film *Charade* (not to be confused with Stanley Donen's film of the same name), which consisted of three pieces originally intended for TV release.

The first story is *Portrait of a Murderer*, about a woman who is murdered by a man whose portrait she has drawn; the second, *Duel at Dawn*, based on a Chekhov story, *The Duel*, was set in 19th-century Austria and concerned a duel fought over a woman; while the third and final story, *The Midas Touch*, was a contemporary comedy about a man who cannot help making money no matter what he does.

Charade was directed by Roy Kellino and, apart from James, who appeared in all three segments, the film starred Pamela (now billed as Pamela Mason rather than Pamela Kellino), Scott Forbes, Paul Cavanagh, Bruce Lester and John Dodsworth. It was described in the *Monthly Film Bulletin* as 'an almost embarrassingly amateurish failure' and brought glory to none of its participants.

Next, James directed but did not appear in a 30-minute featurette called *The Child*, shot for TV, but released the following year (1954) in British cinemas. It was the simple story of a lonely spinster (Pamela Mason) who adopts a lost child (Portland Mason).

In 1953 James made his second film for Carol Reed —a political drama of post-war Berlin called *The Man Between*. Although the script by Harry Kurnitz was not nearly as good as Graham Greene's screenplay for *The Third Man* (whose success *The Man Between* attempted to repeat) James was delighted to be able to work with Carol Reed once again and said: 'The film can perhaps be faulted on a point of structure, but Carol staged the individual sequences better than anyone else could have and also got the best out of his actors.'

The Man Between was followed by *The Story of Three Loves*, made at M.G.M.—another three-in-one package in which James's appearance was confined to the first story (*The Jealous Lover*) directed by Gottfried Reinhardt. It was an unsuccessful attempt on the studio's behalf to recreate James's *The Seventh Veil* characterisation (the story tells of an encounter between a ballet impressario and a ballerina who literally dances herself to death) and made little impression on either the critics or the public. This was followed by yet another repeat performance—as Rommel in *The Desert Rats*—about a British commander and his Australian force at Tobruk. It was made as a sop to the many critics of *Rommel—Desert Fox* who were outraged by that film's sympathetic treatment of Rommel and who

demanded, in return, a film that glorified the home team. There is only one sequence in *The Desert Rats* in which Rommel appears and, naturally, James was asked to repeat his characterisation, but with one difference. In *Rommel—Desert Fox*, the entire cast spoke without German accents. In *The Desert Rats*, however, as the English and the Australians spoke in their own accents, it became necessary for James to acquire a German accent for authenticity.

'Of course, what they should have done,' James said, 'was simply get a German actor to play the rôle. But I didn't want them to do this, because if they had a *real* German playing Rommel, I was afraid his performance would be bound to appear much more credible than my own earlier effort. So I grabbed the part in self-protection.'

Also in the cast were Richard Burton, Robert Newton, Robert Douglas and Chips Rafferty. Robert Wise directed.

His next film was *Julius Caesar* (1953), made at M.G.M. and brilliantly directed (from his own screenplay) by Joseph L. Mankiewicz. Although the film succeeded both commercially and artistically, James felt that Mankiewicz had been somewhat hampered by M.G.M. protocol.

'Department heads were disinclined to defer to the director. This is not surprising since in the big old bad days of the majors, the director might well be the last of the personnel to be enlisted; and the heads of departments always had an eye to Oscar nominations and wanted their work to draw attention to itself.'

James was happy to be cast as Brutus because he had once made a great success in the rôle at the Dublin Gate Theatre. He assumed, wrongly as it turned out, that he would be able to do it again. When he started working alongside Gielgud he fancied that Sir John was overdoing the great voice; but he was to recognise during the course of the shooting of the film that Sir John was spot on, and that his own voice, having been exercised for so long exclusively in movies, was weak and colourless. He became so conscious of this shortcoming that when, not long afterwards, Tyrone Guthrie invited him to spend the next season at the Shakespeare Festival at Stratford Ontario, he jumped at the opportunity. He also placed himself in the hands of a dedicated and relentless voice coach called Mrs. Holmes.

After *Julius Caesar*, the best available offer was for a part in a period adventure story called *Botany Bay*. James was cast as a lightweight Captain Bligh, while Alan Ladd appeared as an unjustly sentenced young American bound for the convict settlement. Romantic interest was provided by Patricia Medina. The director was John Farrow, an Australian hagiologist of great charm (husband of Maureen O'Sullivan, father of Mia).

Then came the CinemaScope revolution and at 20th Century-Fox they concluded that bulky segments of biblical or other history would best lend themselves to the awkward ratio of their overgrown screen. The popular historical comic strip 'Prince Valiant' (created by Harold Foster) seemed to fit the bill. Hathaway was unleashed to direct it much to the dismay of a fine body of stuntmen. James played one of those black knights, the bad Sir Brack, and Robert Wagner was Prince Valiant.

After *Prince Valiant*, he was starred opposite Judy Garland in George Cukor's *A Star Is Born*, one of the very best films of his long and chequered career. He was not, however, Warner Brothers' first choice for the rôle of Norman Maine, Garland's alcoholic actor-husband whose dramatic decline parallels her meteoric rise. The part was first offered to Humphrey Bogart, who turned it down. The studio then approached Cary Grant. But happily it was James they settled for. His performance is every bit the equal of Judy Garland's in intensity; and the scene in which he listens to her 'improvised' version of the 'Somewhere There's a Someone' production number in his living room contains, from him, the greatest piece of *re*-acting ever put on film, and perfectly compliments Garland's exuberance as she desperately attempts to take him out of himself.

James, however, considers William Wellman's 1937 version a better picture as, he says, it is a well-balanced telling of the story, placing the emphasis on the man rather than on the woman.

'If you analyse the plot, incident by incident,' he said, 'you'll see that whatever poignancy is inherent in the basic story, is played off the man. When I first saw our version, I was very disappointed. The four hours of film Cukor had shot had to be reduced by an hour or so, and instead of cutting some of the numbers—such as the entire "Born in a Trunk" sequence which slowed down the narrative irreparably, they cut some of Judy's most touching scenes in the early part of the film—which was a pity as she was quite wonderful in those scenes, better than in the more dramatic ones. Some of my own favourite bits were similarly amputated. Still,' he said, 'Judy at her best was great. When she was on form, usually in the afternoons, she was a marvellous, bright, vital, sharp, witty human being. And Cukor was excellent with her. He loved eccentric actresses. The only male who featured in his anecdotes, and had, evidently, a similar appeal, was John Barrymore.'

From the high-voltage emotion of *A Star Is Born*, James went straight into *20,000 Leagues Under the Sea* for Walt Disney. The film turned out to be one of the most popular of James's career—and one of the most enjoyable. 'It was a splendid film,' he said, 'because it incorporated everything the Disney people do best. The model work and the special effects were outstanding as well as the creative imagination brought to the whole project. As a production it could not have been bettered. In fact, it was a producer's film rather than an actor's or director's film. I recently saw it dubbed into German, and the character I played, Captain Nemo, seemed to me to have improved immeasurably with a thick German accent. Kirk Douglas (who played Ned Land) sounds pretty good in German as well. I was a bit reluctant to accept the part at first because Nemo is basically a serious, dramatic part in a film primarily aimed at children—and I wasn't sure whether I could find the right key. But I'm glad I did it, if only for the happy experience of working in the Disney Studio which, I discovered, was the only studio in Hollywood that didn't have a hierarchy of executives who passed the buck and shifted papers on their desks. It was a happy, outgoing studio, more like a university campus, really, than a motion picture factory. The Disney people seemed more alive than their other Hollywood counterparts—more stimulating, and in general nicer! They all had to know how to draw—that may have had something to do with it.'

In 1955 all that James could find for himself was a part in *Forever Darling*, the memory of which causes him to shudder even now. It used to head the list of films which he would wish to be committed to the incinerator, largely because he regarded his performance in it as his worst ever. But recently he has been able to think, with recurring shudders, of several equally bad. Furthermore he would oppose the destruction of *Forever Darling* on the grounds that any film footage featuring Lucille Ball should be mounted in gold, for he claims that Miss Ball is America's most gifted actress.

The pattern of James's career, it would appear from the evidence, was to alternate rubbish with quality and, true to form, after the woebegone *Forever Darling*, he produced and appeared in a powerful domestic drama called *Bigger than Life* about a schoolteacher who takes a new wonder drug, cortisone, to relieve the pain of an arteries condition; and who, as a result of taking an overdose, becomes mentally unhinged. The director was Nicholas Ray, and the film also starred Barbara Rush and Walter Matthau. Although James's performance was excellent, *Bigger than Life* was not a success, and in London, where it received a critical drubbing, it was labelled 'disgraceful and disgusting' by a team of 30 doctors who saw it shortly before it opened, and who asked 20th Century-Fox to withdraw it from release on the grounds that it may do harm by shaking the public's confidence in the drug. James was amazed at the outcry.

His intention in the film, he said, was 'to portray dramatically the evils of an indiscriminate use of drugs'. He should have, he felt, 'been aided and applauded by the drug industry'.

While the controversy over *Bigger than Life* continued, James set out in 1957, for the Caribbean where he appeared in an indifferent adaptation of Alec Waugh's best-selling novel about inter-racial romance and prejudice, *Island in the Sun*. The theme was watered down to suit the censorship of the time, and despite a cast which included Joan Fontaine, Harry Belafonte, Dorothy Dandridge, Michael Rennie, Joan Collins, Basil Sydney, John Justin and Ronald Squire, Robert Rossen's direction failed to generate much heat. James played Maxwell Fleury, a neurotic, part-coloured son of a plantation owner driven, in the course of the story, to murder. Although it is not one of his more striking performances, and the film, as a whole, was poorly received by the critics, the experience, said James, was 'absolute heaven'. 'We made the film on a couple of islands in the Caribbean,' he said, 'and from a pleasure-loving actor's point of view, it could not have been more enjoyable. As there were five groups of actors who each had their own story, it gave those of us who weren't working in that particular story a great deal of free time to go off on sailing parties and have picnics—or just lie on a beach. I loved that part of it tremendously. But I didn't much like the film when I saw it.'

The following year, in *Cry Terror*, he played an electronics engineer who finds himself involved in an elaborate extortion plot; and after that he went straight into *The Decks Ran Red*, where he was cast as a sea-captain endeavouring to halt a mutiny. Both films were directed by Andrew Stone, and in each James chose to play the hero, leaving the dirty work to Rod Steiger in the first and Broderick Crawford and Stuart Whitman in the second.

In *North by Northwest*, directed by Alfred Hitchcock and starring Cary Grant and Eva Marie Saint, James appeared as Philip Vandamm, a villainous importer and exporter of government secrets, and gave the best performance in the film. 'It was a pretty straightforward part,' he said, 'and I was expected to do pretty straightforward things in it. Except in the last scene when Hitchcock wanted me to get a laugh, which I just couldn't deliver. Otherwise there were no problems and we got on well together, even though he isn't my ideal director. For example, Hitch never expects an actor to help him. And he seldom diverges from his blueprint, regardless of what the human circumstances

might be. One can't complain since it is such a skilful and amusing blueprint.'

In 1959, James next teamed up with Pat Boone, Arlene Dahl and Diane Baker to play Professor Oliver Lindenbrook in Henry Levin's *Journey to the Centre of the Earth* for 20th Century-Fox. 'It could not be as good as *20,000 Leagues Under the Sea*,' James said, 'because at Fox they simply weren't able to achieve the same sort of spectacular special effects that Disney could. But it came out better than I expected and the scenes depicting those giant iguanas and the whirlwind at the centre of the earth were effective, I thought. What didn't work though was our attempt to play the humour which was hinted at in the screenplay (by Walter Reisch and Charles Brackett). When the film opened in London the critics didn't seem to know whether the humour was intended or not. So obviously we failed to pull it off.'

It was clear though that James could play comedy when the script was right—and the following year, in *A Touch of Larceny*, directed by Guy Hamilton and produced by Ivan Foxwell, he delighted his critics and surprised them with his ability to raise a laugh. A comedy about a naval man who concocts a plot to defect to the Russians with some non-existent 'secrets' in order, ultimately, to sue the newspapers who could be counted on to refer to him as a traitor, and, with the resultant damages, to marry Vera Miles, *A Touch of Larceny* was a joyous film—which cannot, alas, be said for *The Marriage-go-round*, a feeble sex item in which a buxom Swedish blonde (Julie Newmar) chooses a University lecturer (James) as her ideal mate. It was written by Leslie Stevens and directed by Walter Lang and was a sorry business indeed. It was, in short, a Broadway-based comedy in which James seemed to be helpless. 'I can play situation comedy,' he says, 'but I'm not the sort of actor who draws laughter easily. If, for example, I look baffled, people don't automatically laugh: they are more likely to yawn.'

In 1960, James performed a two-day stint as Edward Carson, Q.C., the eloquent prosecuting counsel in *The Trials of Oscar Wilde* which he sandwiched between *A Touch of Larceny* and *The Marriage-go-round*. Peter Finch played Wilde, and Nigel Patrick was Sir Edward Clarke. The film, far superior to its rival version *Oscar Wilde*, with Robert Morley as Wilde, was written and directed by Ken Hughes. The excellent cast included Yvonne Mitchell as Mrs. Wilde, Lionel Jeffries as the Marquis of Queensberry and John Fraser as Bosie. It was released a week after the Morley version, and was never shown in the West End of London as no cinema could be found to house it.

James next made an uncredited and ill-advised appearance as a manager of an oil refinery in Ronald

James opening an amateur artists' exhibition—featuring some of his own contributions—during the shooting of *The Deadly Affair*.

Neame's *Escape from Zahrain* with Yul Brynner and Sal Mineo. James's given excuse for this mistake was that he had been asked by an old friend Ronald Neame to do it as a favour. But it is more likely that the boredom of life in Hollywood, which was beginning to get him down, had something to do with it.

A far happier event was *Lolita*, from Nabokov's novel, in which James played Humbert Humbert. (Again he was not director Stanley Kubrick's first choice: Noël Coward was originally offered the rôle but turned it down.) It was the first part James had had since Norman Maine in *A Star is Born* seven years earlier that gave him an opportunity to re-assert himself as one of the screen's great actors. His rapport with Kubrick, who, like Carol Reed, expected and encouraged a creative contribution, was excellent, and the result was a characterisation as memorable as any he has given. As the magazine *Sight and Sound* put it: 'James Mason has been quietly good, or merely quiet for so long in so many films, that it is easy to underestimate his achievement here.'

As James had by now well and truly established the up-down pattern of his career, it came as no surprise to his followers that his next few films should be duds. For the record, they were his and Leslie Stevens's production of *Hero's Island* (U.S. title: *The Land We Love*) set in 1718, and in which he played a pirate in disguise who helps save an island off the Carolinas from marauders; *Tiara Tahiti*, about an officer whose attempts to build a modern hotel in Tahiti are opposed by an erstwhile enemy; and *Torpedo Bay*, a war drama in which the crews of an Italian sub and a British anti-sub—meeting in Tangiers—grow to like each other even though they are enemies.

At this point in James's career he was becoming more of a character actor. At the time of his initial move to the U.S., his intention had been to establish himself as a leading man with whom the audience would happily identify. He reasoned that he would thus achieve such power as was needed to produce the kind of films he fancied. In England, there were more stars than vehicles; in Hollywood, he expected to do better. But having now been there over ten

With authoress Penelope Mortimer during the shooting of *The Pumpkin Eater*.

years he could not help noticing that things had not turned out the way he had intended. The best that a frustrated actor could do at this point was to turn to what was in its early days in the U.S. an exciting medium: live television.

James was a veteran of the B.B.C.'s transmissions from Alexandra Palace prior to World War Two. Actors had then found it a scary experience. But when TV started in the U.S. after the war there was a brave new generation of young men who had worked in no other medium and who were evidently unscareable. James, however, held off until 'Playhouse 90', a series of unrelated 90-minute plays, was launched in Hollywood.

Among the many now well-known American film directors who worked regularly for 'Playhouse 90' was Sidney Lumet, who cast James in two distinctly 'character' parts, the ex-Nazi official in Robert Shaw's *The Hiding Place* and the protagonist in *John Brown's Raid*.

Thus in Part III of James's career, which started with his re-adoption of European domicile, his more interesting rôles turned out to be 'character' rather than 'straight'. But because he was used to living in the style to which Hollywood had accustomed him, he continued to accept leads in films, regardless of the quality of the scripts, in order 'to pay the rent'. 'Had I been a modest bachelor living in a small apartment,' he said, 'I would never have done the rubbish I did. It was sheer economic necessity that forced me into mediocrity. But then this is one of the hazards of the profession and most actors are prone to it.'

His next film was *The Fall of the Roman Empire*, an ineptly written account of the events leading up to that historic event. James played Timonides, a Greek philosopher. The cast included Alec Guinness, Sophia Loren, Christopher Plummer, Stephen Boyd, Anthony Quayle, Mel Ferrer and Eric Porter. The director was Anthony Mann.

He was superb, as Bob Conway, the inwardly bitter but outwardly genial stockbroker friend of Peter Finch and Anne Bancroft, in Jack Clayton's account of Penelope Mortimer's *The Pumpkin Eater*, all about a woman's insecurity and her crumbling marriages. 'The film', said James, 'would have been even better than it was if they had found a means of attaching more sympathy to the woman rather than to the current husband. When reading the book one had felt a deep compassion for the lady; seeing the film, much less so. One of the things that emerged most powerfully in the film (written by Harold Pinter) was the relationship between Peter Finch, who was quite outstanding, and his children. We should, of course, have been much more interested in Bancroft's relationship with the children—as

was the case in the book. But the whole emphasis was somehow changed. Just as in Cukor's *A Star Is Born* emphasis was placed on the woman when it was essentially the man's story that commands attention, so in *The Pumpkin Eater*, I felt that it should have been the woman's story.'

After *The Pumpkin Eater* came *Lord Jim*, in which James played Gentleman Brown, a bible-punching river pirate, and in which he made far more impact than Peter O'Toole in the title rôle. Richard Brooks directed and provided the screenplay, based on the novel by Joseph Conrad.

And without James as the Chinese court official Kam Ling in Henry Levin's 'action spectacular' *Genghis Khan*, the film would have been even more deadly than it was.

Next came *Les Pianos Mécaniques*, which was all about a group of people, and their problems, who were visitors to or residents of Cadaquez on the Costa Brava. It starred Melina Mercouri and Hardy Kruger, and was a failure which not even James— as an author who drinks to forget his troubles— could, in any way, salvage. The film was briefly seen in America, but has not yet been released in Britain. The three films that followed, however, were of a different calibre entirely. First came *The Blue Max*, John Guillermin's absorbing World War One drama of a German pilot's career. It starred George Peppard, and Ursula Andress as a glamorous countess. James played Count von Klugermann, a high-ranking German official. Although the characterisation was similar to several James had undertaken before, it was none the less effective, as was his memorable portrayal of the wealthy James Leamington in Silvio Narizzano's archetypal sixties comedy *Georgy Girl*, which made a star out of Lynn Redgrave.

Sidney Lumet's adaptation of John le Carré's *The Deadly Affair* came next and in it James excelled himself as the seedy Charles Dobbs, an agent who uncovers the facts behind a British government employee's suicide. It also starred Simone Signoret, Maximilian Schell and Harriet Andersson. The climax of the film, which takes place at the Aldwych Theatre during a performance by the Royal Shakespeare Company of Marlowe's *Edward II*, is conceived in the great Hitchcock tradition and is quite stunningly effective.

The Blue Max, *Georgy Girl* and *The Deadly Affair* were all successful. Not so the trio that followed. *Stranger in the House*, a drama in which an alcoholic barrister returns to the profession he has abandoned and solves a murder case, made no impression on the box-office at all. It was based on a novel by Georges Simenon and starred Geraldine Chaplin and Bobby Darin. *Duffy*, a trendy thriller set in the

Mediterranean and in which James played a banker and shipping magnate, was equally forgettable. It starred James Coburn, Susannah York and James Fox, and was directed by Robert Parrish.

The downward thrust continued with *Mayerling*, the famous story of the doomed lovers set in the Vienna of the 1880s—in which James portrayed the Emperor Franz Josef. In the late thirties, an attractive film starring Charles Boyer and Danielle Darieux was made of this subject and Terence Young had long aspired to set up a remake. But he failed to ring the bell. James's mutton-chop whiskers were his most effective contribution. The other losers involved were Omar Sharif and Catherine Deneuve as the tragic lovers, and Ava Gardner as the Empress Elizabeth. All were hopelessly miscast.

In *The London Nobody Knows*, a documentary about 'forgotten' London made by Norman Cohen for British Lion, James served as both guide and narrator before teaming up with Michael Powell to star in and co-produce *Age of Consent*, an outdoor drama set in Australia, about an Australian commercial artist living in New York (James) who decides to give up his successful life in the big city and 'find himself' somewhere along the Great Barrier Reef. He finds Helen Mirren instead.

In the cast was an Australian actress called Clarissa Kaye who became James's second wife in August 1971. (James and Pamela Mason were divorced in September 1964.)

More impressive was his interpretation of Trigorin in Sidney Lumet's version of Chekhov's *The Sea Gull*, with both Simone Signoret (as Arkadina) and Vanessa Redgrave (as Nina) miscast, but with David Warner splendid as the would-be writer Konstantin. It was, however, James's film all the way, and on the strength of his performance, Sir Laurence Olivier invited him to appear in his screen adaptation of the National Theatre production of *The Three Sisters*. But James turned the offer down for financial reasons and in 1970 made *Spring and Port Wine*, Bill Naughton's domestic comedy-drama in which he played Rafe Crompton, the martinet head of an average workaday Lancashire family from Bolton—whose environment and way of life James, personally, knew very well. The film, directed by Peter Hammond and also starring Diana Coupland and Susan George, was not as effective (or as successful) as the play, but James's performance was totally convincing.

In 1970 came a curiosity called *The Yin and the Yang* which was started in Hong Kong, but the production company (Ross Film Productions) kept running out of money.

Unfortunately, *The Yin and the Yang* began a bad period for James, who next went to Italy to begin work on what seemed like a promising idea. The picture, *Die Boss Die Gently*, was to be an Italian and French co-production all about mercenaries in Africa, and was to star Alain Delon. But after three weeks' shooting, Delon and his partner Robert Dorfman, who put up the French part of the money, decided it was not being made properly, so Dorfman bought up the assets and liabilities of the production, including the property itself, as well as James's contract, and by way of recompense he offered him a part in a film called *Cold Sweat* which director Terence Young was to make with Charles Bronson in the South of France. James read the script, which he thought would work well as a suspense drama and be a worthy successor to Terence Young's *Wait Until Dark*, and gladly accepted the substitution. But there followed a spell of rewriting which contrived, somehow, to make it less exciting and less plausible.

Next came a spoof western made in Spain called *Bad Man's River* in which James played a Mexican revolutionary who offers 10,000 dollars to one of the most wanted men in Texas if he will blow up an arsenal used by the Mexican army. Lee van Cleef played this protagonist. To James's deep disappointment the film received a circuit release in Britain. He had hoped that nobody would get to see it.

Kill!, also shot in Spain, and written and directed by Romain Gary, was a thriller about the drug market and corruption in Interpol, the year's popular ingredients. The film also starred Stephen Boyd and Curt Jurgens and was, in James's assessment of it, 'definitely one for the incinerator—if only to clear Gary's hitherto unblemished reputation—well, fairly unblemished'.

Also unsuccessful was *Child's Play*, with Robert Preston and Beau Bridges, which Sidney Lumet directed from Robert Marasco's awkward Broadway play. The story, about the sinister goings on at a Catholic boarding school for boys, always promised more than it delivered, and although James gave one of his most satisfying performances in it, the film was a failure, and it, too, has not been given a West End release.

Child's Play was followed by *The Last of Sheila*, a complicated 'murder game' written by Anthony Perkins and Stephen Sondheim, in which a group of six Hollywood personalities, all present on the fatal night a young woman called Sheila is killed by a hit-and-run driver, are brought together by Sheila's film-producer husband Clinton (James Coburn) on his yacht in the South of France and are made to divest themselves of their innermost secrets and expose their deepest thoughts to each others. Clinton believes one of the guests is responsible for his wife's death and is determined to find out who it is.

James played a jaded movie director, and apart from

James Coburn, the cast included Richard Benjamin, Dyan Cannon, Ian McShane, Joan Hackett and Raquel Welch. It was slickly directed by Herbert Ross. But, despite its gloss and attractive cast, the British critics found it confusing, and it was not a success.

Nor was John Huston's *The Mackintosh Man*, which pivoted around a diamond robbery. James appeared about midway through the film just as the story line began to disintegrate, but he had a couple of good scenes and did the best he could with the material. The film also starred Paul Newman and Dominique Sanda.

The Mackintosh Man was followed by *11 Harrowhouse*, a comedy-adventure about a diamond heist. It was produced by Elliot Kastner and directed by Aram Avakian from a screenplay by Jeffrey Bloom. Apart from James, whose performance as an ageing employee of the diamond syndicate was the best thing in a better-than-average thriller, the film also starred Candice Bergen, Charles Grodin, Trevor Howard and John Gielgud. After *11 Harrowhouse*, which was not the commercial success it deserved to be, James played Dr. Polidori in *Frankenstein: The True Story*. The rest of the cast included Michael Sarrazin, Leonard Whiting, David McCallum, Nicola Paget, Clarissa Kaye and Jane Seymour, with guest stars Michael Wilding and the late Agnes Moorehead. Then, for director Robert Parrish, he made *The Marseille Contract*, a flaccid thriller set in present-day France, and starring Michael Caine and Anthony Quinn. This was quickly followed by an adaptation for Sir Lew Grade of Charles Dickens' *Great Expectations* in which James appears as Magwich. For director Richard Fleischer he then made *Mandingo*, a drama about a slave plantation in America's deep south, starring Susan George.

His latest film is a comedy-thriller once again involving a heist. It is called *Inside Out*, was shot in Berlin and stars Telly Savalas, Robert Culp and Aldo Ray.

Although James has appeared in countless productions that have recouped their costs and even shown a profit, out of his 92 films, only eight have made over a million dollars clear profit: *20,000 Leagues Under the Sea* (the biggest money-maker in which he has starred and which grossed over 11,000,000 dollars in the States alone), *The Blue Max, Georgy Girl, A Star Is Born, Island in the Sun, Journey to the Centre of the Earth, Lolita*, and *The Seventh Veil*, which only cost £92,000. He believes his best film to be *Odd Man Out*, which did not make very much money; and he has a fondness, too, for *20,000 Leagues Under the Sea, A Star is Born*, and *Lolita*. He talks generously about *Stranger in the House* as it provided him with an excellent part,

and feels it is one of the few he would gladly keep 'in some back room' rather than destroy. He admires *The Deadly Affair* which he considers 'an excellent spy story', *The Pumpkin Eater* as it has 'some virtue', *Age of Consent* because it is 'an attractive film', and *The Last of Sheila* 'although you have to listen intelligently to the dialogue which for many people is too much to ask'.

He does not have a favourite rôle, nor does he ever allow a part to obsess him to the extent where he cannot divorce it from reality. 'Acting and real life,' he said, 'make uneasy bedfellows, and I am never in danger of confusing the two. To me acting is a slightly more sophisticated version of a child's "let's pretend". It's simulation and nothing more. If you can simulate well, then you're halfway to being a good actor. If you can't you're not. I do not become personally involved in the characters I play. If, for example, I'm going to do Rommel, or the Emperor Franz Josef, I research the subject as much as time allows me, so that I may come to know the man and his background so well that, if called upon, I could improvise for any situation in which he might find himself.'

Although James has never received an Academy Award (but then neither has Mickey Rooney, Marilyn Monroe, Barbara Stanwyck, Judy Garland—except as a child when she was given a 'baby' statuette for *The Wizard of Oz*—nor, during their working years, Buster Keaton, Greta Garbo, Cary Grant, nor Charlie Chaplin), and has only been nominated twice, for *A Star Is Born* and, as best supporting actor for *Georgy Girl*, no one can question his stature as an actor of great power and individuality. His performances as Norman Maine, Humbert Humbert, Brutus, Trigorin, Johnny (in *Odd Man Out*), Bob Conway (in *The Pumpkin Eater*), Cicero (in *Five Fingers*) and Rafe Crompton (in *Spring and Port Wine*) are testimony enough to his impressive range and versatility.

Even in the plethora of mediocre and downright bad films with which he has been associated, his characterisations have, at least, always been interesting; and that distinctive Mason voice has frequently rescued both himself and his audience from his material.

The magnetism and 'star quality' which James Mason radiated as far back as 1938 in *I Met a Murderer* is still very much in evidence.

All it needs is a good script to liberate it.

With second wife Clarissa in London shortly after their marriage.

James and Clarissa in Monte Carlo with Dr. Berussan.

FILMOGRAPHY

LATE EXTRA

1935

Fox British. *Producer:* Ernest Garside. *Director:* Albert Parker. *Screenplay:* Fenn Sherie and Ingram d'Abbes—*from an original story by* Anthony Richardson. *Director of Photography:* Alex Brice. 69 minutes.

CAST

Virginia Cherrill . . . . *Janet*
James Mason . . . . *Jim Martin*
Alastair Sim . . . . *Mac*
Ian Colin . . . . *Carson*
Clifford McLaglen . . . . *Weinhardt*
Cyril Cusack . . . . *Jules*
David Horne . . . . *Editor*
Antoinette Cellier . . . . *Sylvia*
Donald Wolfit . . . . *Inspector Greville*
Hannen Swaffer . . . . *Himself*

SYNOPSIS

Weinhardt, escaping with the proceeds of a bank robbery, shoots a policeman and succeeds in getting away. The *Daily Gazette* offers a large reward for his capture, which tempts a woman to surrender valuable information she possesses. She is shot down, however, before Jim Martin, *Gazette* reporter, arrives to take down her statement. The young newshound sets about the task of solving the crimes and, following various leads, manages to track down and apprehend Weinhardt in the vaults of a Soho restaurant.

REVIEW

'The newspaper office sequences are convincing, lighting and photography are good and the direction is thoroughly competent. The acting is adequate.'— *Monthly Film Bulletin*

James Mason (1974):
Sample dialogue:
J. M. (*as cub reporter*): IS THAT BLOOD OR IS THAT BLOOD!

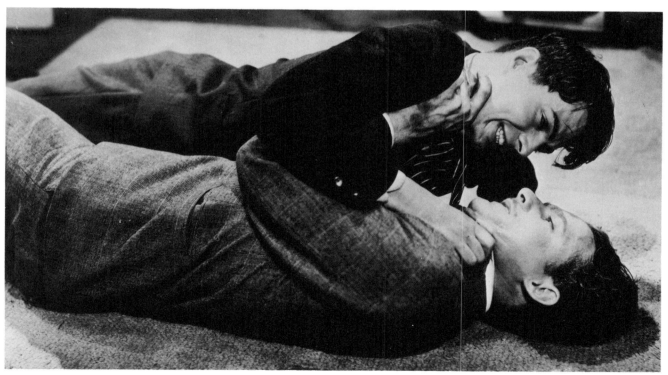

With Ian Colin.

With Virginia Cherrill in *Late Extra*.

TWICE BRANDED

1936

G.S. Enterprises (Radio). *Producer:* George Smith. *Director:* Maclean Rogers. *Screenplay:* Kathleen Butler—*from an original novel 'Trouble in the House' by* Anthony Richardson. 72 minutes.

CAST

Robert Rendel . . . . *Charles Hamilton*
Lucille Lisle. . . . . *Betty Hamilton*
James Mason . . . . *Henry Hamilton*
Eve Gray. . . . . *Sylvia Hamilton*
Mickey Brantford . . . . *Dennis*
Ethel Griffies . . . . *Mrs. Hamilton*
Isobel Scaife. . . . . *Mary*
Paul Blake . . . . *Lord Hugo*

SYNOPSIS

Sentenced to 12 years for unwitting complicity in a large City fraud, Henry Hamilton works out his punishment, eventually returning to the bosom of his family. However, they are unwilling to bear the shame reflected on them should his true identity be revealed, and introduce him to their circle as 'Uncle Charles from South America'.

The gaolbird's son, Henry, embroiled in the toils of the identical crook responsible for his father's downfall, is left 'holding the bag' when the crook sneaks off, but Hamilton senior agrees to shoulder the blame, glad to return to prison where snobbery is unknown and good fellowship exists among the unfortunate inmates.

REVIEWS

'The direction and photography are adequate and straightforward, but too akin to stage technique to be at all outstanding on the screen.'—*Monthly Film Bulletin*

'This study in domesticity and snobbery is written with no little skill. The entertainment to be found in the picture is rich and comprehensive.'—*Kinematograph Weekly*

TROUBLED WATERS

1936

Fox British. *Producer:* John Findlay. *Director:* Albert Parker. *Screenplay:* Gerard Fairlie—*from an original story by* W. P. Lipscomb and Reginald Pound. *Director of Photography:* Roy Kellino. 70 minutes.

CAST

Virginia Cherrill . . . . *June Elkhardt*
James Mason . . . . *John Merriman*
Alastair Sim . . . . *Mac MacTavish*
Raymond Lovell . . . . *Carter*
Bellenden Powell . . . . *Dr. Garthwaite*
Sam Wilkinson . . . . *Lightning*
Peter Popp . . . . *Timothy Golightly*
William T. Ellwanger . . . . *Ezra Elkhardt*

SYNOPSIS

The inhabitants of a small country village in England have gathered together and invested in a moribund mineral spring water business. When a man is killed in a local car crash, the Coroner's jury get together and decide to return a murder verdict in order to get publicity which will put both the village and the mineral water project on the map.

John Merriman, a government agent engaged on trailing a gang of explosives smugglers, discovers the alleged murder to be very much the real thing. By making enquiries and following the leads, he manages successfully to clear up the matter to the general satisfaction of all concerned.

REVIEW

'Action and interest are well-sustained. . . . James Mason plays his part, that of a secret agent, with greater ease than is evinced by Virginia Cherrill.'— *Kinematograph Weekly*

James Mason (1974):

Al Parker (on his knees): OH GOD, GIVE ME ACTORS! This seizure was prompted neither by Miss Cherrill nor myself, but by an actor whose part consisted of one line, a difficult one: A BOTTLE OF APPLEFORD WATER, SIR?

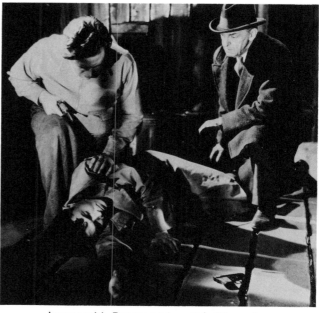

James with Raymond Lovell (with gun).

PRISON BREAKER

1936

A George Smith production released by Columbia-Grand. *Producer:* George Smith. *Director:* Adrian Brunel. *Original Screenplay:* Frank Witty—*from the novel by* Edgar Wallace. 69 minutes.

CAST

James Mason . . . . *Bunny Barnes*
Andrews Engleman . . . . *Stiegelman*
Marguerite Allan . . . . *Veronica*
Ian Fleming . . . . *Stephen Shand*
George Merritt . . . . *Goldring*
Wally Patch . . . . *Villars*
Vincent Holman . . . . *Jackman*
Andrea Malandrinos . . . . . . *Supello*
Tarver Penna . . . . *Macallum*
Neville Brook . . . . *Lord Beldam*
Aubrey Mallalieu . . . . *Sir Douglas Mergin*

SYNOPSIS

Bunny Barnes, a young Secret Service agent, is assigned to prevent an international crook, Stiegelman, from stealing an important treaty. Matters are complicated because Barnes is in love with Stiegelman's daughter Veronica. While following up a clue, Barnes accidentally kills Supello, Stiegelman's 'lieutenant', and is sent to prison on a manslaughter charge. By posing as a warder, he manages a daring escape and heads for London where, with the help of Veronica, he apprehends Stiegelman. As the villains are brought to justice, Barnes and Veronica happily leave together.

REVIEWS

'. . . largely incoherent and improbable . . . weak direction . . . forced portrayal . . . indifferent production quality. Only for the uncritical.'—*The Cinema*
'James Mason, heading a cast of nearly fifty players, presents a daredevil and amusing Barnes . . . and is given all the support he deserves.'—*Monthly Film Bulletin*
'James Mason and Ian Fleming are sound as the friendly rivals but would have been even better had their speaking voices been less toney and the dialogue more free of "stout fellow" sentiment. The continuity is not too clear.'—*Kinematograph Weekly*

James Mason (1974):

Fleming and I must have been influenced more than we knew by the director Adrian Brunel, who had a distinctly toney speaking voice. A nice enthusiastic director. A descendant, perhaps, of the Great Western railway pioneer? I never thought to ask. This is one of the very few films in which I appeared but never saw.

BLIND MAN'S BLUFF

1936

A Present Day/Fox British production released by Apex Film Distributors. *Director:* Albert Parker. *Screenplay:* Cecil Maiden—*from an original play 'Smoked Glasses' by* William Foster and B. Scott-Elder. *Art Director:* W. Ralph Brinton. *Editor:* Cecil Williamson. 72 minutes.

CAST

Basil Sydney . . . . *Dr. Peter Fairfax*
Enid Stamp-Taylor . . . . . *Sylvia Fairfax*
Barbara Greene . . . . *Vicki Sheridan*
James Mason . . . . *Stephen Neville*
Iris Ashley . . . . *Claire*
Ian Colin . . . . *Philip Stanhope*
Wilson Coleman. . . . . . . *Dr. Franz Morgenhardt*
Warburton Gamble. . . . . *Tracy*
'Tuff de Lyle' . . . . *The Dog*

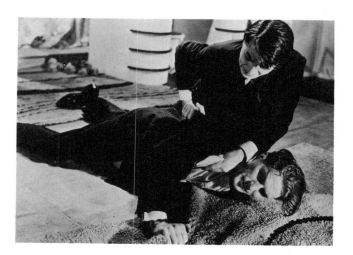

SYNOPSIS

Dr. Peter Fairfax, blinded by an accident, leaves home for Vienna to perfect an invention for making the human body invisible. His blindness is cured but, suspecting that his wife Sylvia is having an affair with Philip Stanhope, who is trying to acquire the invention, he does not reveal this fact on his return except to his laboratory assistant, Stephen Neville. When, through Sylvia, Stanhope gets possession of the formula, Stephen gets it back after a hand-to-hand struggle but refuses to give Sylvia away to her husband. Vicki, co-assistant and in love with the doctor, confesses to the theft for the same reason. Sylvia's elopement with Stanhope, however, loosens the young couple's tongues and Stephen, who is in love with Vicki, yields her to the doctor's care.

REVIEW

'Albert Parker develops his tale with a flood of dialogue but succeeds in holding interest by giving clear cut characterisations.'—*Kinematograph Weekly*

(Top) With Ian Colin.

(Centre) with Barbara Greene.

(Bottom) With Enid Stamp-Taylor and Basil Sydney.

THE SECRET OF STAMBOUL

(Re-issued in 1940 as THE SPY IN WHITE)

1936

A Wainwright production released by General Film Distributors. *Producer:* Richard Wainwright. *Director:* Andrew Marton. *Screenplay:* Richard Wainwright, Howard Irving Young and Noel Langley—*from the novel* Eunuch of Stamboul *by* Dennis Wheatley. 93 minutes.

CAST

Valerie Hobson	*Tania*
Frank Vosper	*Kazdim*
James Mason	*Larry*
Kay Walsh	*Diana*
Peter Haddon	*Peter*
Laura Cowie	*Baroness*
Cecil Ramage	*Prince Ali*
Robert English	*Sir George*
Emilio Cargher	*Renouf*
Leonard Sachs	*Arif*

SYNOPSIS

During a regimental ball, Larry and Peter, two Guards officers, set about Prince Ali, an Eastern potentate, because of his unwelcome attentions to Diana, a girl in love with Larry, and find themselves on the retired list. Diana's father, however, makes some recompense by engaging Larry to become manager of his tobacco depot in Turkey.

While there he falls in love with Tania, a Russian girl, and learns that she is an involuntary accomplice of Kazdim, a sinister Eastern gentleman employed by Prince Ali, now head of an organisation plotting to overthrow the Turkish government. Larry finds his rôle of Sir Galahad a dangerous one and later, when Diana and Peter arrive in Stamboul, they too become involved in Larry and Tania's attempts to save Turkey from the insurgents. After Larry has narrowly escaped from walking into his grave, Tania comes to the rescue and eventually finds a way out from all their difficulties and the villains are brought to justice.

REVIEWS

'No fancy money has been spent on cast, but every member of the acting organisation is thoroughly seasoned . . . worth fitting into double-feature programmes in America.'—*Variety*

'The best part of this film is the staging, most of it authentic, but much of it wasted on the story, the age and novelettish qualities—all of which are unhappily stressed by the indifferent acting and clumsy direction. James Mason overdoes the "white man" stuff as Larry.'—*Kinematograph Weekly*

'A foully acted British thriller. Biologically and cinematically speaking, the film is still in the egg-laying stage.'—*New York Times*

James Mason (1974):
Two things stand out in my memory. I was surrounded by immensely tall actors, those playing the Turkish colonel and the father of Kay Walsh, and Peter Haddon whom the script obliged to be constantly at my side (Frank Vosper shrewdly wore lifts). Also my moustache (would-be Ronald Colman style) kept breaking continuity. But neither of these can excuse overdoing 'the white man stuff'.

With Peter Haddon and Kay Walsh.

THE MILL ON THE FLOSS

1937

A Morgan production released by National Provincial Film Distributors. *Producer:* John Clein. *Director:* Tim Whelan. *Screenplay:* John Drinkwater, Garnett Weston, Austin Melford and Tim Whelan—*from the novel by* George Eliot. 94 minutes.

CAST

Frank Lawton . . . . *Philip Wakem*
Victoria Hopper . . . . *Lucy Deane*
Fay Compton . . . . *Mrs. Tulliver*
Geraldine Fitzgerald . . . . *Maggie Tulliver*
Griffith Jones . . . . *Stephen Guest*
Mary Clare . . . . *Mrs. Moss*
James Mason . . . . *Tom Tulliver*
Athene Seyler . . . . *Mrs. Pullet*
Sam Livesey . . . . *Mr. Tulliver*
Amy Veness . . . . *Mrs. Deane*
Felix Aylmer . . . . *Mr. Wakem*
Eliot Makeham . . . . *Mr. Pullet*
William Devlin . . . . *Bob Jakin*
Ivor Barnard . . . . *Mr. Moss*
David Horne . . . . *Mr. Deane*
O. B. Clarence . . . . *Mr. Gore*
Cecil Ramage . . . . *Luke*

SYNOPSIS

Stephen Tulliver, a mill owner, finds the tranquillity of his business and family life disturbed by an irrigation scheme sponsored by the Lord of the Manor, Sir John Pivart. He is determined to fight for his water rights, but Sir John's solicitor, Wakem, beats him, and the legal contest ends with him becoming servant to Wakem. Tulliver's daughter is loved by Wakem's crippled son Philip, but just as there is the possibility of the feud ending with the death of Tulliver, she is forced into a compromising situation by Stephen Guest, a friend of Philip and fiancé of her childhood friend Lucy.

She is branded as a wanton by her brother Tom and the rest of the community, but Philip's love for her never wanes and they go to their death together when a flood sweeps away part of the village.

REVIEWS

'Really no film at all, but a series of stiff little sequences decorously posed, one after the other, without much concern with their cumulative force, without much thought of dramatic or emotional continuity. It is about as electric, vital and intense as a platter of cold beef and Yorkshire pudding. . . . James Mason is thoroughly acceptable as brother Tom.'—*New York Times*

'The climax is superbly framed, and the same high standard in technical artistry is maintained throughout. A human, poignant story.'—*Kinematograph Weekly*

With Frank Lawton and Geraldine Fitzgerald.

FIRE OVER ENGLAND

1937

An Alexander Korda presentation. A Mayflower-Pendennis production released by United Artists. *Producer:* Erich Pommer. *Director:* William K. Howard. *Screenplay:* Clemence Dane and Sergei Nolbandov—*from the novel by* A. E. W. Mason. *Director of Photography:* James Wong Howe. *Art Director:* Lazare Meerson. *Costumes:* Rene Hubert. *Editor:* John Dennis. 92 minutes.

CAST

Laurence Olivier . . . . *Michael Ingolby*
Flora Robson . . . . *Queen Elizabeth*
Leslie Banks . . . . *Earl of Leicester*
Raymond Massey . . . . *Philip of Spain*
Vivien Leigh . . . . *Cynthia*
Tamara Desni . . . . *Elena*
Morton Selten . . . . *Burleigh*
Lyn Harding . . . . *Sir Richard*
George Thirlwell . . . . *Gregory*
Henry Oscar . . . . *Ambassador*
Robert Rendell . . . . *Don Miguel*
Robert Newton . . . . *Don Pedro*
Donald Calthrop . . . . *Don Escobal*
Charles Carson . . . . *Admiral Valdez*
James Mason . . . . *Ambassador/Envoy*
  (uncredited)

SYNOPSIS

The Virgin Queen, Elizabeth I, is frantic lest Philip of Spain invade her beloved land. Surrounded by a retinue of traitors, Elizabeth turns to Michael Ingolby for aid, knowing that, as his father had been burnt to death by the dreaded Inquisition, he will be only too glad to avenge this deed. Disguised as a renegade, Michael penetrates Philip's Court, learns the names of his English accomplices and the date of the Armada's arrival. Despite being discovered, Michael manages to escape, with the result that he sees the crushing of Spain's Armada, and the breaking of Philip's power.

REVIEWS

'Those who are strong-minded enough to be consistently cynical about glorious pages of our history will be made to squirm more than a little. But for the less critical majority . . . *Fire Over England* will provide a cordial orgy of heart swellings.'—*New Statesman*

'One of the most notable pictures of the year . . . a credit to British Studios. Excellent and intelligent entertainment.'—*Picturegoer*

'We think *Fire Over England* is a very fine film. Its historical setting is good, the dialogue excellent, and the acting excellent also. It might have been more than a fine film but for the very second rate and impossible adventure story which takes the name of A. E. W. Mason's novel in vain.'—*Sight and Sound*

THE HIGH COMMAND

1937

A Fanfare-Wellesley production released by Renown Pictures-A.B.F.D. *Producer:* Gordon Wellesley. *Director:* Thorold Dickinson. *Screenplay:* Katherine Strueby—*from the novel* The General Goes Too Far *by* Lewis Robinson. *Dialogue:* Walter Meade and Val Valentine. *Director of Photography:* Otto Heller. *Music:* Ernest Irving. *Art Director:* R. Holmes Paul. *Editor:* Sidney Cole. 74 minutes.

CAST

James Mason . . . . *Heverell*
Lionel Atwill. . . . . *Major-General Sir*
 John Sangye, V.C.
Lucie Mannheim . . . . . . *Diana Cloam*
Steve Geray . . . . *Martin Cloam*
Leslie Perrins . . . . *Carson*
Allan Jeayes . . . . *H.E. the Governor*
Michael Lambart . . . . *Lorne*
Kathleen Gibson . . . . *Belinda*
Tom Gill . . . . *Daunt*
Wally Patch . . . . *Crawford*

SYNOPSIS

Following an ambush in Ireland in 1921, Major Sir John Sangye, V.C., and a civilian, Challoner, find themselves the sole survivors. Challoner accuses Sangye of being the father of his wife's child and draws a revolver. Sangye, however, is too quick and kills him, but Carson, the medical officer, discovers Sangye's secret.

Sixteen years later, Sangye, now a General, is in command of a West African Garrison to which Carson is attached. Sangye's step-daughter, Belinda, is with him and Carson knows that she is really the General's own daughter. Carson makes a play for her. Heverell, Carson's cousin and brother officer, is having an affair with Diana, wife of Martin Cloam, a trader, but Cloam erroneously believes that Carson is Diana's lover.

Later, Carson is found murdered and suspicion falls on Heverell. During the ensuing court-martial, Heverell's counsel rakes up the past and it is revealed that Carson has been blackmailing Sangye, who, however, suspects Cloam and brings about his eventual confession and death, and incidentally, his own, thereby freeing an innocent man and shielding his own daughter from scandal.

REVIEWS

'It is much to the credit of Thorold Dickinson that he has made an interesting, and, at times, very dramatic film.'—*Spectator*

'There is a tendency to divert interest with trifling and somewhat over-pukka incidentals. James Mason is good as Heverell.'—*Kinematograph Weekly*

'But for Lionel Atwill's performance and some quite realistic West African atmosphere, the film would be a negligible novelettish affair. The story is rather far-fetched.'—*Film Weekly*

James Mason 1974:

The original working title was *The General Goes Too Far*. Either Atwill's position of power in the set-up, or Dickinson's artistic predilection, resulted in an enormous number of close-ups of the General. Amiable Hungarian humorist, Steve Geray, who was playing rather a thankless part, got us referring to the film as *The General Has No Legs*.

With Lucie Mannheim.

CATCH AS CATCH CAN

(Re-issued in 1947 as ATLANTIC EPISODE)

1937

Fox British. *Director:* Roy Kellino. *Screenplay:* Richard Llewellyn—*from an original story by* Alexander George. 71 minutes.

CAST

James Mason . . . . *Robert Leyland*
Viki Dobson . . . . *Barbara Standish*
Eddie Pola . . . . *Tony Canzari*
Finlay Currie. . . . . *Al Parsons*
John Warwick . . . . *Eddie Fallon*
Margaret Rutherford . . . . *Maggie Carberry*
Paul Blake . . . . *Cornwallis*
Jimmy Mageean. . . . . *Ben*
Paul Sheridan . . . . *Fournival*
Zoe Wynn . . . . *Mrs. Kendal*

SYNOPSIS

Barbara Standish, the impecunious heroine of the story, decides to earn herself some money by smuggling jewels from France to America aboard a transatlantic liner. However, her attempts are thwarted by Robert Leyland, U.S. Customs agent, who does not give her away but suggests she travel back to Europe and return the jewels. Three separate crooked factions endeavour to secure the loot, and one of these unsavoury gentlemen, Chicago gangster Tony Canzari, meets a sticky end. Finally, in a burst of gunplay that transforms the normally tranquil vessel into something approaching a madhouse, matters are satisfactorily sorted out.

REVIEWS

'The film has interest, but is slow . . . James Mason makes an attractive hero.'—*Monthly Film Bulletin*
'The attempt to establish American character and atmosphere fails by a long chalk . . . James Mason and Viki Dobson are not too good as the lovers.'—*Kinematograph Weekly*

James Mason (1974):
BUT there was also the great Margaret Rutherford!

Margaret Rutherford and Paul Sheridan.

THE RETURN OF THE SCARLET PIMPERNEL

1937

A London Film production released by United Artists. *Producer:* Arnold Pressburger. *Director:* Hans Schwartz. *Screenplay:* Lajos Biro, Arthur Wimperis and Adrian Brunel—*from the novel by Baroness Orczy. 94 minutes.*

CAST

Barry K. Barnes	*Sir Percy Blakeney*
Sophie Stewart	*Marguerite Blakeney*
Margaretta Scott	*Theresa Cabarries*
James Mason	*Jean Tallien*
Francis Lister.	*Chauvelin*
Anthony Bushell	*Sir Andrew ffoulkes*
Patrick Barr	*Lord Hastings*
David Tree	*Lord Denning*
Henry Oscar	*Robespierre*
Hugh Miller.	*de Calmet*
Allan Jeayes	*Judge*
O. B. Clarence	*de Marre*
George Merritt	*Chief of Police*
Evelyn Roberts	*Prince of Wales*
Esmé Percy	*Richard Sheridan*
Edmund Breon	*Colonel Winterbottom*

SYNOPSIS

In order to induce Sir Percy Blakeney, the Scarlet Pimpernel, to come to France, Chauvelin sends a pretty young actress, Theresa, to England to ask for his help in rescuing her lover, Tallien, whose life is threatened by the guillotine. She meets Sir Percy in Brighton where he is playing cricket, but it is only when his wife, Lady Blakeney, is kidnapped that he agrees to sail for France with his men. After a series of escapes and recaptures, with Sir Percy donning many different disguises, Tallien is saved and the evil Robespierre brought to justice.

REVIEWS

'. . . same old Guillotine square . . . same old aristocrats dying with incredible grace, same old extra women knitting and cackling obscenely as the heads fall . . . same old British melodrama laid on with fine British unrestraint. Credit is due both to director and cast for betraying so few signs of ennui.'—*New York Times*

'Though the melodramatic romance begins to date and the dice seem to be loaded impossibly for the hero in his tight corners, this is, on the whole, brisk, glowing entertainment.'—*News Chronicle*

'The tempo of the film is very properly accelerated and intrigues, perils and escapes flow continuously across the screen, but the film would have been stronger and even more exciting had the Pimpernel been less "demn'd elusive".'—*The Times*

'For something concerned with such exciting topics [the picture] is curiously mild in tone.'—*Sunday Express*

With Francis Lister.

I MET A MURDERER

1939

A Gamma production released by Grand National Pictures. *Producers:* Roy Kellino, Pamela Kellino and James Mason. *Director:* Roy Kellino. *Screenplay:* Pamela Kellino and James Mason—*from an original story by* Pamela Kellino. *Director of Photography:* Roy Kellino. *Music:* Eric Ansell. *Editor:* Fergus Macdonnell. 78 minutes.

CAST

James Mason	*Mark Warrow*
Pamella Kellino	*Jo*
Sylvia Coleridge	*Martha Warrow*
William Devlin	*Warrow*
Peter Coke	*Horseman*
Esma Cannon	*Hiker*
James Harcourt	*Cart Driver*

SYNOPSIS

Mark Warrow, a young and ambitious farmer, lives with his nagging and ill-tempered wife Martha on their small farm. Because of an argument concerning her drunken brother, Martha shoots Mark's dog, and Mark, incensed at this action, shoots her and buries her in the garden. Her brother, however, becomes suspicious and Mark runs away, managing to evade the police for many days.

One night he meets Jo, a girl novelist, who is touring the countryside in her motor-caravan. He joins her

and for several weeks they are ideally happy with their undeclared love for each other. Later Mark realises that she has guessed his true identity and is using the experience for the novel she is writing. Before any plans can be made, the police arrive to investigate a tramp seen lurking in the woods and question Jo. Mark hides with Jo's revolver and the police, thinking that the tramp is the missing murderer because Jo's holster is empty, begin a full-scale hunt. Mark is chased across country towards the sea where, watched by Jo from the headland, he plunges into the water but slowly loses his strength and disappears beneath the waves.

REVIEWS

'Mason's performance is the strong thread of the whole thing . . . the very sincerity of the talented trio who made it gives the picture a novelty and distinction above its strict merits. Not merely does it get away from studio conventions in a refreshing way, but it has something individual and rather precious which no studio with all its efficiencies could have given it. The Kellino-Mason team should be encouraged—for its potentialities as well as its courage.'—*Sunday Express*

'Though it tries too hard for its own artistic good—and often with remarkable smoothness—to look "professional", the picture is streaked with enough amateurishness to pretty well guarantee its commercial failure. There are also some downright poor things in it . . . yet this is one of the fairly few movies I have seen in years in which it was clear that its makers knew and cared and in general had lively, sensible ideas how each shot should follow the next, and what in the way of emotion, atmosphere, observation and psychological weight and progression each shot and each group of shots should contain. I also thought it graceful, gallant, resourceful, and in every way satisfying and encouraging in its broken field run through the problems of cost . . . it is better and more enjoyable than most studio pictures.—James Agee, *The Nation*

'A grimly engaging picture . . . the sort one welcomes from newcomers—imaginatively conceived, beautifully photographed and adequately played. We should have a few such experimentalists on this side of the water.'—*New York Times*

With Pamela Kellino.

THIS MAN IS DANGEROUS

(Alternative title THE PATIENT VANISHES)

1941

A Rialto production released by Pathé. *Producer:* John Argyle. *Director:* Lawrence Huntington. *Screenplay:* John Argyle and Edward Dryhurst—*from the novel* They Called Him Death *by* David Hume. 82 minutes.

CAST

James Mason . . . . *Mick Cardby*
Mary Clare . . . . *Matron*
Margaret Vyner . . . . *Mollie Bennett*
Gordon McLeod . . . . *Inspector Cardby*
Frederick Valk . . . . *Dr. Moger*
Barbara Everest . . . . *Mrs. Cardby*
Barbara James . . . . *Lena Morne*
G. H. Mulcaster . . . . *Lord Morne*
Eric Clavering . . . . *Al Meason*
Brefni O'Rorke . . . . *Dr. Crosbie*
Michael Rennie. . . . . *Inspector*

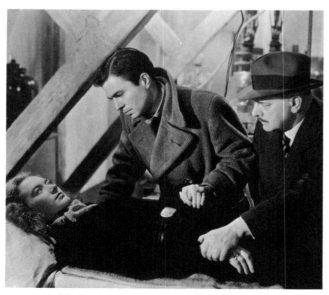

With Barbara James and Gordon McLeod.

SYNOPSIS

When a policeman is found murdered in Hyde Park, Mick, Detective Inspector Cardby's private detective son, discovers that Lord Morne's daughter, Lena, has been kidnapped. The distracted father, who dare not contact the police for fear of blackmailers, offers Mick £1,000 to get his daughter back alive. With the help of his pretty secretary Mollie, Mick tracks the criminals down to a nursing home in the country. The gang, however, escapes taking Lena with them. After a series of adventures, Mick then trails them to a large house in North Wales where, due to the intervention and quick thinking of his father, he is saved and Lena is rescued.

REVIEWS

'Maintains the excitement throughout . . . all the required ingredients for arresting melodrama. . . . James Mason . . . an admirable portrayal.'—*The Cinema*

'An excellent thriller with a good story, well told and full of action and excitements.'—*Monthly Film Bulletin*

James Mason (1974):

Sample dialogue: Frederick Valk, the splendid Czech actor who played the heavy (about to suspend me in the rat-infected hold of his ship): KROOD METTODS, KARDBEE, BUT I TINK YOO VILL FINE DEM EFFEKTEEF.

HATTER'S CASTLE

1941

Paramount British. *Producer:* Isadore Goldsmith. *Director:* Lance Comfort. *Screenplay:* Rodney Ackland—*from the novel by* A. J. Cronin. *Director of Photography:* Max Green. *Music:* Horace Shepherd. *Art Director:* James Carter. *Editor:* Douglas Robertson. 102 minutes.

CAST

Robert Newton . . . . *James Brodie*
Deborah Kerr . . . . *Mary Brodie*
Beatrice Varley . . . . *Mrs. Brodie*
James Mason . . . . *Dr. Renwick*
Emlyn Williams . . . . *Dennis*
Henry Oscar . . . . *Grierson*
Enid Stamp-Taylor . . . . *Nancy*
Anthony Bateman . . . . *Angus Brodie*
June Holden . . . . *Janet*
Brefni O'Rorke . . . . *Foyle*
George Merritt . . . . *Gibson*
Lawrence Hanray . . . . *Dr. Lawrie*
Roddy Hughes . . . . *Gordon*
Claude Bailey . . . . *Paxton*
Stuart Lindsell . . . . *Lord Winton*
Mary Hinton . . . . *Lady Winton*
Ian Fleming . . . . *Sir John Latta*
David Keir . . . . *Perry*
Aubrey Mallalieu . . . . *Clergyman*

SYNOPSIS

James Brodie, a ruthless and cruel but successful hatter, lives with his ailing wife, their daughter Mary and young son Angus in a large mansion called Hatter's Castle. While they live in fear of him, Brodie finds some solace in his mistress, a barmaid named Nancy, and is persuaded to give her former lover, Dennis, a position in his shop. Dennis meets

James as Dr. Renwick.

Mary and plans to marry her and gain her inheritance. Mary is in love with Dr. Renwick but is attracted by Dennis who contrives to have the doctor barred from the house. When Brodie discovers Mary's interest in Renwick, he throws her out and she catches the midnight train to Glasgow. Dennis, who is also on the train, tells her that he no longer wants anything to do with her, especially now that Brodie has gone bankrupt, and Mary jumps off the train. Later the train crashes and Mary is believed dead.

With Beatrice Varley and Deborah Kerr.

With Deborah Kerr.

With Robert Newton.

One day, when Renwick is attending Mrs. Brodie who is dying of cancer, she tells him that she has had a letter from Mary, but that it has been destroyed. Then, when Mrs. Brodie dies, and Nancy leaves Brodie, the hatter becomes totally deranged and pins all his hopes on Angus winning a scholarship. Angus, fearing his father's wrath if he fails the exam, is found to have cheated and, in despair, commits suicide. Brodie, realising that he has been the cause of his death, curses the symbol of his vanity, Hatter's Castle, and razes the house to the ground, burying himself and the body of Angus. Mary learns what has happened and attends the funeral. While she is shunned as an outcast by the local inhabitants, Renwick leads her out of the church to a new-found freedom and a life together.

REVIEWS

'*Hatter's Castle* was a film worth making, but it suffers from the initial disadvantage of following a story so ham that all Rodney Ackland's skill in scenario and dialogue cannot animate it.'—Dilys Powell, *Sunday Times*

'Some of the finest British acting since Charles Laughton left these shores.'—*Daily Express*

'Melodramatic to a degree, there's not a foot of this film which isn't interesting . . . full of good acting.'—*Sunday Express*

'One of the best films ever made anywhere.'—*Daily Mail*

'Robert Newton's Brodie . . . a stunning tour de force which will be remembered for longer than many better pictures.'—C. A. Lejeune, *Observer*

James Mason (1974):

Interesting running skirmish between Newton and the producer I. Goldsmith. The latter, presumably having made a deal with an American distribution company, insisted there be no local British accents. This was taken to include the essential Scottish and Goldsmith was at pains to control Newton's. As I remember, Goldsmith's own accent was mid-European with an American taint. Though Newton was obliged to accept the no accent regulation, he thought it was a safe bet that Goldsmith could not really tell the difference. Every so often some sneak would let on that Newton was cheating and thus reactivate the skirmish.

THE NIGHT HAS EYES

(U.S. title TERROR HOUSE)

1942

An Associated British Picture production released by Pathé. *Producer:* John Argyle. *Director:* Leslie Arliss. *Screenplay:* Alan Kennington—*from an original story by* Alan Kennington. *Director of Photography:* Gunther Krampf. *Art Director:* Duncan Sutherland. 79 minutes.

CAST

James Mason . . . . *Stephen Deremid*
Wilfred Lawson . . . . *Sturrock*
Mary Clare . . . . *Mrs. Ranger*
Joyce Howard . . . . *Marian Ives*
Tucker McGuire . . . . *Doris*
John Fernald . . . . *Barry Randall*

SYNOPSIS

At the end of term, Marian Ives and her flirtatious friend Doris, the games-mistress, set out for the Yorkshire moors where Marian's great friend Evelyn disappeared a year before and was never seen again. They become caught in a storm and are given shelter

by Stephen Deremid, a music composer who had been wounded in Spain but now lives the life of a recluse with his housekeeper, Mrs. Ranger, and her husband, Sturrock.

Marian and Stephen fall in love, but he thinks that he is a killer and would kill Marian in one of his fits. Marian stumbles on a clue which throws light on the disappearance of Evelyn, and nearly suffers the same fate herself before the mystery is finally solved and she gets the man of her choice.

REVIEWS

'There is some ingenuity and not a little cinematic skill in this British film which shows by the quality of its dialogue that it aims at being something more than an ordinary "thriller".'—*The Times*

'The direction and production are too stagey to get the most out of quite a good plot. James Mason and Joyce Howard do their best as the hero and heroine.'—*Monthly Film Bulletin*

'Forthright direction, powerful leading portrayal, plenty of light relief. James Mason paints a powerfully melodramatic portrait of the alleged killer.'—*Today's Cinema*

James Mason (1974):

In the days when fog was thought to be a necessary ingredient of the British thriller, how much the more so when the action took place on Dartmoor! But it is really very boring stuff. Our cameraman was a perfectionist, Gunther Krampf. He had to see that the fog remained consistent through every scene of that last exciting sequence. If too thick, the doors of the stage had to be opened to release some of it; if too thin, more waiting while the fog men laid it on with their bellows, Gunther gazing at it steadfastly through his little square of dark glass.

The moor was constructed on a relatively small sound stage. Two leading characters were to walk into the distance upon it. So what do you do when you do not have much distance to play around with? You use midgets. I always had assumed that Krampf was the first man to hit upon this device. You carry Wilfred Lawson and Mary Clare as far as

With Jane Howard.

JAMES MASON
WILFRID LAWSON
MARY CLARE

THE NIGHT HAS EYES

with
JOYCE HOWARD

AN ASSOCIATED BRITISH
PRODUCTION
Produced by JOHN ARGYLE
Directed by LESLIE ARLISS

you can on this small set; then you cut back to a tight three shot of myself and Joyce Howard and John Fernald watching them disappear into the distance; and when you cut back to Lawson and Clare they have been replaced by midgets and consequently appear to be much farther away. Hey presto!

Lately, however, someone told me that Hitchcock used the same device on *The Lady Vanishes*. The great art director Vishinsky constructed in false perspective a seemingly long railway station in, again, a rather small sound stage, this time at Islington. The far end of the platform was peopled with midgets. Yes, it sounds like a Hitchcock invention.

ALIBI

1942

A Corona production released by British Lion. *Associate Producer:* Herbert Smith. *Producer:* Josef Somlo. *Director:* Brian Desmond Hurst. *Screenplay:* Messrs. R. Carter, Juttke and Companeez—*from the novel by* Marcel Achard. *Director of Photography:* Otto Heller. *Music:* Jack Beaver. *Art Director:* Walter Murton. *Costumes:* Molyneux of London. *Editor:* Alan Jaggs. And Clarie Wear's Embassy Orchestra. 82 minutes.

CAST

Margaret Lockwood	*Hélène Ardouin*
Hugh Sinclair	*Inspector Calas*
James Mason	*André Laurent*
Raymond Lovell	*'Winkler'*
Enid Stamp-Taylor	*Dany*
Hartley Power	*Gordon*
Jane Carr	*Delia*
Rodney Ackland } Edana Romney }	*'Winkler's' Assistants*
Elisabeth Welch	*Singer*
Olga Lindo	*Madame Laureau*
Muriel George	*Madame Brettonet*
George Merritt	*Bourdille*
Judy Gray	*Josette*
Philip Leaver	*Dodo*
Derek Blomfield	*Gerrard*

SYNOPSIS

In pre-War Paris, Hélène runs the smartest night-club in town where the star turn is a mind-reader, 'Professor Winkler'. One evening he recognises an enemy in the audience and, after the show, follows him in his car and shoots him as he is trying to escape. 'Winkler' then turns up at Hélène's flat and offers her 20,000 francs to say that he was with her from 2 a.m. onwards. Being in financial difficulties she agrees, and although the suspicion falls on 'Winkler' his alibi is strong.

The police, however, think that Hélène is lying and hope to force the truth from her by using one of their men, André Laurent, to court and make her fall in love with him. Then, by pretending he is suspect and arrested, she will tell the truth to save her lover from wrongful punishment. All goes well with this plan except that the couple really do fall in love. Hélène confesses that 'Winkler's' alibi is false to the police inspector, who admits that Laurent is one of his men. Hélène is naturally furious and rushes off to the station followed by Laurent, who tells her that he can explain everything. Accepting his explanation, Hélène buys two tickets instead of one.

REVIEWS

'Margaret Lockwood, fresh and lovely in a difficult part, does extremely well; so does up-and-coming James Mason, a good looker with a nice style of his own.'—*Sunday Express*

'The only mystery in *Alibi* is why they bothered to make the thing at all.'—C. A. Lejeune, *Observer*

'On the whole, a goodish melodrama well directed and with one or two first rate moments of suspense.' —Dilys Powell, *Sunday Times*

With Margaret Lockwood.

With Hugh Sinclair and Margaret Lockwood.

With Margaret Lockwood.

SECRET MISSION

1942

A Marcel Hellman/Excelsior production released by General Film Distributors. *Producer:* Marcel Hellman. *Director:* Harold French. *Screenplay:* Anatole de Grunwald and Basil Bartlett—*from an original story by* Shaun Terence Young. *Director of Photography:* Bernard Knowles. *Special Effects:* Percy Day, Desmond Dickinson and John Mills. *Music:* Mischa Spoliansky. *Art Director:* Carmen Dillon. *Editor:* E. B. Jarvis. 94 minutes.

With Hugh Williams.

CAST

Hugh Williams . . . . *Peter Garnett*
Carla Lehmann . . . . *Michele de Carnot*
James Mason . . . . *Raoul de Carnot*
Roland Culver . . . . *Red Gowan*
Michael Wilding . . . . . . *Nobby Clark*
Nancy Price . . . . *Violette*
Percy Walsh . . . . *Fayolle*
Anita Gombault . . . . . . *Estelle*
David Page . . . . *Child René*
Betty Warren . . . . *Mrs. Nobby Clark*
Nicholas Stuart . . . . *Captain Mackenzie*
Brefni O'Rorke . . . . *Father Jouvet*
Karel Stepanek . . . . *Major Lang*
F. R. Wendhausen . . . . . *General von Reichmann*
John Salew . . . . *Captain Grune*
Herbert Lom . . . . *Medical Officer*
Beatrice Varley . . . . *Mrs. Donkin*
Yvonne Andre . . . . *Martine*
Stewart Granger . . . . . . *Sub-Lieutenant Jackson*
Oscar Ebelsbacher . . . . . *Provost Officer*

SYNOPSIS

Major Peter Garnett, Captain Raoul de Carnot, Captain Red Gowan and Private Nobby Clark, all of British Intelligence, are sent to discover the strength of German defences in Occupied France. They are landed on the French coast and get to the appointed village without arousing suspicion. The information they require is only at German Headquarters, so with forged instructions from Ribbentrop, Garnett and Red get inside posing as champagne merchants. The Germans are deceived long enough for Garnett to uncover the information he is after, but soon the hunt is on.

By means of the French Resistance movement, information is relayed to British paratroops who

With Carla Lehmann.

Hugh WILLIAMS
James MASON
Michael WILDING
Carla LEHMANN

Secret Mission

A MARCEL HELLMAN
PRODUCTION

NANCY PRICE
ROLAND CULVER

Directed by HAROLD FRENCH
Produced by MARCEL HELLMAN

GENERAL FILM DISTRIBUTORS

descend on the German H.Q. and destroy the fortifications, munitions and reinforcement regiments, but Raoul, whose country home has acted as a base for the team, is killed as the Intelligence men are escaping. His sister, Michele, with whom Garnett has fallen in love, refuses to accompany him back to England as she feels that she must continue to help the Resistance movement until the Germans have left her country.

REVIEWS
'This film should have made a story full of excitement and suspense. Instead it lacks pace and direction, and, in some instances, sincerity in acting.'—*Monthly Film Bulletin*
'The story is simple. What makes it effective is the adroit blending of suspense with humour. Good work by James Mason and Michael Wilding.'—*Evening Standard*
'Hugh Williams, Carla Lehmann, James Mason and, in particular, Nancy Price conjure up exciting and, at times, witty entertainment.'—*Sunday Express*

James Mason (1974):
One of my early death scenes featured in this film. As I was passing away, the fact that I was supposed to be a French Resistance hero caused the sound track to reverberate with 'La Marseillaise'.

THUNDER ROCK

1942

A Charter Film production released by M.G.M. *Producer:* John Boulting. *Director:* Roy Boulting. *Screenplay:* Jeffrey Dell and Bernard Miles—*from an original play by* Robert Ardrey. *Director of Photography:* Mutz Greenbaum. *Music:* Hans May. *Art Director:* Duncan Sutherland. *Editor:* Roy Boulting. 112 minutes.

With Michael Redgrave.

CAST

Michael Redgrave . . . . *David Charleston*
Barbara Mullen . . . . *Ellen Kirby*
James Mason . . . . *Streeter*
Lilli Palmer . . . . *Melanie Kurtz*
Finlay Currie . . . . *Captain Joshua*
Frederick Valk . . . . *Dr. Kurtz*
Frederick Cooper . . . . *Briggs*
Sybilla Binder . . . . *Anne-Marie*
Jean Shepeard . . . . *Mrs. Briggs*
Barry Morse . . . . *Robert*
George Carney . . . . *Harry*
Miles Malleson . . . . *Chairman of Directors*
Bryan Herbert . . . . *Planning*
James Pirrie . . . . *New Pilot*
A. E. Matthews . . . . *Mr. Kirby*
Olive Sloane . . . . *Woman Director*
Tommy Duggan⎫
Tony Quinn   ⎭ . . . . . . *Office Clerks*
Harold Anstruther . . . . . . *British Consul*
Alfred Sangster . . . . *Director*

SYNOPSIS

David Charleston, British author and journalist, is disenchanted with what is happening in Europe during the years before the war and, to escape the world of which he despairs, takes up the post of lighthouse keeper at Thunder Rock. Not even the outspoken comments of his friend Streeter can persuade him to take any further interest in the world he has forsworn.

At the lighthouse he attempts to escape from the complexities of modern life by living in a dream world peopled by some of the men and women who were shipwrecked nearly a century before nearby.

With Michael Redgrave (extreme left) and Andreos Malandrinos (next to James, as carabiniere).

MICHAEL
REDGRAVE
BARBARA
MULLEN
in The CHARTER FILM PRODUCTION of
THUNDER ROCK
by Robert Ardrey
and JAMES
MASON
with LILLI
PALMER

Directed and Edited by ROY BOULTING
Produced by JOHN BOULTING
Screen Play by Jeffrey Dell and Bernard Miles
Cert. A.
Distributed by
METRO-GOLDWYN-MAYER PICTURES LTD.

From the construction of the lives of these ghostly companions he draws inspiration and, whilst attempting to reprove them for their lack of faith, finds his own regeneration, once more able to face the real world by means of his own enlightenment.

REVIEWS

'If I thought it wouldn't keep too many people away, I'd call it a work of art. Boldly imaginative in theme and treatment, it has many signs of just those distinctions which have lifted British films so high.'—*Sunday Express*

'*Thunder Rock* is a compromise between stage and screen, with the screen honourably losing.'—*New Statesman*

'A really intelligent film, more moving in parts than anything this country's studios have produced before, and more interesting, technically, than anything since *Citizen Kane*.'—*Manchester Guardian*

'What a stimulus to thought it is . . . this good, brave, outspoken, unfettered picture. I like it very much.'—C. A. Lejeune, *Observer*

THE BELLS GO DOWN

1943

An Ealing Studio production released by United Artists. *Associate Producer:* S. C. Balcon. *Producer:* Michael Balcon. *Director:* Basil Dearden. *Screenplay:* Roger MacDougall—*from the novel by* Stephen Black. *Director of Photography:* Ernest Palmer. *Music:* Roy Douglas. *Art Director:* Michael Relph. *Editor:* Mary Habberfield. 90 minutes.

CAST

Tommy Trinder. . . . . *Tommy Turk*
James Mason . . . . . . *Ted Robbins*
Philip Friend. . . . . . *Bob*
Mervyn Johns . . . . . *Sam*
Billy Hartnell. . . . . . *Brookes*
Finlay Currie. . . . . . *District Officer MacFarlane*
Philippa Hiatt . . . . . *Nan*
Meriel Forbes . . . . . *Susie*
Beatrice Varley . . . . *Ma Turk*
Norman Pierce. . . . . *Pa Robbins*
Muriel George . . . . . *Ma Robbins*
Julien Vedey . . . . . . *Lou Freeman*
Richard George . . . . *P.C. O'Brien*
Victor Weske . . . . . *Peters*
Leslie Harcourt . . . . *Alfie Parrott*
Leslie Brook . . . . . . *June*
Frederick Culley. . . . *Vicar*
Stanley Lothbury . . . *Verger*
Johnnie Schofield . . . *Milkman*

SYNOPSIS

Bob and Nan, a young East London couple, postpone their marriage due to the outbreak of war. Bob joins the Auxiliary Fire Service, attached to the local fire station, under the guidance of Station Officer MacFarlane and Leading Fireman Ted Robbins. Other new recruits include Tommy, a greyhound enthusiast, and Sam, a petty dockside thief.

Although the professionals look down upon the amateurs and try to break their backs with discipline, they all acquit themselves with honours when the Blitz falls on London.

Bob and Nan get married and set up home, only for Bob to watch it burn down while he plays water in the opposite direction on a warehouse; meanwhile Nan has her child in the middle of the road. Tommy

With Philip Friend (left), Muriel George and Norman Pierce.

With (left to right) Tommy Trinder, Philip Friend and Finlay Currie.

dies in a fruitless attempt to save his chief, MacFarlane, and Sam fishes a policeman, who has been trying to catch him, out of the dock basin on the end of a boathook. Later, Bob and Nan decide to christen their child Tommy, after Tommy Turk whom they had both admired and respected.

REVIEWS
'A first-rate picture.'—*Evening Standard*
'A good, honest comedy-melodrama.'—*Kinematograph Weekly*
'A sound and most creditably handled tale.'—*News Chronicle*

James Mason (1974):
This was my only appearance in an Ealing film. Although there was nothing special about this film, except technical ingenuity and Trinder's cheeky personality, I am glad to have worked momentarily in a British movie-making régime that was never bettered. Its stars were Sir Michael Balcon and Sir Alec Guinness.

THE MAN IN GREY

1943

A Gainsborough production released by General Film Distributors. *Producer:* Edward Black. *Director:* Leslie Arliss. *Screenplay:* Margaret Kennedy and Leslie Arliss—*from the novel by* Lady Eleanor Smith. *Director of Photography:* Arthur Crabtree. *Musical Director:* Louis Levy. *Music:* Cedric Mallabey. *Art Director:* Walter Murton. *Costumes:* Elizabeth Haffenden. *Editor:* R. E. Dearing. 116 minutes.

CAST

Margaret Lockwood . . . . *Hesther Shaw*
James Mason . . . . *Marquis of Rohan*
Phyllis Calvert . . . . *Clarissa Rohan*
Stewart Granger . . . . *Peter Rokeby*
Helen Haye . . . . *Lady Rohan*
Raymond Lovell . . . . *Prince Regent*
Nora Swinburne . . . . *Mrs. Fitzherbert*
Martita Hunt . . . . *Miss Patchett*
Jane Gill-Davis . . . . *Lady Marr*
Amy Veness . . . . *Mrs. Armstrong*
Stuart Lindsell . . . . *Lawrence*
Diana King . . . . *Jane Seymour*
Ann Wilton . . . . *Miss Edge*
Celia Lamb . . . . *Louisa*
Lupe Maguire . . . . *Sally*
Beatrice Varley . . . . *Gipsy*
Harry Scott . . . . *Toby*
Drusilla Wills . . . . *Cook*
Gertrude Maesmore Morris . . . *Lady Bessborough*
Hargrave Pawson . . . . *Lord Craven*
James Carson . . . . *Gervaise*
Roy Emmerton . . . . *Gamekeeper*
Babs Valerie . . . . *Molly*
Wally Kingston . . . . *Old Porter*
Glynn Rowland . . . . *Lord Mildmay*
Patrick Curwen . . . . *Doctor*
Lola Hunt . . . . *Nurse*
Mary Naylor . . . . *Blennerhasset*
Ruth Woodman . . . . *Polly*
A. E. Matthews . . . . *Auctioneer*
Kathleen Boutall . . . . *Amelia*

With Margaret Lockwood.

SYNOPSIS

When the home of the Rohans is being sold up, Lady Clarissa Rohan meets a young airman from Jamaica, Rokeby, who tells her that his mother's ancestor was in love with the nineteenth-century Clarissa Rohan; and in flashback we see . . .

Hesther Shaw, left in poverty by her father, is befriended by a rich girl, Clarissa, at their school in Bath. Hesther elopes with a young ensign and Clarissa leaves school to become immersed in a loveless marriage with the wealthy Lord Rohan, a Regency buck, who merely wants an heir. Four years later Clarissa hears that Hesther is an actress and goes to the theatre where she again befriends her by employing her as a governess to her child. Clarissa also finds herself attracted to Rokeby, the young actor playing opposite Hesther.

Hesther and Lord Rohan fall in love and, when she becomes his mistress, Hesther schemes to oust Clarissa from the house by encouraging the romance between Clarissa and Rokeby. When they decide to elope together to Jamaica, where Rokeby can claim his inheritance, Clarissa is persuaded by the Prince Regent to return to Rohan and avoid a scandal. Later, however, Clarissa falls ill and Hesther, furious that her plans have been upset, allows her to catch a cold and die. When Rokeby learns the truth about Hesther he succumbs to an ungovernable rage and thrashes her to death.

Back in the present day, Lady Clarissa Rohan leaves the sale arm in arm with the modern Rokeby, looking forward to a happier life than their ancestors.

REVIEWS

'James Mason, too sentimental an actor for this sort of thing, is in a vile temper throughout and one sympathises. My feelings are expressed by the Clarissa of the film: "I don't think I can bear this. I can't! I really can't!"'—*New Statesman*

'A film that has every chance of interesting you as a good novel. It is never likely to get into a list of the world's ten best films, but provides a remarkably pleasant way of spending an evening.'—C. A. Lejeune, *Observer*

'Good, escapist, colourful melodrama. Novelettish, but nice. James Mason makes the most of the sadistic marquis.'—*Evening Standard*

'*The Man in Grey* is a less painful melodrama than many of its U.S. counterparts.'—*Time* magazine

James Mason (1974):

The great theatre critic James Agate, who was then writing on films, sensibly headed his review BOSH AND TOSH.

THEY MET IN THE DARK

1943

A Marcel Hellman/I.P./Excelsior production released by General Film Distributors. *Producer:* Marcel Hellman. *Director:* Karel Lamac. *Screenplay:* Anatole de Grunwald and Miles Malleson—*based on a scenario by* Basil Bartlett, Victor MacClure and James Seymour *from an original story* The Vanishing Corpse *by* Anthony Gilbert. *Director of Photography:* Otto Heller. *Music:* Ben Frankel. *Art Director:* Norman Arnold. *Editor:* Terence Fisher. 104 minutes.

CAST

James Mason . . . *Commander Heritage*
Joyce Howard. . . *Laura Verity*
Tom Walls . . . . *Christopher Child*
Phyllis Stanley . . *Lily Bernard*
Edward Rigby . . *Mansel*
Ronald Ward . . . *Carter*
David Farrar . . . *Commander Lippinscott*
Karel Stepanek . . *Riccardo*
Betty Warren . . . *Fay*
Walter Crisham . *Charlie*
George Robey. . . *Pawnbroker*
Peggy Dexter . . . *Bobby*
Ronald Chesney . *Max [Mouth Harmonica Player]*
Finlay Currie . . . *Merchant Captain*
Brefni O'Rorke . . *Inspector Burrows*
Jeanne de Casalis *Lady with Dog*
Patricia Medina . *Mary, Manicurist*
Eric Mason . . . . *Benson, Illusionist*
Herbert Lomas . . *Van Driver*
Charles Victor . . *Pub Owner*
Robert Sansom . . *Petty Officer Grant*
Alvar Lidell . . . . *Boothby, Radio Announcer*

SYNOPSIS

Enemy agents plant false orders on Commander Heritage which result in the loss of ships and his dismissal from the Service. Heritage goes at night to a lonely cottage in which he expects to find the girl who may have been used by the enemy to decoy him. Finding the cottage initially empty, he is surprised by Laura Verity, and runs off. Laura, a Canadian who has just arrived to visit her uncles at the cottage, explores upstairs and finds a murdered girl. She fetches the police, only to find that the body has been removed.

The following day at the police station, Laura meets Heritage, who is enquiring about a missing girl, and recognises him as the man she saw in the dark. Although Laura suspects Heritage as the murderer, she tells him that the murdered girl had in her hand a scrap of paper with the words 'Child's Agency' on it. At first separately and then, trusting him, together, they investigate the theatrical concern and become increasingly suspicious of Child and his associates. Eventually they manage to prove that the agency is a cover for a spy network and is responsible for both his dismissal and the murdered girl. The mystery solved, Heritage is reinstated and marries Laura, who joins the Wrens.

REVIEWS

'Fair entertainment with goodish moments.'—*Daily Express*
'A neat spy piece . . . exciting if not particularly original.'—Dilys Powell, *Sunday Times*
'James Mason is sound, and the rest of the cast make the most of an exciting, if familiar adventure story.'—*Evening Standard*
'Some of the individual scenes have character and show observation, but the pattern, as a whole, is derivative and unconvincing. Mr. James Mason does his best as a naval officer.'—*The Times*

James Mason (1974):

The producer was Marcel Hellman, whom no actor or director could forget because he was always on the sound stage breathing down our necks. On the other hand, he was well liked by the crews because he gave them each a share of the profits, a splendid idea. I do not know how many of Marcel's films ran into profits.

CANDLELIGHT IN ALGERIA

1943

A George King production released by British Lion. *Producer and Director:* George King. *Screenplay:* Brock Williams and Katherine Strueby—*from an original story by* Dorothy Hope. *Director of Photography:* Otto Heller. *Musical Director:* Jack Beaver. *Music:* Roy Douglas and James Turner. *Songs: 'It's Love', words and music by* Muriel Watson and Jack Denby; *'Flamme d'Amour', music by* Hans May, *lyric by* Alan Stranks; *all French lyrics by* G. Arbib, *sung by* Christiane de Murin. *Art Director:* Norman Arnold. *Editors:* Terence Fisher and Winifred Cooper. 85 minutes.

With Carla Lehmann.

CAST

James Mason	*Alan Thurston*
Carla Lehmann	*Susan Ann Foster*
Raymond Lovell	*Von Alven*
Enid Stamp-Taylor	*Maritza*
Walter Rilla	*Doktor Muller*
Pamela Stirling	*Yvette*
Lea Seidl	*Senior Sister*
Hella Kurty	*Maid*
Leslie Bradley	*Henri de Lange*
MacDonald Parke	*American*
Michel Morel	*Commissioner of Police*
Albert Whelan	*Kadour*
Meinhart Maur	*Schultz*
Paul Bonifas	*French Owner*
Harold Berens	*Toni*
Richard George	*Matthews*
Bart Norman	*General Mark Clark*
John Slater	*1st American Officer*
Berkeley Schultz	*1st Commando Officer*
Jacques Metadier	*Old French Officer*
Graham Penley	*Pierre*
Richard Mollainas	*French Sergeant*
Cecile Chevreau	*Nun*
Cot d'Ordan	*Hotel Manager*
Paul Sheridan	*1st Plain-clothes Man*

SYNOPSIS

At the time when Eisenhower's deputy, General Mark Clark, and other Allied leaders were to meet on a lonely stretch of the Algerian coast to arrange the North African landings, a piece of film, because it showed the exact position, became highly important to the Germans.

The film, captured from an enemy agent, is cached in a German colony in Algiers and Doktor Muller hopes that a British agent sent to recover it, Alan Thurston, will lead him to it. An American girl, Susan Ann, and a French street girl, Yvette, help Thurston, who finally manages to shoot his way out of the Casbah and warn the Allied officers on the

With Carla Lehmann.

coast, thereby saving the lives of the French patriots who have been instrumental in signalling a British submarine as a prelude to the invasion.

REVIEWS

'A British film which has the slickness, tense pace of many American productions plus a restraint and beauty of its own.'—*Daily Mail*

'Not a particularly good film. . . I didn't believe a word of it.'—*Sunday Express*

'Will neither detract much from nor add much to the English motion-picture tradition for good melodrama. James Mason, a Cambridge edition of a 1935 Clark Gable, acquits himself admirably as a British agent. Carla Lehmann's American slang is all pretty ridiculous.'—*New York Times*

'Goes all out for romance and thrills, and gets them. This is the sort of English film that a few years ago would have been dreadfully second rate; but since then we have learned a lot. The total result is a streamlined affair.'—*New Statesman*

'A thrilling story. James Mason suggests a welterweight Clark Gable.'—*Evening Standard*

James Mason (1974):

This film topped the popularity polls in Bulgaria in one or more of the immediately post-war years. I, who saw the film, find this interesting.

With Carla Lehmann.

FANNY BY GASLIGHT

(U.S. title MAN OF EVIL)

1944

A Gainsborough production released by General Film Distributors. *Producer:* Edward Black. *Director:* Anthony Asquith. *Screenplay:* Doreen Montgomery—*from the novel by* Michael Sadleir. *Director of Photography:* Arthur Crabtree. *Musical Director:* Louis Levy. *Music:* Cedric Mallabey. *Art Director:* John Bryan. *Costumes:* Elizabeth Haffenden. *Editor:* R. E. Dearing. 108 minutes.

CAST

Phyllis Calvert	*Fanny Hopwood*
James Mason	*Lord Manderstoke*
Wilfrid Lawson	*Chunks*
Stewart Granger	*Harry Somerford*
Jean Kent	*Lucy Beckett*
Margaretta Scott	*Alicia*
Nora Swinburne	*Mrs. Hopwood*
Cathleen Nesbitt	*Kate Somerford*
Helen Haye	*Mrs. Somerford*
John Laurie	*William Hopwood*
Stuart Lindsell	*Clive Seymore*
Amy Veness	*Mrs. Heaviside*
Ann Wilton	*Carver*
Guy le Feuvre	*Dr. Lowenthall*
Ann Stephens	*Fanny as a child*
Gloria Sydney	*Lucy as a child*

SYNOPSIS

Fanny, illegitimate daughter of a cabinet minister, Clive Seymore, is brought up in the 1870s by foster parents in a saloon-cum-nightclub atmosphere. When her father is killed in a brawl by Lord Manderstoke, Fanny goes to her real father's house to become a servant, and there learns the facts surrounding her birth. However, when Alicia, Lord Manderstoke's mistress, discovers that her husband is the father of Fanny, she threatens him with a public scandal unless he grants her a comfortable divorce. Faced with ruin, Clive Seymore commits suicide.

Harry Somerford, Seymore's secretary, is in love with Fanny who, not wishing to hinder Harry's career and disapproved of by his sister and mother,

With Stewart Granger.

With Stewart Granger, Phyllis Calvert and Jean Kent.

leaves the house and goes to live in Islington. Harry manages to locate her, however, and they agree on a trial marriage for a year. They set up house and go to Paris for a holiday. Once again the evil presence of Lord Manderstoke falls on Fanny's life and he quarrels with Harry and challenges him to a duel. Manderstoke is killed, and Harry is seriously wounded. Despite Harry's sister, who again tries to break up the lovers, Fanny restores their happiness by her constant bedside vigil and the promise of their coming marriage.

REVIEWS

'A pleasant, carefully made British movie . . . [only] James Mason puts some colour into the part of a Victorian rake. He gives more than a hint of what he could do if real demands were made on his intel-

ligence and talent.'—*News Chronicle*

'The film has been made with a delighted feeling for period. . . . James Mason might well belong to the rough-and-tumble of 19th century night life . . . [but] the characters appear novelettish. *Fanny by Gaslight* is aesthetically correct where it might have been passionate.'—Dilys Powell, *Sunday Times*

'It has all the essentials of roaring Victorian melodrama. Mr. Mason, improving in every rôle, offers a fascinating study in evil. Anthony Asquith's direction has authenticity and style.'—*Daily Telegraph*

'The acting is serviceable without any very great range of emotion. Mr. Mason, as the horrid Lord Manderstoke, comes nearest, perhaps, to a sketch for a life-size figure. The film is hardly likely to excite the *cinemanes*, but it will have its admirers.'—C. A. Lejeune, *Observer*

HOTEL RESERVE

1944

Produced and released by R.K.O.-Radio. *Producer:* Victor Hanbury. *Directors:* Victor Hanbury, Lance Comfort and Max Greene. *Screenplay:* John Davenport—*from the novel* Epitaph for a Spy *by* Eric Ambler. 89 minutes.

With Lucie Mannheim.

With Clare Hamilton.

CAST

James Mason . . . *Peter Vadassy*
Lucie Mannheim . *Madame Suzanne Koche*
Raymond Lovell . *Monsieur Robert Duclos*
Julien Mitchell . . *Monsieur Beghin*
Clare Hamilton . . *Miss Mary Skelton*
Martin Miller . . . *Herr Walter Vogel*
Herbert Lom . . . *Monsieur André Roux*
Frederick Valk . . *Herr Emil Schimler*
Ivor Barnard . . . *The Chemist*
Valentine Dyall . . *Mr. Warren Skelton*
Patricia Medina . *Madame Odette Roux*
David Ward . . . . *Monsieur Henri Asticot*
Hella Kurty . . . . *Frau Hilda Vogel*
Anthony Shaw . . *Major Anthony Clandon-Hartley*
Lawrence Hanray *Police Commissaire*
Patricia Hayes . . *Jacqueline*
Josef Almas . . . . *Albert*
Ernest Ulman . . . *Man in Black*
Mike Johnson . . . *Old Man*
Hugo Schuster . . *Inspector Fournier*
Henry T. Russell . *Gendarme*
John Baker . . . . . *Policeman*

SYNOPSIS

Peter Vadassy, an Austrian refugee, is spending a holiday, along with other guests, at the Hotel Reserve in the South of France. His hobby is photography and, after leaving a film for developing with the local chemist, he is interrogated by the police on charges of espionage. Baffled, Peter declares that he has only been photographing lizards, but the photographs show the new naval fortifications at Toulon. The police accept his explanations but charge him with the task of finding out who had accidentally changed cameras with him at the hotel.

Hoping to qualify for French citizenship, Peter has no alternative other than to comply with the request and sets about, albeit rather clumsily, to find the culprit. He is ridiculed by the other guests, any of whom may be the guilty person, and finds little solace with the police. In the moment he imagines to be his triumph, Peter is re-arrested and the spy escapes. This, however, is exactly what the police

James as the young doctor in *Hotel Reserve*.

desire and they follow the spy to his gang near the docks. A roof-top drama ensues with the spy meeting his death at the hands of Peter.

REVIEWS

'There is neither humour nor suspense . . . Mr. James Mason's sympathetic playing of the hero does all that can be done for the colourless simpleton.'—*The Times*

'A light-hearted affair about a young Austrian medical student played gaily enough by Mr. James Mason.'—*Sunday Times*

'In this adaptation of *Epitaph for a Spy* they have altered the plot without any other purpose, it seems, than to confuse. James Mason is at his worst in this sort of part.'—*News Chronicle*

'The story has been adapted from Eric Ambler's *Epitaph for a Spy* to no great profit.'—*Observer*

James Mason (1974):

Eric Ambler's early heroes were a feckless breed, and I had concluded that if Ambler films were to be made these heroes should be converted into either vulnerable heroines or funny men—like Bob Hope in *The Cat and the Canary*. Otherwise it would be hard for them to retain the audience's sympathy (e.g. Joseph Cotton in *Journey into Fear*). But of course when I was asked to play this Ambler hero in the film version of *Epitaph for a Spy*, through arrogance or despair, I evidently did not apply this ruling to myself. Consequently my Ambler hero was the most feckless and unsympathetic that ever appeared on screen. Belatedly I apologise to Ambler. I note also that, starting with *The Light of Day (Topkapi)* his protagonists have been so fortified with humour, that the playing of them must now be richly rewarding.

A PLACE OF ONE'S OWN

1945

A Gainsborough production released by Eagle-Lion Distributors. *Producer:* R. J. Minney. *Director:* Bernard Knowles. *Screenplay:* Brock Williams—*from the novel by* Osbert Sitwell. *Director of Photography:* Stephen Dade. *Music:* Louis Levy. *Art Director:* John Elphick. *Editor:* Charles Knott. 92 minutes.

CAST

Margaret Lockwood . . . *Annette*
James Mason . . . . *Mr. Smedhurst*
Barbara Mullen . . . . . . *Mrs. Smedhurst*
Dennis Price . . . . *Dr. Selbie*
Helen Haye. . . . . *Mrs. Manning-Tutthorn*
Michael Shepley. . . . . *Major Manning-Tutthorn*
Dulcie Gray . . . . *Sarah*
Moore Marriott . . . . . *George*
O. B. Clarence. . . . . . *Perkins*
Helen Goss. . . . . *Barmaid*
Edie Martin . . . . *Cook*
Gus McNaughten. . . . . *P.C. Hargreaves*

SYNOPSIS

Mr. and Mrs. Smedhurst, a middle-aged couple, retire from their business and buy a fine old country house and engage a charming young companion, Annette, to help them. Her arrival, however, marks the beginning of strange occurrences which centre on Annette, and the reputedly haunted house starts to live up to its reputation. Their neighbours explain that the spirit of a dead girl, who was murdered some forty years previously, still haunts the house. The Smedhursts are still sceptical, even when Annette is suddenly and inexplicably stricken ill and confined to bed. A specialist is called in but can offer no remedy and Annette grows weaker, constantly asking for a Dr. Marsham, a doctor who attended the dead girl. One night, Dr. Marsham arrives and sees Annette, whom he believes is the dead girl. In the morning Annette is cured, but there is no trace of the doctor. When a police inspector informs Mr.

With Dennis Price (left).

With Moore Marriott, Margaret Lockwood and Barbara Mullen.

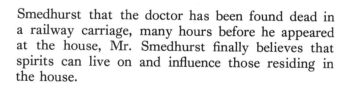

With Dennis Price and Helen Goss.

Smedhurst that the doctor has been found dead in a railway carriage, many hours before he appeared at the house, Mr. Smedhurst finally believes that spirits can live on and influence those residing in the house.

REVIEWS

'I must confess that the situation and its weird solution, even although expected, made my flesh creep and gave me the authentic chill up the spine that every good ghost story should. The dialogue no doubt owes its distinction to its distinguished author (Osbert Sitwell) while the Victorian settings are not only authentic, but charming.'—*Evening Standard*

'*A Place of One's Own* is a fine piece of work . . . a gripping, marvellous, outstanding, eerie, perky, beautiful, lovely, and different film . . .'—C. A. Lejeune, *The Observer*

'James Mason projects his romantic profile into a study of baffled middle-age and very good he is . . . this is a polished period piece, agreeably acted and directed.'—*Sunday Express*

'. . . that unusual thing in the cinema, a ghost story which develops simply and naturally without resort to the violence of melodrama . . . one comes away from the film with an impression of elegance which has not so far been frequent in the British cinema.'—Dilys Powell, *Sunday Times*

'A well-acted, well-told ghost story. James Mason puts up another first-rate performance. An artistic and gripping picture.'—*Daily Mirror*

THEY WERE SISTERS

1945

A Gainsborough production released by General Film Distributors. *Producer:* Harold Huth. *Director:* Arthur Crabtree. *Screenplay:* Roland Pertwee— *from the novel by* Dorothy Whipple. *Director of Photography:* Jack Cox. *Music:* Louis Levy. *Art Director:* David Rawnsley. *Costumes:* Yvonne Caffin. *Editor:* Charles Knott. 115 minutes.

CAST

Phyllis Calvert	*Lucy*
James Mason	*Geoffrey*
Hugh Sinclair	*Terry*
Anne Crawford	*Vera*
Peter Murray Hill	*William*
Dulcie Gray	*Charlotte*
Barrie Livesey	*Brian*
Pamela Kellino	*Margaret*
Ann Stephens	*Judith*
Helen Stephens	*Sarah*
John Gilpin	*Stephen*
Brian Nissen	*John*
David Horne	*Mr. Field*
Brefni O'Rorke	*Coroner*
Roland Pertwee	*Sir Hamish Nair*
Amy Veness	*Mrs. Purley*
Thorley Walters	*Channing*
Joss Ambler	*Blakemore*
Roy Russell	*Lethbridge*
Edie Martin	*Cook*
Dora Sevening	*Janet*
Helen Goss	*Webster*

With Phyllis Calvert.

SYNOPSIS

Three sisters, Lucy, Charlotte and Vera, live at home and lead normal social lives until all three of them marry. The years pass, and while Lucy is still happy with the kindly and sympathetic William although the death of their daughter has left them childless, Vera has grown hard and capricious though still married to the well-intentioned but ill-used Brian. Charlotte, the 'mother' of the three sisters, has married Geoffrey, outwardly a successful businessman but in his private life a sadist, who by refined cruelties is slowly breaking Charlotte's spirit. Lucy tries to save Charlotte by arranging for her to see a psychologist, but Vera, preoccupied with one of her young men, fails to keep the appointment which would have kept Geoffrey at home. He returns, sends the psychologist away and treats his wife so badly that she is forced to run out of the house, throwing herself under a car. At the inquest Lucy gives damn-

With Pamela Kellino.

With Phyllis Calvert.

With Phyllis Calvert.

With Pamela Kellino.

ing evidence against Geoffrey who is left shunned by his friends, while Lucy and William find themselves the guardians of Geoffrey's two children.

REVIEWS

'There is a warm atmosphere of kindliness in the picture of an attempt to show how families live. But it is never real and seems to have been made with all the emotions carefully plotted for the box-office beforehand . . . the hero [is] played by James Mason as though he were suffering from a succession of Victory hangovers.'—*Sunday Express*

'Powerful and emotionally exciting domestic drama. . . . James Mason acts with sinister subtlety.'—*Kinematograph Weekly*

'James Mason gives another very fine performance . . . a tragic story beautifully told.'—*Picture Show*

'The merit of this long and intelligent film lies in the skill with which it establishes the personalities of the sisters . . . the acting throughout has strength and sincerity.'—*The Times*

James Mason (1974):

We could never figure out why the character I played, who in early days had seemed innocuous, though hearty, turned into such a beast in later life. To satisfy me, motivation-wise, I had to tell myself that the sister whom I had married (Dulcie Gray) had a heavy hand in the kitchen, provoking antagonism and dyspepsia.

THE SEVENTH VEIL

1945

A Theatrecraft/Sydney Box/Ortus production released by General Film Distributors. *Producer:* Sydney Box. *Director:* Compton Bennett. *Original Story and Screenplay:* Muriel and Sydney Box. *Director of Photography:* Reginald H. Wyer. *Music:* Ben Frankel. *Art Director:* James Carter. *Editor:* Gordon Hales. 94 minutes.

CAST

James Mason . . . . *Nicholas*
Ann Todd . . . . *Francesca Cunningham*
Herbert Lom . . . . *Dr. Larson*
Hugh McDermott . . . . . . *Peter Gay*
Albert Lieven . . . . *Maxwell Leyden*
Yvonne Owen. . . . . *Susan Brook*
David Horne . . . . *Dr. Kendal*
Manning Whiley . . . . . . *Dr. Irving*
Grace Allardyce . . . . *Nurse*
Ernest Davies. . . . . *Parker*
John Slater . . . . *James*
Arnold Goldsborough⎰
Muir Mathieson ⎱ . . . *Conductors*

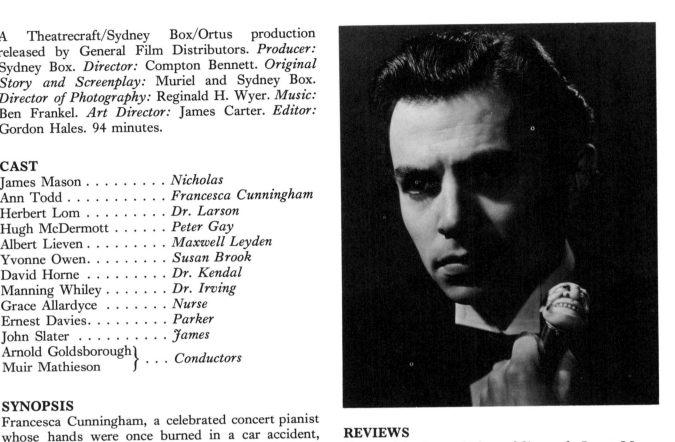

SYNOPSIS

Francesca Cunningham, a celebrated concert pianist whose hands were once burned in a car accident, suffers from acute depression, and attempts suicide by trying to drown herself. She is saved and confined to a sanatorium where Dr. Larson, a psychiatrist, places her under narco-hypnotic treatment.

Step by step she reveals her past life to him. As a child she had been caned on the hands by a brutal headmistress and, consequently, was unable to pass her musical exams the following day. Left as an orphan, she went to live with her guardian, Nicholas, who cultivated her musical talents, but strongly disapproved of her attraction to a popular band-leader, and took her away to Paris where she made a successful début. Back in London she fell in love with a portrait artist, but Nicholas, incensed at the prospect of losing her, stole her lover's car and crashed it with the result that, in the flames, her hands were burned. Learning the true circumstances of her depression, Dr. Larson is successfully able to convince her that her talent and ability have not been lost, and reunites her with the man she really loves—Nicholas.

REVIEWS

'A surprisingly good piece of film craft. James Mason registers another hit as a fascinating brute. A winner all the way.'—*Daily Mirror*

'It seems to be that *The Seventh Veil* belongs to a type of film which the British film industry has never previously achieved. . . . It is an example of the intelligent, medium-priced picture made with great technical polish which has represented for Hollywood the middle path between the vulgar and the highbrow.'—*Spectator*

'Smooth, competent and admirably acted . . . a popular film that does not discard taste and atmosphere; a melodrama that held me for every moment of its running time.'—*Daily Mail*

'I don't think that, in the end, its mixture of analysis and old-fashioned drama comes off. Partly owing to the music, I found *The Seventh Veil*, for three-quarters of the way, enjoyable.'—*New Statesman*

'Mr. Mason suggests a passion for art that is strong and selfless.'—*The Times*

With David Horne and Yvonne Owen.

With Albert Lieven.

With Ann Todd.

James Mason (1974):
This was Sydney Box's and Ann Todd's film. But director Compton Bennett and I also profited from its success. 'Welcome' mats were spread for us in Hollywood.

THE WICKED LADY

1945

A Gainsborough production released by Eagle-Lion Distributors. *Producer:* R. J. Minney. *Director:* Leslie Arliss. *Screenplay:* Leslie Arliss—*from the novel* The Life and Death of the Wicked Lady Skelton *by* Magdalen King-Hall. *Director of Photography:* Jack Cox. *Music:* Louis Levy. *Art Director:* John Bryan. *Editor:* Terence Fisher. 104 minutes.

CAST

Margaret Lockwood	*Barbara Worth, later Lady Skelton*
James Mason	*Captain Jackson*
Patricia Roc	*Caroline*
Griffith Jones	*Sir Ralph Skelton*
Enid Stamp-Taylor	*Henrietta Kingsclere*
Michael Rennie	*Kit Locksby*
Felix Aylmer	*Hogarth*
David Horne	*Martin Worth*
Martita Hunt	*Cousin Agatha*
Amy Dalby	*Aunt Doll*
Beatrice Varley	*Aunt Moll*
Helen Goss	*Mistress Betsy*
Francis Lister	*Lord Kingsclere*
Emrys Jones	*Ned Cotterell*

SYNOPSIS

In the days of Charles II, Sir Ralph Skelton, the local squire, makes arrangements to marry Caroline the girl he has cared for since she was orphaned. Her cousin, Barbara Worth, arrives and Caroline has to stand aside while the more brilliant and cunning Barbara becomes Lady Skelton instead.

Barbara soon finds county life boring and turns to a life of crime for excitement. She becomes a highway robbery expert and has a passionate affair with a fellow highwayman, Captain Jerry Jackson. Robbery leads to murder and eventual discovery of the rôle she is playing by Hogarth, the family retainer, who keeps her secret on condition she reforms.

While Sir Ralph now realises that he really loves Caroline, Kit Locksby, who met and fell in love with Barbara on her wedding day, asks Caroline to marry him. Barbara, however, falls sincerely in love with Kit and determines also to take him away from Caroline. Through Barbara's treachery Jerry Jackson is nearly hanged at Tyburn but cunningly manages to escape. Barbara, however, after committing more crimes in order to achieve happiness, cannot escape the tragedy which ultimately befalls her.

REVIEWS

'Inept to the point of exasperation. James Mason [is] so embarrassed yet so competent that he aroused at once both admiration and sympathy.'—*Tribune*

'The only time the picture comes alive is when Mr. James Mason is on the screen.'—*The Listener*

'An artfully compounded bromide. [The cast] do their turns with the embarrassed gravity and hesitant timing of participants in a family charade.' —*News Chronicle*

'The hoary, the tedious and the disagreeable are married with an infelicity rare even in costume.'— *Sunday Times*

'Mr. James Mason brings a fine swagger of indifference and bravado to the part, and the wonder is that a film with so many exciting ingredients should, in performance, prove so dull.'—*The Times*

'The dialogue is atrocious, and this is frankly not my stoup of romantic wine.'—*Daily Sketch*

'A mixture of hot passion and cold suet pudding. Never misses bathos.—*Manchester Guardian*

With Margaret Lockwood.

ODD MAN OUT

1947

A Carol Reed/Two Cities production released by General Film Distributors. *Producer and Director:* Carol Reed. *Assistant Producer:* Filippo del Giudice. *Screenplay:* F. L. Green and R. C. Sherriff—*from the novel by* F. L. Green. *Director of Photography:* Robert Krasker. *Music:* William Alwyn. *Art Director:* Ralph Brinten. *Décor:* Roger Furse. *Editor:* Fergus McDonell. 116 minutes.

CAST

James Mason . . . . *Johnny McQueen*
Robert Newton . . . . *Lukey*
Robert Beatty . . . . *Dennis*
F. J. McCormick . . . . *Shell*
Fay Compton . . . . *Rosie*
Beryl Measor . . . . *Maudie*
Cyril Cusack . . . . *Pat*
Dan O'Herlihy . . . . *Nolan*
Roy Irving . . . . *Murphy*
Maureen Delany . . . . *Theresa*
Kitty Kirwan . . . . *Granny*
Min Milligan . . . . *Housekeeper*
Joseph Tomelty . . . . *Cabby*
W. G. Fay . . . . *Father Tom*
Arthur Hambling . . . . *Alfie*
Kathleen Ryan . . . . *Kathleen*
Denis O'Dea . . . . *Head Constable*
William Hartnell . . . . *Fencie*
Elwyn Brook Jones . . . . *Tober*
Other parts played by Anne Clery, Maura Milligan, Eddie Byrne, Maureen Cusack.

With Robert Newton.

SYNOPSIS

Johnny, the idealist leader of an illegal political organisation in Northern Ireland, has escaped from prison while serving a sentence for gun-running. Needing funds, he organises a raid on a linen mill. During the raid he is shot and badly wounded. Left by his comrades, who panic, Johnny, from then onwards, is mercilessly pursued by the police throughout the city.

Wounded and bleeding, Johnny is befriended by some and spurned by others. He tries to contact Kathleen, the girl who loves him, but the police are watching. She manages, however, to contact some of his friends and Johnny finds himself being painted by an artist, who sees in him all the pain-crazed emotions he has wanted to portray, and operated upon by a medical student who has never graduated. His one idea is to get to the docks and on to a ship. On the way there he meets Kathleen and realises, for the first time, her great unselfish love for him. The police are quickly closing in and, when Johnny and Kathleen sense the hunt has ended, Kathleen fires a gun to draw an answering volley of bullets which kill them both.

REVIEWS

'Another superb picture for British studios to be proud of. Directed with creative brilliance and dynamic force by Carol Reed, it deals starkly and absorbingly with desperate happenings between tea-time and midnight in the rain and snow of what is obviously Belfast . . . it will be reckoned among the first half dozen films of 1947.'—*Daily Herald*

'The acting is equal in strength to the directing. This is not, however, in spite of Mr. Mason's admirable playing, the kind of film which depends on any one performance. It lives through the efforts of the humblest members of the cast in the tradition of good French films, and the best kind of theatrical repertory.'—*The Times*

'The truth is that Mr. Green's story moves but it never advances. The characters go round-and-round like people on a merry-go-round always ending where they started, with the same side towards the spectator. They are like some obstinate plants; they live but refuse to grow. In five minutes they are firmly established; you know as much about them, and as

little, in two hours. But see it for the fine acting of James Mason and Robert Newton . . . see it for its photography and décor . . . and see it for strong, imaginative direction that needed only a little more material to achieve something of a masterpiece.'—*Daily Telegraph*

'The early reels are exciting and beautiful—purely in movie terms they are the best—yet they fail all but entirely to communicate the revolutionary edge that is so well got in F. L. Green's novel; in that respect, John Ford's *The Informer* was better. The story seems merely to ramify too much, to go on too long, and, at its unluckiest, to go arty. Most unfortunately, the central character, effectively, yet monotonously played by James Mason, is given too little remaining life of his own. Yet, detail by detail *Odd Man Out* is made with great skill and imaginativeness and with a depth of ardour that is very rare in contemporary films.'—James Agee, *The Nation*

'A most intriguing film. And even if you can't perceive its wherefores, you should find it a real experience. As the fugitive, Mr. Mason gives a terrifying picture of a wounded man. But the oblique dramatic construction as the picture draws towards the end, neglects the responsibility of dramatising the movements of his mind.'—*New York Times*

James Mason (1974):
I think this was a great film, perhaps Carol Reed's best; certainly it was mine.

With F. J. McCormick.

THE UPTURNED GLASS

1947

A Triton production released by General Film Distributors. *Producers:* Sydney Box and James Mason. *Director:* Lawrence Huntington. *Screenplay:* Jno P. Monaghan and Pamela Killino—*from an original story by* Jno P. Monaghan. *Director of Photography:* Reginald Wyer. *Music:* Bernard Stevens. *Art Director:* Andrew Mazzei. *Editor:* Alan Osbiston. 86 minutes.

With Pamela Kellino.

With Brefni O'Rorke.

CAST

James Mason	*Michael Joyce*
Rosamund John	*Emma Wright*
Pamela Kellino	*Kate Howard*
Ann Stephens	*Ann Wright*
Henry Oscar	*Coroner*
Morland Graham	*Clay*
Brefni O'Rorke	*Dr. Farrell*
Jane Hylton	*Miss Marsh*
Susan Shaw	*Student*
Richard Afton	*Mate*
Peter Cotes	*Questioner*
Cyril Chamberlain	*Doctor*
Jno P. Monaghan	*Driver*
Maurice Denham	*Policeman*
Beatrice Varley	*Mother*

SYNOPSIS

Michael Joyce, a brilliant Harley Street brain specialist, murders the woman he thinks responsible for the death of the girl he loved. Realising he must dispose of the body, his perfect crime meets with problems, however, for with the body in the back of his car, he runs into fog-bound roads and is stopped by a doctor who asks for a lift to see a child who has suffered a head-fracture as a result of a car accident.

Torn between fear of discovery and his desire to help the child, he helps the doctor, operates on the child and performs a miraculous cure. The doctor notices the body in the back of the car and tells Michael that he is mad. Michael, stunned by this diagnosis which he believes could be true, drives away and throws himself over a cliff.

REVIEWS

'Mr. James Mason is given no opportunity to display his talents.'—*The Times*

'*The Upturned Glass*, with James Mason in the fullest sense of the term a ladykiller, should please practically everybody. As a piece of starry virtuosity, it is bound to enchant the section of the feminine public that would be happy, at any time, to be killed by Mr. Mason. It should satisfy those who know a

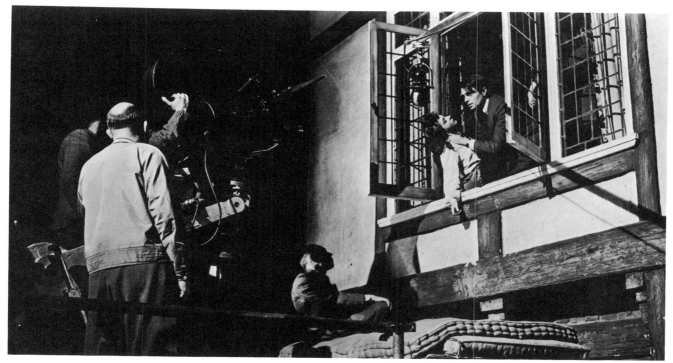

Shooting *The Upturned Glass* with Pamela Kellino.

thoroughly well-made well-acted middleweight entertainment when they see one, and find Mr. Mason's scowl, frown and general air of suffering intelligence always interesting to watch.'—*Daily Mail*

'Loyal admirers of the star (James Mason) will certainly not be disappointed. Moreover, whether or not you are of the Masonic legions, tribute is due to a fine performance of the kind he does best—that of permanent mental turmoil. Miss Kellino misses the full strength of a wicked woman; otherwise the acting is beyond reproach.'—*Daily Herald*

'As smooth-running a piece of its kind as we could wish for.'—*New Statesman*

'An interestingly made, and an unusual, exceedingly well acted film.'—*News Chronicle*

'The film is not always quick enough for a thriller, but it is exciting and unusual.'—*Sunday Graphic*

'It is always a high day for the professional critic . . . when a mind in which he has had confidence justifies itself publicly as a good mind—and *The Upturned Glass* will make the many people who trusted in James Mason's astuteness very happy.'—C. A. Lejeune, *Observer*.

James Mason (1974):

This film was set up by that wily Sydney Box. His sister Betty Box and I were co-producers. I thought we did rather well considering that the thing was a spur of the moment operation designed to take advantage of the freak success of *The Seventh Veil*.

It was an important moment for both of us. She sailed with her tide and became the most sensible and industrious producer in the British industry, and is now one of its few survivors. I consciously missed my tide and set off, but without regrets, to a programme of daft adventure in the United States.

CAUGHT

1949

An Enterprise production released by M.G.M. *Producer:* Wolfgang Reinhardt. *Director:* Max Ophüls. *Screenplay:* Arthur Laurents—*from the novel* Wild Calendar *by* Libbie Block. *Director of Photography:* Lee Garmes. *Music:* Frederich Hollaender. *Editor:* Robert Parrish. 88 minutes.

CAST

James Mason . . . . *Larry Quinada*
Barbara Bel Geddes . . . . *Leonora Ohlrig*
Robert Ryan . . . . *Smith Ohlrig*
Frank Ferguson . . . . *Dr. Hoffman*
Curt Bois . . . . *Franzi*
Ruth Brady . . . . *Maxine*
Natalie Shaefer . . . . *Dorothy Dale*
Art Smith . . . . *Psychiatrist*
Sonia Darrin . . . . *Miss Chambers*
Bernadine Hayes . . . . *Mrs. Rudecki*
Ann Morrison . . . . *Miss Murray*
Wilton Graff . . . . *Gentry*
Jim Hawkins . . . . *Kevin*
Vicki Raw Stiener . . . . *Lorraine*

With Robert Ryan.

SYNOPSIS

Leonora fulfils her ambitions and marries a fabulously wealthy man called Smith Ohlrig, who, she soon realises, has a cruel and vicious nature, and who beats her mercilessly. She leaves him and takes a job as a receptionist to a doctor, Larry Quinada. But her inexperience upsets Larry, and when Ohlrig promises her a new start she returns home—only to find that their intended second honeymoon is to be in the company of her husband's executives, and that she has been duped again.

Larry takes her back as his receptionist (she promises to apply herself to the job more seriously) and their attraction grows for each other. But when Leonora discovers she is pregnant, she decides that the security provided by Ohlrig will, at least, enable her child to get a better start in life, and once again she returns to her husband. Larry and Ohlrig meet and the truth is revealed. Ohlrig admits he has never loved Leonora, but refuses to divorce her unless she gives him custody of the child. Leonora, however, is unwilling to accept these conditions, and has no choice now but to remain married. Ohlrig then has a fatal heart-attack.

Leonora is rushed to hospital shortly afterwards, but her baby, which is premature, dies.

With her ordeal finally over—she and Larry are now able to marry.

REVIEWS

'This is a dull film for anybody. It will be particularly depressing to women who have come to regard an annual vicarious beating from Mr. Mason as essential to a full and happy life.'—*Daily Mail*

'*Caught* is *awful*. It is a turgid, gloomy piece of nonsense.'—*Daily Express*

'At moments a faint suggestion of *Citizen Kane* stirs in the sets of magnificence and megalomania, but it dies away, and little, save conventional melodrama, is left.'—*The Times*

'Somewhere along the way (James) decided he could play the part of a kind and gentle doctor. Of course he can't. Every time he appears with the girl (Barbara Bel Geddes) she steals a scene from him, and every time he appears with the brutal husband (Robert Ryan) he steals one too. In fact, the only time poor James is safe on the screen is when he is

With Barbara Bel Geddes.

by himself. And even then he isn't very interesting. Nevertheless . . . it is quite the best made bad story I ever remember seeing.'—*Daily Herald*
'This little-publicised movie was a financial failure, but I think it is the most interesting and emotionally complex of Ophüls's American pictures.'—Pauline Kael, *Kiss Kiss, Bang Bang*

James Mason (1974):
The film was accorded a 'Sneak Preview' in Pasadena, an area where wealthy people reside. The 'cards' were the greatest the theatre manager had ever seen. The cards referred to, circulated among the audience, contained a brief questionnaire, the answers to which were supposed to show how the big public might be expected to respond at the time of the film's release. Enterprise, the company that made *Caught*, were so delighted by the Pasadena reception that they saw no point in exposing it to further preview adjudications, although the release date was three months ahead. For everyone concerned with the making of the film these were three months of euphoria, a great time for signing contracts with an upping of salaries. Things returned to normal when the film opened in New York. No-one came to see it.

With Barbara Bel Geddes (left).

MADAME BOVARY

1949

An M.G.M. production. *Producer:* Pandro S. Berman. *Director:* Vincente Minnelli. *Screenplay:* Robert Ardrey—*from the novel by* Gustave Flaubert. *Music:* Miklos Rozsa. *Art Director:* Cedric Gibbons. 114 minutes.

CAST

Jennifer Jones . . . . *Emma Bovary*
James Mason . . . . *Gustave Flaubert*
Van Heflin . . . . *Charles Bovary*
Louis Jourdan . . . . *Rodolphe Boulanger*
Christopher Kent . . . . . *Léon Dupuis*
Gene Lockhart . . . . *J. Homais*
Frank Allenby . . . . *Lhereux*
Gladys Cooper . . . . *Mme. Dupuis*
John Abbott . . . . *Mayor Tuvache*
Henry Morgan . . . . *Hyppolite*
George Zucco . . . . *Dubocage*
Ellen Corby . . . . *Félicité*
Eduard Franz . . . . *Roualt*
Henri Letondal . . . . . . *Guillaumin*
Esther Somers . . . . *Mme. Lefrançois*
Frederic Tozere . . . . . . *Pinard*
Paul Cavanagh . . . . *Marquis d'Andervilliers*
Larry Sims . . . . *Justin*
Dawn Kinney . . . . *Berthe*
Vernon Steele . . . . *Priest*

SYNOPSIS

Gustave Flaubert, a novelist, finds himself forced to defend a leading character in a French court of law and proceeds to tell the story of his novel, *Madame Bovary*.

Emma Roualt, endowed with an ardent temperament and great beauty, spends her formative years in a convent and then on her father's poor farm. Her desperately dull life is interrupted by Charles Bovary, who falls in love with Emma and offers her marriage. She accepts, but soon realises her husband's devotion is not enough to satisfy her. She takes a lover, Léon Dupuis, but his mother sends him away and she becomes involved in another affair which, once again, leaves her embittered. By accident she meets Léon again and renews their affair, but, with her creditors pressing for money, she can take no more, and commits suicide.

REVIEWS

'This adaptation of Flaubert's classic emerges from its manhandling in better shape than one might expect. . . . Our own James Mason is seen little, but booms throughout in a totally unnecessary running commentary. The film inspires no emotional reaction whatsoever, and is considerably too long. But I found it sufficiently easy on the eye and ear to atone for the posterior cramp I endured.'—*Evening Standard*

'Mr. James Mason, who, for most of the time, has to be content to be a disembodied voice, appears at the beginning and the end as Flaubert himself defending his novel from the charges brought against it. If the judges had seen this film instead of reading the book, they would certainly have wondered what all the fuss was about.'—*The Times*

'Entertaining, though Flaubert might not recognise himself or his characters. . . . James Mason a flatulent Flaubert.'—*Sunday Express*

'A creditable attempt.'—*Daily Mail*

'Nonsense, nonsense. The acting comes under the general heading of arch, and the decoration gets almost hysterically "period".'—*Daily Herald*

'Put the book out of your mind, and the film is well worth while . . . James Mason makes a brief appearance as Flaubert [and] performs this unnecessary chore with earnest sincerity.'—*Daily Express*

James Mason (1974):
Having detested this film on its first release, I nevertheless watched quite a lot of it when it came our way recently on TV. The role of Flaubert was indeed lazily and unimaginatively played but the flatulence escaped me.

THE RECKLESS MOMENT

1949

A Columbia production. *Producer:* Walter Wanger. *Director:* Max Ophüls. *Screenplay:* Henry Garson and R. W. Soderborg—*from the novel* The Blank Wall *by* Elizabeth Sanxay Holding. *Director of Photography:* Burnett Guffey. *Music:* Morris Stoloff. *Art Director:* Gary Odell. *Editor:* Gene Havlick. 82 minutes.

CAST

James Mason . . . . *Martin Donnelly*
Joan Bennett . . . . *Lucia Harper*
Geraldine Brooks . . . . *Beatrice Harper*
Henry O'Neill . . . . *Mr. Harper*
Sheppard Strudwick . . . . *Ted Darby*
David Blair . . . . *David Harper*
Roy Roberts . . . . *Nagle*
Frances Williams . . . . *Sybil*

With Joan Bennett.

SYNOPSIS

Attractive Lucia Harper warns her pretty 17-year-old daughter, Beatrice to have nothing more to do with Ted Darby, a handsome scoundrel. However, Beatrice sees him again in the Harper boathouse, and, in a scuffle, Ted falls to his death after having been hit by Beatrice with a flashlight. Lucia discovers the body and hides it in the marshes. Martin Donnelly, confederate of an unscrupulous thug called Nagle, appears to blackmail Lucia for some foolish letters her daughter wrote to the dead man. Lucia can only obtain a portion of the money she is supposed to raise for the letters, but Martin assures her she will only have to pay half the amount as he will not accept his share. Lucia tells Donnelly the true story of Darby's death when another man is apprehended for the crime. She goes home only to have Nagle confront her with the demand for money. Donnelly arrives and the two men struggle until Donnelly kills Nagle, but is desperately wounded himself. Donnelly crashes his car and, just before he dies, tells the police that he killed both Darby and Nagle. Lucia is now free of the nightmare that has been haunting her.

REVIEWS

'Mr. Mason takes ably enough the few chances that come his way, but the film belongs to Miss Joan Bennett; her performance matches the intelligence of Max Ophüls's direction.'—*The Times*

'There wasn't a moment, not even a reckless moment, when I wasn't enthralled. I think this is a really first-class film. Max Ophüls's direction is splendid.'—*Evening Standard*

'A thoroughly fresh treatment of a thoroughly average piece of melodramatic cake. The film wins your surrender by swift, sure narrative and solidly pleasurable detail. James Mason brings to a tough part a sympathy and quality which should not go unacknowledged.'—*News Chronicle.*

'Comes near to being outstandingly good. James Mason is given his first distinguished rôle since he went to the States.'—*Manchester Guardian*

With Joan Bennett.

'There are times when James Mason is hardly recognisable . . . gone is all that smouldering sex . . . the passion [Mason] displays is pale pink and utterly unconvincing. A dreary, sluggish film that's best forgotten.'—*News of the World*

'The reckless moments are many. I had one when I went to see the film.'— *Daily Worker*.

James Mason (1974):

The occasion of another dramatic preview. But this time *sans* euphoria. There was a limited number of theatres in the environs of Los Angeles where film producers might preview 'unmarried' prints (picture and sound track not yet cohabiting the same strip of film). The theatre on this occasion was some place much less respectable than Pasadena. Let's say Redondo.

The film broke down at about the halfway point. The audience, already incompletely gripped, now faced a hiatus of ten minutes while the projectionists stuck the film together again. They entertained themselves with an exchange of loud and critical witticisms, When the lights again dimmed and the film re-emerged on the screen, the sound-track no longer synchronised with our lip movements. (It was 'out of sync'.) Cue for further witticisms and a further hiatus. The second half of the film when it re-captured sync failed to recapture a depleted audience. Ophüls, the director, and Walter Wanger, the producer, were both present and doubtless the experience shortened their lives.

EAST SIDE, WEST SIDE

1949

An M.G.M. production. *Producer:* Voldemar Vetluguin. *Director:* Mervyn LeRoy. *Screenplay:* Isobel Lennart—*from the novel by* Marcia Davenport. *Director of Photography:* Charles Rosher. *Music:* Miklos Rozsa. *Art Directors:* Cedric Gibbons and Randall Duell. *Editor:* Harold F. Kress. 108 minutes.

With Ava Gardner.

CAST

Barbara Stanwyck	*Jessie Bourne*
James Mason	*Brandon Bourne*
Van Heflin	*Mark Dwyer*
Ava Gardner	*Isabel Lorrison*
Cyd Charisse	*Rosa Senta*
Nancy Davis	*Helen Lee*
Gale Sondergaard	*Nora Kernan*
William Conrad	*Lt. Jacobi*
Raymond Greenleaf	*Horace Elcott Howland*
Douglas Kennedy	*Alec Dawning*
Beverly Michaels	*Felice Backett*
William Frawley	*Bill the Bartender*
Lisa Golm	*Josephine*
Tom Powers	*Owen Lee*

SYNOPSIS

When Isabel Lorrison returns to New York, the oft-patched-up marriage of wealthy socialite Brandon Bourne and his wife Jessie takes another setback. Brandon is involved in a brawl with one of her admirers, and only the help of a model, Rosa, saves him from complete public disgrace. Jessie goes to thank Rosa and learns that Mark Dwyer, a former policeman whom Jessie has admired since childhood, is returning home, now a war hero, and will be the guest of honour at a party that night. Although the Bournes are both invited, Brandon fails to come home and Jessie goes alone. Mark and Jessie find themselves attracted to each other. In the morning Brandon begs forgiveness and offers to take her on holiday.

Before they go, Isabel contrives to induce Jessie to divorce her husband, but her threats prove fruitless. Then, when Brandon fails to catch the train and Jessie phones Isabel's apartment, Brandon answers and tells her that Isabel has been murdered. Mark steps in to solve the murder and manages to prove that Brandon was not the murderer. Once again Brandon seeks Jessie's forgiveness, but she now realises her love for him is dead.

With Cyd Charisse.

With Cyd Charisse.

REVIEWS

'Soap suds . . . the square of the triangle equals zero.'
—*Evening Standard*

'The language spoken by James Mason in his latest effort isn't especially foreign, but might as well be since he has taken to speaking his lines in a new kind of voice—as if muffled in fold after fold of felting.'—C. A. Lejeune, *Observer*.

'The dialogue is that odd mixture of sentimentality, pretentiousness and wit that always goes down well on the American stage and screen.'—*Daily Telegraph*

'A glossy, reasonable piece of entertainment.'—*Sunday Pictorial*

James Mason (1974):

Lejeune observed correctly that my voice sounded muffled in the films of this era. I think that this was partly because subconsciously I did not want my presence to be detected; partly because I may have been trying out a mid-Atlantic accent. Soon after these disasters I righted myself, at least in this respect. That is, I saw clearly that in each film I must aim specifically at the accent of the character I was playing, English, American or whatever.

ONE WAY STREET

1950

A Universal-International production released by General Film Distributors. *Producer:* Leonard Goldstein. *Associate Producer:* Sam Goldwyn Jr. *Director:* Hugo Fregonese. *Original Screenplay:* Lawrence Kimble. *Director of Photography:* Maury Gertsman. *Music:* Frank Skinner. *Art Director:* Bernard Herzbrun and Al Ybarra. *Editor:* Milton Carruth. 79 minutes.

CAST

James Mason	*Doc Matson*
Marta Toren	*Laura*
Dan Duryea	*Wheeler*
William Conrad	*Ollie*
King Donovan	*Grieder*
Jack Elam	*Arnie*
Tito Renaldo	*Hank Torres*
Basil Ruysdael	*Father Moreno*
Rodolpho Acosta	*Francisco Morales*
Margarito Luna	*Antonio Morales*
George Lewis	*Captain Rodriguez*
Robert Espinoza	*Santiago*
Emma Roldan	*Catalina*
Jose Dominguez	*Blas*
Julia Montoya	*Juanita*
Marguerite Martin	*Frasca*

SYNOPSIS

Doc Matson, a disillusioned man and bullet-removing expert, has become involved with a criminal gang comprising the wounded boss, Wheeler, and his henchmen, Ollie and Grieder. When another member, Arnie, brings in the stolen money for a share out, Matson tells them that he has given Wheeler a deadly poison and, unless they allow him to leave with the money and Wheeler's girlfriend Laura, he will not telephone the name of the antidote.

Matson and Laura escape to Mexico where he wants comfort and respectability—but not Laura, whom he took from Wheeler as an act of vanity. Laura loves Matson, however, and when their small plane is forced down near a village, Matson accepts the situation and they settle down to a tranquil life. Encouraged by the local priest, Matson builds a makeshift hospital. But when an incident is reported in the national newspapers, Matson, fearing that Wheeler (who in fact had only been given an aspirin) will try and seek revenge, decides to return the money and contacts the gang. At the meeting place, Ollie, suspecting a double-cross, shoots Wheeler—and Matson shoots Ollie in self-defence. As Matson leaves the building to join Laura on the other side of the street, he slips in front of a car and is killed.

REVIEWS

'An arid, pointless little film, not worth the bother of making.'—*Daily Mail*

'Mr. Mason brings to the part the casual, off-hand manner it demands; but there are times when the one-way street seems inordinately long.'—*The Times*

'It is said that James Mason chooses his own parts; and if this is true I have to report that he is a glutton for punishment.'—*Daily Herald*

'James Mason, whose acting range now seems confined to giving passable imitations of a somnabulist, appears in *One Way Street*—a haywire crime piece.' —*News Chronicle*

'The film starts promisingly, then tails into one of the dullest most stupid films of the year.'—*Sunday Pictorial*

'Hugo Fregonese (the director) gives freshness and distinction to the story—and in many respects this is the best job Mason has done in America.'—*Evening News*

James Mason (1974):

I never encountered anyone who saw this film, other than studio personnel. It must have been a left-over project from some previous régime, for you'd think that Universal would no longer have afforded the floor space for this sort of pretentious melodrama, having recently struck a rich seam of box-office gold which included Donald O'Connor and that talking donkey, Pa and Ma Kettle and acres of 'Tits and Sand'. Not to mention Abbott and Costello.

With Marta Toren.

With Marta Toren.

PANDORA AND THE FLYING DUTCHMAN

1951

A Dorkay/Romulus production released by Independent Film Distributors. *Producer, Director and Writer:* Albert Lewin. *Director of Photography:* Jack Cardiff. *Music:* Alan Rawsthorne. *Art Director:* John Bryan. *Editor:* Ralph Kemplen. Technicolor. 122 minutes.

CAST

James Mason . . . . *Hendrick van der Zee*
Ava Gardner . . . . *Pandora Reynolds*
Nigel Patrick . . . . *Stephen Cameron*
Sheila Sim . . . . *Janet Fielding*
Harold Warrender . . . . . *Geoffrey Fielding*
Mario Cabre . . . . *Juan Montalvo*
John Laurie . . . . *Angus*
Pamela Kellino . . . . *Jenny Ford*
Patricia Raine . . . . *Peggy Ford*
Margarita d'Alvarez . . . . . *Señora Montalvo*
Marius Goring . . . . *Reggie Demarest*
La Pillina . . . . *Spanish Dancer*
Abraham Sofaer . . . . *Judge*
Francisco Igual . . . . *Vincente*
Guillermo Beltran . . . . . *Barman*
Lila Moinar . . . . *Geoffrey's Housekeeper*
Phoebe Hodgson . . . . . . *Dressmaker*
John Carew . . . . *Priest*
Edward Leslie . . . . *Doctor*
Christina Forbes . . . . . . *Nurse*

SYNOPSIS

Pandora Reynolds, a beautiful American girl, joins a colony of wealthy people living on the coast of Spain. She is comparatively unmoved when a young playboy commits suicide because of her, and although unable to return the love of any man, she impulsively agrees to marry a young racing driver, Stephen Cameron. Their engagement is announced, but Pandora is distracted by a yacht moored outside the harbour. She swims out and introduces herself to the owner, a mysterious and troubled Dutchman, Hendrick van der Zee, and, to her surprise, finds herself falling in love.

Hendrick, however, is the Flying Dutchman, a man condemned to roam the seas, but allowed to live the life of a human for six months every seven years. If, however, he can win the love of a girl who is willing to die for him, his sins will be expiated.

Hendrick realises that Pandora is just such a girl, but discourages the romance by feigning indifference. She, however, is infatuated with him and neglects her fiancé, while a former lover, a bull-fighter named Juan, tries to recapture her attentions by staging a brilliant and dangerous bullfight. Stephen, to demonstrate *his* courage, attempts to break a land speed record on the sand, but crashes the car. He is unhurt and later, at a party, is unaware that Pandora and Hendrick have slipped away. Juan now realises that his rival is not Stephen but Hendrick, and stabs the Dutchman. But Hendrick cannot be killed.

Events, though, take their pre-determined course, and Pandora and the Flying Dutchman find themselves united forever in a suicide pact.

REVIEWS

'Mason gets very little help from Miss Ava Gardner whose acting consists of a succession of star poses, or from a script of incredible pretentiousness which every now and again sets Mr. Mason reciting what Miss Gardner insists on calling a "pome" . . . a verdict that it would do for the general public and would make the sophisticated laugh would probably not be far from the mark.'—*The Times*

With Ava Gardner.

'The eye is more than satisfied . . . but . . . beauty by itself doesn't make an entertaining film, and there is little doubt that this one, though it has a hundred qualifications, drags abominably. Mr. Mason's silences are nearly infinite . . . it's all very beautiful but a sad disappointment.'—*Evening Standard*

'Conspicuous in its confident assumption of scholarship and in its utter poverty of taste and imagination. James Mason correctly interprets a man who obviously needs a rest after being chivvied about the world for two or three centuries.'—C. A. Lejeune, *Observer*

'Not a complete success . . . one admires the intensity of Mr. Mason's acting, but one is not moved.'—*Daily Telegraph*

James Mason (1974):
Only two features of this film now stand up when, these many years later, it unwinds itself for late night televiewers: the superb cinematography of Jack Cardiff, and the resultant embellishment of Ava Gardner's great natural beauty.

ROMMEL—DESERT FOX

(U.S. title THE DESERT FOX)

1951

A 20th Century-Fox production and release. *Producer:* Nunnally Johnson. *Director:* Henry Hathaway. *Screenplay:* Nunnally Johnson—*from the biography* Rommel *by* Desmond Young. *Director of Photography:* Norbert Brodine. *Music:* Daniele Amfitheatrof. *Art Directors:* Lyle Wheeler and Maurice Ransford. *Special Effects:* Fred Sersen. *Editor:* James B. Clark. 89 minutes.

CAST

James Mason . . . . *Rommel*
Cedric Hardwicke. . *Dr. Karl Strolin*
Jessica Tandy . . . . *Frau Rommel*
Luther Adler . . . . . *Hitler*
Everett Sloane. . . . *General Burgdorf*
Leo G. Carroll. . . . *Field Marshal von Rundstedt*
George Macready . . *General Fritz Bayerlein*
Richard Boone. . . . *Aldinger*
Eduard Franz . . . . *Colonel von Strauffenberg*
Himself . . . . *Desmond Young*
William Reynolds. . *Manfred Rommel*
Charles Evans . . . . *General Shultz*
Walter Kingsford . . *Admiral Ruge*
John Hoyt . . . . . . *Keitel*
Don de Leo . . . . . *General Maisel*
Robert Coote. . . . . *British Medical Officer*
Richard Elmore . . . *Rommel's Driver—Africa*
John Vosper . . . . . *Major Walker*
Sean McClory . . . . *Jock*
Dan O'Herlihy. . . . *Commando Captain*
Scott Forbes . . . . . *Commando Colonel*
Victor Wood . . . . . *British Doctor*
Lester Matthews . . *British Officer*
Mary Carroll . . . . . *Maid*
Paul Cavanagh. . . . *Colonel von Hafaker*
Lumsden Hare. . . . *Doctor*
Jack Baston . . . . . *Jodl*
John Goldsworthy . *Stulpnagel*
Carleton Young . . . *German Major*
Freeman Lusk . . . . *German Surgeon*

SYNOPSIS

Field Marshal Rommel, the Desert Fox, is commander of the crack Afrika Korps whose brilliant tactics have earned him the respect of both friend and foe, even though he is hampered by the lack of promised supplies from Hitler. When the tide is turning at El Alamein, Rommel disobeys the Fuehrer's orders and pulls his men out of the battle. Still suffering from jaundice, Rommel returns to Germany to be hospitalised and mentions his loss of confidence in Hitler to his friend, Dr. Strolin.

Rommel recovers his strength and makes a tour of the Atlantic defences, which are disappointing, and, as Hitler has assumed total command of the defence of Europe against the expected invasion in the spring, he visits his wife, Lucie Maria, and their son, Manfred. Later, when Strolin sounds him out anew on his attitude towards Hitler, Rommel is emotionally torn between his oath of loyalty to his country and his own better judgement.

With the invasion now in progress, Rommel learns that three members of an anti-Hitler plot have been caught. He is now committed to the conspiracy to kill Hitler but is wounded by British bombers while driving his car. The plot is carried through, but Hitler miraculously escapes and in the ensuing interrogation of suspects, the name of Rommel is mentioned. Rommel's position is now critical, and when a delegation from Hitler informs him that he should remedy the situation himself, to save his wife and son from any possible recriminations, he commits suicide by shooting himself.

REVIEWS

'This film does as much to revive the discredited legend of an efficient, wise and above all gentlemanly military caste as if it had been made by the Propaganda Department of the Wehrmacht itself . . . for all Mr. Mason's chest-puffing and under-lip biting, Rommel resolutely remains a very dull fellow.'—*Evening Standard*

'This is not really a war picture. It is an outline of a dramatic feud, stretched on a warlike canvas.'—*Evening News*

'The romantic legend that Rommel was the British Army's favourite general grows with the years . . . [and] . . . with 20th Century-Fox's version of that biography, the whole silly fiction is carried to its final absurdity. James Mason, with a military haircut

With Leo G. Carroll.

and a competent starring performance, supplies the final touch of glamour.'—*Daily Mail*

'James Mason plays the part of our most famous enemy. He does it stolidly, coldly, and with dignity.' —*Daily Herald*

'Brilliantly made, fiendishly well-acted, tremendously exciting, but there were moments when I wanted to stand up and throw hand grenades at the screen. It made me *that* angry.'—*Daily Express*

James Mason (1974):

I am often asked where this film was shot. The real battle scenes were extracted from David MacDonald's documentary *Desert Victory* which Twentieth Century had bought for this specific purpose. And the rest of it was shot at Borrego Springs in the Californian Desert. To my chagrin the best sequence in the film preceded the credit titles and showed the unsuccessful commando raid on Rommel's headquarters, in which Rommel himself did not show. I do not know where they made this sequence.

Referring back to the matter of accents brought up in my comment on *East Side, West Side,* it was clear in *Rommel—Desert Fox* that German accents would be out of place, since the entire cast consisted of British and American actors pretending to be Germans. A year and a half later *The Desert Rats* was made, a riposte to *Rommel—Desert Fox*, also about the African campaign in World War II. This time the characters were supposed, with one exception, to be British and spoke with their local accents, be they Welsh or Australian. The exception was myself in a brief reappearance in the part of Rommel, a circumstance which explains the rather crummy German accent which I felt obliged to affect.

FIVE FINGERS

1952

A 20th Century-Fox production and release. *Producer:* Otto Lang. *Director:* Joseph L. Mankiewicz. *Screenplay:* Michael Wilson—*from the book* Operation Cicero *by* L. C. Moyzisch. *Director of Photography:* Norbert Brodine. *Music:* Bernard Herrmann. *Art Directors:* Lyle Wheeler and George W. Davis. *Special Effects:* Fred Sersen. *Editor:* James B. Clark. 108 minutes.

CAST

James Mason . . . . *'Cicero'—Ulysses Diello*
Danielle Darrieux . . . . . *Countess Anna*
Michael Rennie . . . . . . *George Travers*
Walter Hampden . . . . . *Sir Frederic*
Oscar Karlweis . . . . . . *Moyzisch*
Herbert Berghorf . . . . . *Col. von Richter*
John Wengraf . . . . *Von Papen*
A. Ben Astar . . . . *Siebert*
Roger Plowden . . . . . . *MacFadden*
Michael Pate . . . . *Morrison*
Ivan Triesault . . . . *Steuben*
Hannelore Axman . . . . . *Von Papen's Secretary*
David Wolfe . . . . *Da Costa*
Larry Dobkin . . . . *Santos*
Nestor Paiva . . . . *Turkish Ambassador*
Antonio Filauri . . . . . . *Italian Ambassador*
Richard Loo . . . . *Japanese Ambassador*

SYNOPSIS

Cicero, valet to the British Ambassador in Ankara, Sir Frederic, offers to sell top-secret information to the Germans. The deal is agreed and Cicero contacts a former employer, Countess Anna, to offer her a life of ease and wealth if she will look after his money and rent a house for his 'business'. She agrees, but refuses any romantic involvement with him.

While the various authorities are concerned over security Cicero builds up a considerable sum with the Countess. Sir Frederic requests Whitehall to send an agent, and even though George Travers arrives and questions everybody, Cicero continues selling information unperturbed. Eventually Travers discovers, by breaking the German codes, that the leak is from the British Embassy, and questions Cicero, telling him that the Countess has left for Switzerland that morning. Realising his money has gone as well, Cicero steals further documents and letters, including the invasion plans—'Operation Overlord'—and boards a train for Istanbul.

In the train Cicero, 'protected' by German agents who want to kill him after they have the plans, and Travers who wants him alive, reads a letter from Anna to Sir Frederic denouncing him as a spy. Meanwhile, the German Embassy receives a letter from Anna stating that Cicero is a British plant. With the price for the 'Overlord' plans raised to £100,000, Cicero manages to escape both the British and Germans and flees to Rio de Janeiro.

While dining in comfort in Rio, Cicero's banker arrives and informs him that a Countess has been arrested in Switzerland with a large sum of money, and that his banknotes are forgeries. Altogether, Cicero had sold the Germans thirty-five top secrets, but they had never acted on any of them!

With Danielle Darrieux.

With Oscar Karlweis.

REVIEWS

'. . . a smoothly turned comedy which, in its cynical zest, reminds one of the vintage Lubitsch pictures during the thirties. James Mason plays the Albanian valet improbably but entertainingly as a Satanic Jeeves whose valeting seems to have been studied at Winchester or Balliol.'—*Daily Mail*

'. . . that *Five Fingers* is not a conventional cloak-and-dagger thriller is due to a silken performance by James Mason. All in all I think you will enjoy it.'—*Evening Standard*

'The film is an exciting and accurate account of how a shabby little embassy servant bamboozled the British Secret Service, and pulled off the smartest espionage coup of all time.'—*Daily Express*

'James Mason did very well in *The Desert Fox*, but he is even better in *Five Fingers*, one of the best spy films ever made. A pulse-raising thriller.'—*Daily Mirror*

'Highly entertaining, thanks to a polished script, Joseph Mankiewicz's direction and fine acting all round.'—*Daily Telegraph*

'An absorbing and wonderfully entertaining film that is helped a great deal by a shrewd, witty and talented performance by James Mason.'—*Daily Sketch*

'James Mason gives a firm, suave, delightfully amusing performance, in every way excellent according to the demands of the script.'—*Evening News*

James Mason (1974):

Even though Michael Wilson may have been accorded sole screenplay credit, valuable refinements and jokes were added by Director Mankiewicz. I have not seen the film recently, but I used firmly to hold the view that of sensible spy films, as opposed to the ritualistic or nonsensical, *Five Fingers* was the best.

101

LADY POSSESSED

1952

A Portland Pictures production released by Republic. *Producer:* James Mason. *Directors:* William Spier and Roy Kellino. *Screenplay:* Pamela Kellino and James Mason—*from the novel* Del Palma *by* Pamela Kellino. *Director of Photography:* Karl Struss. *Music:* Nathan Scott. *Art Director:* Frank Arrigo. *Editor:* Arthur Roberts. 86 minutes.

CAST

James Mason . . . . *Del Palma*
June Havoc. . . . . *Jean Wilson*
Stephen Dunne . . . . *Tom Wilson*
Fay Compton . . . . *Madame Brune*
Pamela Kellino. . . . . *Sybil*
Steven Geray. . . . . *Dr. Stepanek*
Diana Graves . . . . *The Medium*
Odette Myrtil . . . . *Mrs. Burrows*

SYNOPSIS

Del Palma, a popular pianist, takes his critically ill wife Madeleine from a nursing home against the doctor's orders, and she dies. The scene is overheard by another patient, Jean Wilson, and recorded in her subconscious mind. Tom Wilson, her husband, rents a country house for her convalescence, which turns out to belong to Del Palma. Jean finds Del Palma's clothes, painting and pets and, unhinged by her illness, begins imagining that she is destined to take the place of Del Palma's dead wife.

Tom fails to understand his wife who, encouraged by her frivolous friend Sybil, makes a play for Del Palma who, in turn, responds to her understanding of his situation. He invites Jean to go with him on a trip to the Continent, but before they can leave, Tom has a showdown with him. Del Palma now realises that Jean is insanely obsessed and brutally rejects her. She tries to commit suicide by throwing herself

under a train. But Tom rescues her and promises that her sanity will return now that she has managed to rid herself of her infatuation for Del Palma.

REVIEWS

'A bleak little drama of neuroses. This dreary and meaningless twaddle is based, we are candidly told, upon a novel entitled *Del Palma* by Pamela Kellino. Since Miss Kellino and Mr. Mason take credit for writing the script, the much celebrated couple have only themselves to blame.'—*New York Times*

'Another unfortunate venture . . . clumsily tackled . . . and remains on an absurd and novelettish level. James Mason is bad but fascinating.'—*Monthly Film Bulletin*

'Sordid and unpleasant. Mason sings three tunes in a hoarse croon. [His] vocalising is as unpleasant as the rest of the film.'—*Variety*

'Weird, utterly fantastic melodrama.'—*New York Daily News*

James Mason (1974):

In trying to find something good to say about this misadventure, I can think only of the old Bedford Theatre which at that time was still in working order and served as the background for certain sequences. A little jewel of a theatre with the most romantic associations. My next visit took place many years later when I took the audience for a tour of inspection in *The London Nobody Knows*. The bulldozers, surprisingly, had not yet been set on her; and there the poor thing stood, uncared for and deprived of her finery, melancholy and somewhat unstable.

With June Havoc.

THE PRISONER OF ZENDA

1952

An M.G.M. production. *Producer:* Pandro S. Berman. *Director:* Richard Thorpe. *Screenplay:* John L. Balderston and Noel Langley—*adaptation by* Conrad Salinger *from the novel by* Anthony Hope. *Director of Photography:* Joseph Ruttenberg. *Music:* Alfred Newman. *Art Directors:* Cedric Gibbons and Hans Peters. *Editor:* George Boemler. Technicolor. 100 minutes.

CAST

Stewart Granger . . . . . *Rudolph Rassendyll, King Rudolph V*
Deborah Kerr . . . . *Princess Flavia*
Louis Calhern . . . . . . *Colonel Zapt*
Jane Greer . . . . *Antoinette de Mauban*
Lewis Stone . . . . *The Cardinal*
Robert Douglas . . . . . *Michael, Duke of Streslau*
Robert Coote . . . . . . *Fritz von Tarlenheim*
Peter Brocco . . . . *Johann*
Francis Pierlot . . . . . *Josef*
James Mason . . . . . . *Rupert of Hentzau*

SYNOPSIS

Rudolph Rassendyll, an Englishman on holiday in Ruritania, is entertained by the King on the eve of his coronation. The King's half-brother Michael, who covets both the throne and the woman who is going to share it, Princess Flavia, arranges with his unscrupulous henchman, Rupert of Hentzau, for the King to be drugged, and so prevent his appearance at the forthcoming ceremonies.

When the King is found comatose, his loyal followers persuade Rudolph, whose looks are similar to the King's, to impersonate him. At the palace ball after the coronation, Rudolph finds himself deeply drawn to Princess Flavia, and, when the real King is kidnapped, Rudolph continues his masquerade.

When the King is found to be held captive at Michael's castle, Rudolph prepares to swim the moat and release him. Inside the castle, however, a jealous fight develops between Rupert and Michael and the latter is killed. Rudolph appears and begins fighting with Rupert until Rudolph eventually manages to lower the drawbridge for the rescue party, leaving Rupert to escape by diving into the moat. With the King safe and Rudolph about to return to England, Flavia is tempted to go with him. But, born with the responsibilities of being Queen, she decides to stay and forsake her love for Rudolph.

REVIEWS

'This new technicolour version is by far the best I have seen. The dialogue is civilised, the story moves fast and plausibly enough to command a suspension of disbelief, the sets and costumes are gorgeous.'— *Daily Telegraph*

'A likeable adventure. James Mason is a quietly effective villain.'—*People*

'James Mason may be miscast, but I don't think he is bad. The splendours of the court are made up of just so many extras and yards of this and that.'—Dilys Powell, *Sunday Times*

'Mr. Mason looks suitably sinister wearing an innocent shade of baby blue and the sneeriest sneer in the Balkans.'—*Star*

James Mason (1974):

I thought the costumes were ghastly.

With Robert Douglas.

With Stewart Granger and fencing instructor Jean Heremans.

With Stewart Granger.

With Stewart Granger.

FACE TO FACE

(THE SECRET SHARER episode)

1952

A Huntington Hartford production released by R.K.O. *Producer:* Huntington Hartford. *Director:* John Brahm. *Screenplay:* Aeneas MacKenzie—*from the story by* Joseph Conrad. *Director of Photography:* Karl Struss. *Music:* Hugo Friedhofer. *Art Director:* Edward Ilou. *Editor:* Otto Meyer. Second episode entitled *The Bride Comes to Yellow Sky.* 90 minutes (complete film).

CAST

James Mason . . . . *The Captain*
Michael Pate . . . . *The Swimmer*
Gene Lockhart . . . . *Captain Archbold*
Albert Sharpe . . . . *1st Mate*
Sean McClory . . . . *2nd Mate*
Alec Harford . . . . *Ship's Cook*

With Gene Lockhart.

SYNOPSIS

Out of the fog that hangs over an Oriental port, a Swimmer draws close to the rope ladder dangling from an anchored ship and pulls himself aboard. The Captain, who has observed this, questions the Swimmer and learns that he is a fugitive from a killing on another ship anchored nearby. The Swimmer confesses he was responsible, but with extraordinarily extenuating circumstances. The Captain's sympathies go out to the man, and thereafter he tries to prevent him from being sacrificed to what he believes is an unjust and too-literal application of the law.

REVIEWS

'Mixed with the measured Conrad pace is suspense and extremely able acting.'—*Variety*

'*The Secret Sharer*, in spite of a good performance by James Mason, never comes at all to life . . . the ship settings are artificial, the adaptation is action-less and dialogue-ridden . . . direction slack and uninventive. As a whole *Face to Face* cannot be considered more than a worthy but uninspired effort.'—*Monthly Film Bulletin*

'The two co-features are separate, but fail to stand firmly on their own feet . . . too much talk . . . the stories become laboured. Literary audiences may possibly find the experiments interesting.'—*Kinematograph Weekly*

James Mason (1974):

On the plus side, the film introduced me to John Brahm, who had brought with him, on immigration to the U.S.A., a lovable personality and the best traditions of European theatre (notably the Burgtheater of Vienna). In Hollywood his most successful period had been that in which his fine hand for melodrama had applied itself to *The Lodger, Hangover Square*, etc., at Twentieth Century.

CHARADE

1953

A Portland production released by Monarch. Three episodes entitled *Portrait of a Murderer, Duel at Dawn* and *The Midas Touch. Producer:* James Mason. *Director:* Roy Kellino. *Original Screenplay:* James Mason and Pamela Mason. 83 minutes.

CAST

James Mason	*The Murderer*
	Major Linden
	Jonah Watson
Pamela Mason	*The Artist, Pamela*
	Baroness Tanslan
	Lilly
Scott Forbes	*Captain Stamm*
Paul Cavanagh	*Col. Heisler*
Bruce Lester	*Capt. van Buren*
John Dodsworth	*Lt. Meyerdorf*
Judy Osborne	*Dotty*
Sean McClory	*Jack Stuydevant*
Vince Barnett	*Berg*

With Pamela Mason.

SYNOPSES

Portrait of a Murderer

When Pamela, an attractive but disillusioned young Englishwoman living in a cheap Paris studio, sketches the face of a man she has seen leaving the flat next door, she is unaware that he has, in fact, murdered her girlfriend. He returns to the scene of the crime, however, and Pamela falls under his spell. But as he is a pathological case, he strangles her before anything can develop between them.

Duel at Dawn

An officer of the Austrian army in the 1880s, Major Linden, wins the hand of a beautiful woman, the Baroness Tanslan, from another admirer, Capt. Stamm. The jealous lover forces Linden to agree to a duel, the conditions of which favour Stamm. Linden, however, manages to turn the tables on Stamm but the Baroness, believing Linden has been killed, is only just prevented from committing suicide.

The Midas Touch

Jonah Watson, a likeable, lucky and shrewd fellow, makes a small fortune in New York but, after an argument with a theatrical producer, decides to sail for England and start life over again, this time without money. He takes a position as a valet and falls in love with a servant, Lilly, a cockney girl. In order to please her and to make a better life for them both, he returns to New York and, true to his never-failing good fortune, becomes successfully involved in business deals.

REVIEWS

'An intriguing if somewhat amateur piece.'—*Star*

'Is it good? I don't think so. Too much Masonary for me.'—*Daily Sketch*

'I only hope the Masons had as much fun in making the film as I had in watching it. . . . will evoke gales of laughter wherever it is played.'—*News of the World*

James Mason (1974):

I had hoped that this curiosity would be lost without trace.

With Pamela Mason.

With Pamela Mason and Bruce Lester.

THE MAN BETWEEN

1953

A London Films/B.L.P.A./Carol Reed production released by British Lion. *Producer and Director:* Carol Reed. *Associate Producer:* Hugh Perceval *Screenplay:* Harry Kurnitz—*from the novel* Susanne in Berlin *by* Walter Ebert. *Director of Photography:* Desmond Dickinson. *Music:* John Addison. *Art Director:* André Andrejew. *Editor:* A. S. Bates. 101 minutes.

CAST

James Mason . . . . *Ivo Kern*
Claire Bloom . . . . *Susanne Mallison*
Hildergarde Neff . . . . *Bettina*
Geoffrey Toone . . . . *Martin*
Aribert Waescher . . . . *Halendar*
Ernst Schroeder . . . . *Kastner*
Dieter Krause . . . . *Horst*
Hilde Sissak . . . . *Lizzi*
Karl John . . . . *Inspector Kleiber*

SYNOPSIS

Susanne Mallison arrives in post-War Berlin to stay with her brother Martin, a British Army doctor, and his German wife Bettina. She quickly becomes aware, however, of mysteries and tension which surround her sister-in-law, who is followed by a boy cyclist and threatened on the 'phone by Germans. On a sightseeing tour of the Eastern sector, Bettina nervously introduces Susanne to Ivo Kern, a former lawyer now engaged in black-market activities and enticing the inhabitants of West Berlin wanted by the Eastern authorities over to their side.

Against Bettina's wishes, Susanne goes skating with Ivo and invites him home for a meal. When Susanne tells Bettina, she learns that Bettina is married to Ivo, whom she thought dead but was now black-mailing her to help capture Kastner, a man wanted by the East. Martin informs the police, who set a trap for Ivo, but the boy cyclist foils the plot by warning him.

One day Susanne is mistaken for Bettina and kid-napped to the East. Ivo, though, is touched by Susanne's faith that there is something good in his character, and helps her to escape. In so doing, he realises he is in love with her. They are chased through the city in the back of a laundry van but, just as the escape seems certain, Ivo, to save Susanne, leaps from the van and is shot by the police as the vehicle speeds across the border.

REVIEWS

'This is a cold-hearted film about people with cold feet, and hardly once in its long journey, does the warmth of sentiment, the heat of passion or the torrid temperature of real excitement melt its frigid atmosphere. Before I saw *The Man Between* I looked forward to the partnership of Bloom and Mason. I regret to report that they do not light any fires. As a romantic screen pair they are a frost.'—*Daily Express*

With Hildegarde Neff.

'A drama of intrigue, violence, and on the girl's part romantic first love, is played out against the ruins and tenements of the city with all the style and atmosphere that a brilliant director can give it. The acting is, for the most part, very fine.'—*Daily Telegraph*

'Miss Bloom and Mr. Mason are so shatteringly, ecstatically good that I certainly believed in everything that they said.'—*Evening Standard*

'Skilled as a piece of film-making, yet how empty! The script never really gets going—nor do the characters, except perhaps Mr. Mason's kidnapper.' —*New Statesman*

'Mason turns in one of his most careful performances.'—*Time* magazine

'A brilliant blend of performance and intrigue . . . Mason performs with conviction [and] polish.'— *Daily Mirror*

James Mason (1974):

This film became very big on television in the U.S. In the cinema one demands of a thriller that the narrative thread be ever taut. The American televiewer makes no such demands since continuity is destined to be shattered by commercial interruption. Thus it often happens that what has been hitherto regarded as a failure in the cinemas will be a hit on the Late Late Show. And vice versa.

With Claire Bloom.

THE STORY OF THREE LOVES

1953

An M.G.M. production. *Producer:* Sidney Franklin. *Directors of Photography:* Charles Rosher and Harold Rosson. *Choreography:* Frederick Ashton. *Music:* Miklos Rozsa. *Art Directors:* Cedric Gibbons, Preston Ames, Edward Carfagno and Gabriel Scognamillo. *Editor:* Ralph E. Winters. Technicolor. 122 minutes.

The Jealous Lover
Director: Gottfried Reinhardt. *Screenplay:* John Collier.

Mademoiselle
Director: Vincente Minnelli. *Screenplay:* Jan Lustig and George Froeschel—*from an original story by* Arnold Phillips.

Equilibrium
Director: Gottfried Reinhardt: *Screenplay:* John Collier—*from an original story by* Ladislav Vajda and Jacques Maret.

CAST
The Jealous Lover
James Mason . . . . *Charles Coutray*
Moira Shearer . . . . *Paula Woodward*
Agnes Moorehead. . . . . *Aunt Lydia*

Mademoiselle
Ethel Barrymore. . . . . *Mrs. Pennicott*
Leslie Caron . . . . *Mademoiselle*
Farley Granger . . . . *Tommy*
Ricky Nelson. . . . . *Tommy (12 years)*
Zsa Zsa Gabor . . . . *Girl at Bar*

Equilibrium
Pier Angeli . . . . *Nina*
Kirk Douglas. . . . . *Pierre Narval*
Richard Anderson . . . . *Marcel*

SYNOPSES
The Jealous Lover
Among the passengers on board a liner crossing the Atlantic is a brilliant ballet impresario, Charles Coutray. Two young men ask him why he has presented only one performance of his ballet *Astarte* and their question prompts him to remember the night Paula Woodward inspired it. Finding her dancing alone in his theatre, he had become totally moved by her creation. But when she refused to continue, he wrongly assumed it was because of a jealous lover. Nevertheless, he insisted that she return to his studio to dance for him so that he could capture her movements on a sketch pad. It was the last time she was to dance, for, having ignored her doctor's advice never to dance again, she left Coutray's studio later that night, and died.
After her death Coutray staged the ballet just once more—to allow her to see it from a world beyond. *Astarte* was her dance of death.

Mademoiselle
Another of the ship's passengers is Mademoiselle, a studious French governess travelling with a bored little rich boy called Tommy. Through the magic power of a Mrs. Pennicott, Tommy is transformed for a few hours into a handsome young man who spends an idyllic evening with Mademoiselle. The magic spell over, Tommy returns to his former self, while the governess meets another attractive young man. This time, however, he is real.

Equilibrium
Looking out across the seas is yet another passenger —Pierre, a former trapeze artist who once gave up a brilliant career after believing himself to be responsible for the death of his female partner. After the

With Moira Shearer.

tragedy, however, he met Nina, a quiet, disillusioned young woman whom he rescued from committing suicide, and whom he trained as his new partner. But now that they are finally ready to audition and perform a dangerous new stunt, he realises he has fallen in love with Nina and decides to give up the business entirely, preferring to concentrate on their new-found love for each other rather than on the dangerous world of the circus.

REVIEWS
'A trilogy of stories which succeeds in proving that Hollywood love is too often mushy.'—*Sunday Express*

'Up to the elbows in soap-suds.'—*Evening Standard*

'James Mason plays the impresario very well. A colourful feast of romance.'—*Daily Mirror*

'Mr. Mason contributes one of his familiar studies of ill-mannered brusqueness—but that does not matter. The story, for what it is worth, is Miss [Moira] Shearer's.'—*The Times*

'All tastes are served in this beautiful picture.'—*Star*

With Moira Shearer.

113

THE DESERT RATS

1953

A 20th Century-Fox production and release. *Producer:* Robert L. Jacks. *Director:* Robert Wise. *Screenplay:* Richard Murphy. *Director of Photography:* Lucien Ballard. *Music:* Leigh Harline. *Art Directors:* Lyle Wheeler and Addison Hehr. *Special Effects:* Ray Kellogg. *Editor:* Barbara McLean. 88 minutes.

CAST

Richard Burton	*Captain MacRoberts*
James Mason	*Rommel*
Robert Newton	*Bartlett*
Robert Douglas	*General*
Torin Thatcher	*Barney*
Chips Rafferty	*Smith*
Charles Tingwell	*Lieutenant Carstairs*
Charles Davis	*Pete*
Ben Wright	*Mick*
James Lilburn	*Communications Man*
John O'Malley	*Riley*
Ray Harden	*Hugh*
John Alderson	*Corporal*
Richard Peel	*Rusty*
Michael Pate	*Captain Currie*
Frank Pulaski	*Major O'Rourke*
Charles Keane	*Sergeant Donaldson*
Pat O'Moore	*Jim*
Trevor Constable	*Ginger*
Albert Taylor	*Jensen*
John Wengraf	*German Doctor*
Arno Frey	*Kramm*
Alfred Ziesler	*Von Helmholtz*
Charles Fitzsimons	*Fire Officer*

SYNOPSIS

Tobruk, 1941. An English Captain MacRoberts is appointed to serve with the 9th Australian Division, and is given charge of a newly arrived detachment of inexperienced troops. His discipline antagonises the men, but in the ranks he finds an old friend, Bartlett, an alcoholic ex-schoolteacher and self-confessed coward. During the Afrika Korps' first attack on the defences of Tobruk, MacRoberts foresees Rommel's strategy and sets a trap. MacRoberts is promoted to Lieut.-Col. and leads the Australians on night commando raids behind enemy lines.

Following one such raid, MacRoberts is captured and taken to a field hospital where he meets Rommel, himself wounded, and they discuss 'this little hell-hole, Tobruk'. Finally MacRoberts escapes back to his lines and hears that the British relief force is reported to be advancing. He leads an attack on the Germans occupying a hill and digs in. There is, however, no further news of the relief forces and, when they prepare to repel another attack themselves, MacRoberts orders his men to retreat. To his surprise, his troops refuse to leave their posts and the German tanks have begun to retreat. With the sound of bagpipes leading the relief forces, the siege of Tobruk is over.

REVIEWS

'In detail the film is terribly wrong, in sentiment tolerably right.'—*Daily Herald*

'*The Desert Rats* is well done, with exciting passages during a raid behind the enemy lines and a finely confident performance by Richard Burton . . . James Mason once again suavely plays The Desert Fox.'—*Sunday Times*

'History into Hokum.'—*Evening Standard*

'Good entertainment.'—*Evening News*

'Nearly, but not quite a successful film, *The Desert Rats* does, nevertheless, leave to posterity a working record of Australian and British gallantry.'—*Spectator*

'Well done, with exciting passages.'—Dilys Powell, *Sunday Times*

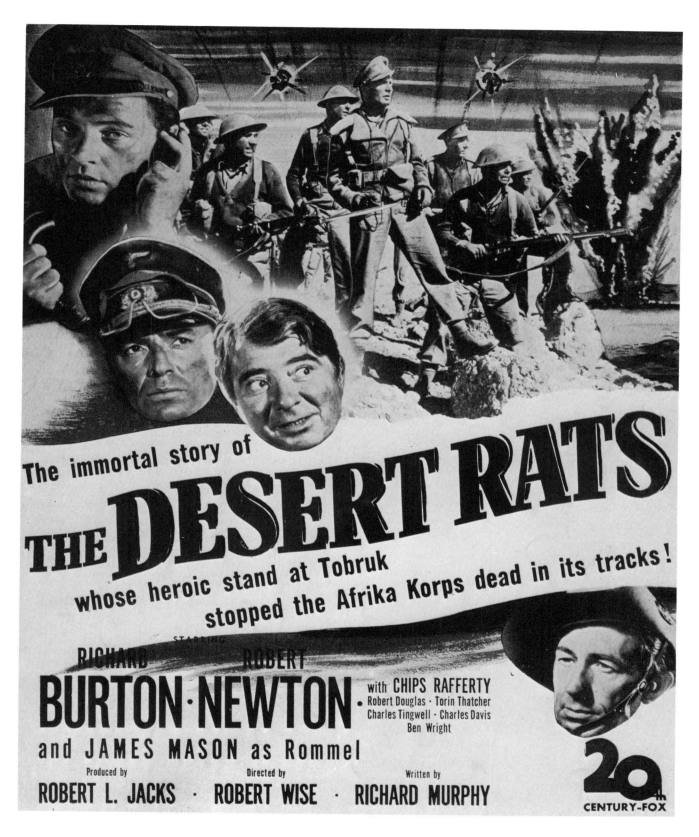

The immortal story of **THE DESERT RATS** whose heroic stand at Tobruk stopped the Afrika Korps dead in its tracks!

STARRING

RICHARD **BURTON** · ROBERT **NEWTON**

with CHIPS RAFFERTY
Robert Douglas · Torin Thatcher
Charles Tingwell · Charles Davis
Ben Wright

and JAMES MASON as Rommel

Produced by
ROBERT L. JACKS · Directed by ROBERT WISE · Written by RICHARD MURPHY

20th CENTURY-FOX

'A first rate war film that does Britain proud. I have only one complaint. This film is so good it should have been British.'—*Daily Mirror*

'James Mason presents, in miniature, another of his endearing impersonations of Rommel.'—*Manchester Guardian*

JULIUS CAESAR

1953

An M.G.M. production. *Producer:* John Houseman. *Directed and adapted by* Joseph L. Mankiewicz— *from the play by* William Shakespeare. *Director of Photography:* Joseph Ruttenberg. *Music:* Miklos Rozsa. *Art Directors:* Cedric Gibbons and Edward Carfagno. *Editor:* John Dunning. 121 minutes.

CAST

James Mason . . . . *Brutus*
Marlon Brando . . . . *Mark Antony*
Louis Calhern . . . . *Julius Caesar*
John Gielgud. . . . . *Cassius*
Edmond O'Brien . . . . *Casca*
Greer Garson . . . . *Calpurnia*
Deborah Kerr . . . . *Portia*
George Macready . . . . *Marullus*
Michael Pate . . . . *Flavius*
Richard Hale. . . . . *Soothsayer*
Alan Napier . . . . *Cicero*
William Cottrell. . . . . *Cinna*
John Hardy. . . . . *Lucius*
John Hoyt . . . . *Decius Brutus*
Tom Powers . . . . *Metellus Cimber*
Jack Raine . . . . *Trebonius*
Ian Wolfe. . . . . *Ligarius*
Lumsden Hare. . . . . *Publius*
Morgan Farley. . . . . *Artemidorus*
Victor Perry . . . . *Popilius Lena*
Douglas Watson. . . . . *Octavius Caesar*
Douglas Dumbrille . . . . *Lepidus*
Rhys Williams. . . . . *Lucilius*
Michael Ansara . . . . *Pindarus*
Dayton Lummis. . . . . *Messala*
John Lupton . . . . *Varro*
Preston Hanson . . . . *Claudius*
John Parrish . . . . *Titinius*
Joe Waring . . . . *Clitus*
Stephen Roberts. . . . . *Dardanius*
Thomas Browne Henry . . . . *Volumnius*
Edmund Purdom . . . . *Strato*

SYNOPSIS

Julius Caesar has become the virtual dictator of Rome in 44 B.C, Cassius, the leader of a group of conspirators who wish to see him destroyed, enlists

With Deborah Kerr.

the aid of a highly respected figure, Brutus, who admires Caesar as a friend but regards his ambitions as a threat to Rome. Brutus joins the conspiracy and, in his garden, meets the other members who agree to assassinate Caesar on the Ides of March.

Calpurnia, Caesar's wife, awakens to an ill-omened dream of the assassination and begs her husband not to go to the Senate. Caesar refuses this advice, however, and goes to the Senate where he is stabbed to death, first by Casca, then by the others and finally Brutus. When Brutus explains his actions to the citizens of Rome, they are ready to hail him as successor. But Mark Anthony also addresses the crowd and turns them against Brutus by stressing, out of loyalty to his friendship with Caesar, the good deeds of the late Emperor.

With Caesar's nephew and heir, Octavius, Mark Antony pursues the escaped plotters who have mustered their forces in Asia Minor. The two armies clash and the conspirators are routed. Cassius realises there is no escape and orders his slave to kill him, and Brutus throws himself upon his sword. Mark Antony then eulogises his vanquished foe, calling him the noblest Roman of them all, for, while the others had murdered Caesar out of envy and greed, Brutus sincerely believed he was acting for the good of Rome.

REVIEWS

'It is maddening to be forced to admit it, but it has been left to Hollywood to make the finest film version of Shakespeare yet to be seen on our screens. . . . James Mason is a highly intelligent rather than a noble Brutus. He is at his best in the famous quarrel scene with Cassius. At other times he tends to a certain verbal monotony. Nevertheless it is a fine and stern performance.'—*News Chronicle*

With John Gielgud.

'It has taken Hollywood all these years to discover that *Julius Caesar* is one of the most exciting gangster stories ever to be conceived by the wit of man and that Shakespeare was not only the first, but the best script writer that ever lived. . . . Oddly enough the defects lie in too many characters speaking Shakespeare like Shakespeare. Astonishingly, James Mason is one of the worst offenders, despite the undoubted dignity which he gives to Brutus.'—*Evening Standard*

'*Julius Caesar* is not only the best Shakespeare Hollywood has ever done. That would be a thorny bouquet. It is also the best theatre that the Americans have ever sent to Britain. . . . The film's biggest flop is James Mason. He tries so hard to be the noblest Roman of them all, he sometimes forgets the sordid business of acting. Only in the Forum scene does he really open his mouth with effect.'—*Sunday Express*

'A breath-taking film. James Mason gives sincerity and attraction (if not quite enough sense of deep-felt vacillation) to his part of Brutus. Maybe Shakespeare on film can be done better than this. It has not been done better so far.'—*Daily Express*

'Socko Shakespeare, seven stars, boffo B.O.'—*Variety*

'James Mason gives an intense brooding performance that effectively combines the poetic and the prosaic.'—*Time* magazine

'James Mason gives the least impressive of the major performances.'—*Manchester Guardian*

'A great picture. Mr. Mason's Brutus is as finely done [as Gielgud's Cassius and Marlon Brando's Mark Antony].'—*Sunday Chronicle*

'James Mason's Brutus is the performance of a man who has played Shakespeare in the theatre; the voice is well-modulated, the lines finely thought; the character is not imposed on the player, but created by him. I have long thought that Mr. Mason was a far more accomplished actor than he has been allowed to appear in the cinema, and this sympathetic Brutus is the proof.'—Dilys Powell, *Sunday Times*

James Mason (1974):

My vote was with the anti-Masons. It seemed to me that the only faultless performance was that of Eddie O'Brien as Casca.

With Edmund Purdom.

BOTANY BAY

1953

A John Farrow/Paramount production released by Paramount. *Producer:* Joseph Sistrom. *Director:* John Farrow. *Screenplay:* Jonathan Latimer—*from the novel by* Charles Nordhoff and James Norman Hall. *Director of Photography:* John F. Seitz. *Music:* Franz Waxman. *Art Directors:* Hal Pereira and Joseph McMillan Johnson. *Editor:* Alma Macrorie. Technicolor. 94 minutes.

CAST

Alan Ladd	*Hugh Tallant*
James Mason	*Captain Paul Gilbert*
Patricia Medina	*Sally Monroe*
Cedric Hardwicke	*Governor Phillip*
Murray Matheson	*Rev. Mortimer Thynne*
Malcolm Lee Beggs	*Nick Sabb*
Noel Drayton	*Spencer*
Jonathan Harris	*Tom Oakley*
Dorothy Patten	*Mrs. Garth*
John Hardy	*Nat Garth*

SYNOPSIS

Among the prisoners of a convict ship heading for Botany Bay in 1787 is Hugh Tallant, an American medical student unjustly convicted as a highwayman. His repeated efforts to escape arouse the violent hostility of the brutal Captain Gilbert, and the two men become rivals for the only attractive woman aboard, Sally Monroe.

On their arrival, the humanitarian Governor, Phillip, sympathises with Tallant but is unable to help him secure his release. Gilbert tricks Tallant into a last attempt to escape, planning to have him arrested and condemned to death afterwards. An attack by aborigines, however, kills Captain Gilbert, and Tallant's services during an outbreak of the plague earn him a welcome pardon, leaving him free to settle down with Sally.

James in danger of his life in *Botany Bay*.

120

With Patricia Medina.

REVIEWS

'For boys and ghouls.'—*Evening Standard*

'This adventure tale is utter balderdash.'—*Daily Herald*

'Mason is a pale shadow of Charles Laughton, while Alan Ladd is definitely no Clark Gable.'—*Daily Express*

'James Mason makes a fetching younger version of Captain Bligh.'—*Time* magazine

'A grim, completely humourless affair.'—*Daily Graphic*

'Not a pleasure cruise, but by gosh! it grips.'—*Daily Mirror*

'A sadly feeble film, though Mr. James Mason gives a good performance.'—*Spectator*

'Mason gives a considerable impression of natural evil in a performance that is almost a tour de force . . . [but] it is a poorly written film.'—*News Chronicle*

James Mason (1974):

Having been fascinated by the Alan Ladd phenomenon, I now had the opportunity to study it at close quarters. It turned out that he had the exquisite coordination and rhythm of an athlete, which made it a pleasure to watch him when he was being at all physical. Paramount, to whom he was under contract, had selected his rôles shrewdly and had taken pains to disguise the fact that he was rather short. When Farrow offered me a part in this film I first extorted a promise that I would not be made to take my shoes off, or walk in a trench, when working with Ladd, for this, I had been told, was obligatory when tall or tallish actors were juxtaposed with Ladd. Farrow told me not to worry; this film, he said, was to be the last which Ladd's contract with Paramount called for and thus the company would now be less insistent about the preservation of his image.

THE CHILD

1954

A Monarch Film Corporation production. *Producer:* Roy Kellino. *Director:* James Mason. *Screenplay:* Inigo Jones. 30 minutes.

CAST

Portland Mason . . . . *Sally*
Pamela Mason . . . . *Janet*
Sean McClory. . . . . *Reverend Smith*
Judy Osborne . . . . *Mrs. Starr*

SYNOPSIS

In 1908 Janet, a lonely middle-aged spinster, reluctantly bids farewell to a young relative, a schoolboy, who has spent a brief holiday with her.

Janet, who is the author of children's adventure stories, longs for the company of children, and one day is surprised to see a little girl playing in her garden. The child is hungry and inadequately clothed, and Janet takes her into the house, determined to keep her. The next day police enquire throughout the neighbourhood and call at Janet's house. She conceals the fact that she is hiding the child. Later, the local parson calls and tells Janet that Mrs. Starr, a widow and the mother of the missing Sally, is not only heart-broken but a very sick woman.

Janet visits Mrs. Starr and is so overcome by the woman's anguish and her own sense of guilt that she later takes Sally to the police station. Returning home full of grief, she prays for resolution and courage to face a bleak and lonely future. The neighbours, who have learnt the truth, become hostile towards her. It is then that Mrs. Starr calls, but in place of expected anger her attitude towards Janet is one of pity and forgiveness. She explains that she has to go away to a sanatorium and asks Janet to take care of the child. Naturally, Janet is overjoyed.

REVIEWS

'A pleasant little short.'—*Daily Express*
'Portland Mason has an engaging manner, a dreadful American accent and a remarkable paucity of dialogue considering her reputation for precocity.'—*Evening News*
'The picture is rather silly, but I was grateful for Portland.'—*Daily Sketch*
'Portland Mason is quite a charmer . . . the picture is fine.'—*Star*

With Portland.

Pamela and Portland Mason.

'A nice little film . . . as harmless as a cup of lukewarm milk.'—*Manchester Guardian*
'Fortunately it is very short.'—*Sunday Chronicle*

PRINCE VALIANT

1954

A 20th Century-Fox production and release. *Producer:* Robert L. Jacks. *Director:* Henry Hathaway. *Screenplay:* Dudley Nichols—*from King Features Syndicate's* Prince Valiant *by* Harold Foster. *Director of Photography:* Lucien Ballard. *Music:* Franz Waxman. *Art Directors:* Lyle Wheeler and Mark-Lee Kirk. *Costumes:* Charles le Maire. *Editor:* Robert Simpson. CinemaScope. Technicolor. 100 minutes.

CAST

James Mason	*Sir Brack*
Janet Leigh	*Aleta*
Robert Wagner	*Prince Valiant*
Debra Paget	*Ilene*
Sterling Hayden	*Sir Gawain*
Victor McLaglen	*Boltar*
Donald Crisp	*King Aguar*
Brian Aherne	*King Arthur*
Barry Jones	*King Luke*
Mary Philips	*Queen*
Howard Wendell	*Morgan Todd*
Tom Conway	*Sir Kay*
Sammy Ogg	*Small Page*
Neville Brand	*Viking Warrior Chief*
Ben Wright	*Seneschal*
Jarma Lewis	*Queen Guinevere*
Robert Adler	*Sir Brack's Man-at-arms*
Ray Spiker	*Gorlock*
Primo Carnera	*Sligon*
Basil Ruysdael	*Old Viking*
Fortune Gordon	*Strangler*
Percival Vivian	*Doctor*
Don Megowan	*Sir Launcelot*
Richard Webb	*Sir Galahad*
John Dierkes	*Sir Tristram*
Carleton Young	*Herald*
Otto Waldis	*Patch Eye*
John Davidson	*Patriarch*
Lloyd Aherne Jr.	*Prince Valiant, age 12*
Lou Nova	*Captain of the Guards*
Hal Baylor Mickey Simpson	*Prison Guards*
Eugene Roth	*Viking*

James as Sir Brack.

SYNOPSIS

Prince Valiant, son of the exiled King Aguar of Scandia, is sent to Camelot to seek King Arthur's help to overthrow the usurper Sligon. On the way, he narrowly escapes a mysterious Black Knight whom he overhears plotting to deliver Aguar and his family to Sligon in return for aid in overthrowing King Arthur. As a reward for this information, King Arthur allows Valiant to become a squire to Sir Gawain, although another Knight of the Round Table, Sir Brack, asks for his services.

Later, Prince Valiant receives a summons for help from his father but, in answering the quest, finds himself ambushed by the Black Knight whom he discovers is Sir Brack. Together with Princess Aleta,

With Robert Wagner.

who is in love with Valiant, he is taken to Scandia where Sligon throws him into a dungeon with his parents. He manages to escape, however, and with the aid of the faithful Boltar and other loyal Vikings, Valiant succeeds in burning down the castle and killing Sligon. He returns to Camelot and challenges Sir Brack to a duel. After a close-fought contest, Sir Brack is defeated and King Arthur rewards Prince Valiant by knighting him.

REVIEWS

'*Prince Valiant* is a sumptuous but naive costume adventure . . . anachronistic, foolish, nonsensical, but fun.'—*Daily Express*

'James Mason as the traitor knight alone has dignity. He also seems to have his tongue in his cheek.'—*Sunday Express*

'James Mason plays the Black Knight with misplaced determination in this undeniably energetic farrago.' —*Spectator*

'. . . a preposterous film? Of course—but what a show-piece for CinemaScope with its pageantry and wonder of stereophonic sound . . . the only player rash enough to make himself conspicuous is James Mason . . . he tries hard to create a personality but I doubt if the laudable effort was worthwhile.'—C. A. Lejeune, *Observer*

'. . . splendidly photographed and costumed . . . deliciously comic.'—*Star*

'It is simple for me to recommend this majestically mad picture to all connoisseurs of Hollywood enormity.'—*News of the World*

James Mason (1974):

I was not amused by this 'energetic farrago'. CinemaScope and other giant screens of varying ratios had been introduced in order to con potential cinemagoers into the illusion that entertainment offered in the cinema was to be bigger, better and more spectacular than anything to which their little black and white television box could ever aspire. To the film makers themselves the big screens were just one more obstacle that stood in the way of making good films. They would have to ride out another era of bosh and tosh before dimension became once more irrelevant.

A STAR IS BORN

1954

A Transcona Enterprises production released by Warner Brothers. *Producer:* Sidney Luft. *Associate Producer:* Verne Alves. *Director:* George Cukor. *Screenplay:* Moss Hart—*based on a screenplay by* Dorothy Parker, Alan Campbell and Robert Carson *from an original story by* William A. Wellman and Robert Carson. *Director of Photography:* Sam Leavitt. *Art Director:* Malcolm Bert. *Art Direction and Costumes for 'Born in a Trunk':* Irene Sharaff; *Music and Lyrics:* Leonard Gershe. *Musical Director:* Ray Heindorf. *Original Music:* Harold Arlen. *Dances created and staged by* Richard Barstow. *Editor:* Folmar Blangsted. CinemaScope. Technicolor. 154 minutes.

CAST

Judy Garland . . . . . . *Esther Blodgett/Vicki Lester*
James Mason . . . . . . *Norman Maine*
Jack Carson . . . . *Matt Libby*
Charles Bickford . . . . *Oliver Niles*
Tom Noonan . . . . . . *Danny McGuire*
Lucy Marlowe . . . . . *Lola Lavery*
Amanda Blake . . . . . *Susan*
Irving Bacon . . . . . . *Graves*
Hazel Shermet . . . . . *Miss Wheeler*
James Brown . . . . . . *Glen Williams*

SYNOPSIS

Norman Maine, a popular but alcoholic actor, stumbles on stage drunk at a Hollywood premiere and is tactfully helped off by an ambitious show-

With Judy Garland.

girl called Esther Blodgett. Later that night, Maine meets Esther at a nightclub, and, after hearing her sing, assures her she has 'star quality' and promises to help her make a career for herself in pictures.

As Vicki Lester, a studio-chosen name, Esther is groomed step by step under Maine's solicitous eye. She begins by playing small parts until, finally, in a starring rôle, she becomes a sensational success. Esther and Maine marry, but while her career flourishes, his declines rapidly—a situation further aggravated by his continuous drinking.

Maine becomes exceedingly morose and earns himself the reputation of being unemployable; and when Esther wins an Oscar, he drunkenly interrupts the presentation ceremony to make an embarrassing, truculent and self-pitying speech.

His health deteriorates, and, in time, he agrees to go to a sanitorium where he is temporarily helped. But after a row with Libby, the studio's malicious publicity chief, he starts drinking again and vanishes for three days. Only an appeal by Esther in court saves him from being sent to prison on a drunken driving charge.

Determined to restore her husband's health, Esther informs her studio boss, Niles, that she intends to give up her career and look after Maine. But Maine overhears this, and rather than allow his wife to sacrifice her career, commits suicide by swimming out to sea.

Esther is grief-stricken and turns her back on the world of show-business. But she is soon persuaded to return to the life she knows and loves, and accepts an invitation to appear at a charity show where she proudly announces herself as 'Mrs. Norman Maine'.

REVIEWS

'James Mason's playing of the great star debauched, drunken, held up for a time by the love of the little girl he has helped from obscurity into the headlines is magnificent.'—*Sunday Express*

'It must be made clear at once that *A Star Is Born* is not a great film but a great show . . . the performances are fine. Mr. Mason's is a fine, mordant bit of acting.'—C. A. Lejeune, *Observer*

'The Warners and Mr. Cukor have really gone to town in giving this hackneyed Hollywood story an abundance of fullness and form . . . Mr. Cukor gets

With Judy Garland.

With Henry Kulky.

performances from Miss Garland and Mr. Mason that make the heart flutter and bleed. . . . It is something to see, this *Star Is Born.'—New York Times*

'A Star Is Born' triumphs in spite of its producer's blatant and largely futile insistence that Miss Garland should appear unchanged by the passage of time . . . Mr. Mason gives the best "modern" screen performance of his life.'—*News Chronicle*

'James Mason does a magnificent job of making his part credible.'—*Daily Worker*

'James Mason has never acted so magnificently. . . . Only in her two biggest moments does Judy Garland find the task just beyond her.'—*Evening News*

'Mason is flawless . . . one of the best things he has ever done.'—*Star*

'James Mason seems even more brilliant than memory paints of Mr. March (in the 1937 version) . . . this is easily the finest performance of his career.'—*Daily Telegraph*

'One cannot imagine Mason's romantic bitterness better seized.'—*New Statesman*

'An inordinately long film . . . and there were times when I was glad that the expectation of life would probably allow me to see it all the way through— even if I did emerge with hardened arteries and white hair . . . the total effect is of something small, blown up to impossible dimensions. James Mason is at his admirably grating best.'—*Financial Times*

'The honours of *A Star Is Born* rest with the stars it presents.'—*The Times*

James Mason (1974):

I saw this again recently on Television Suisse Romande and was filled with admiration, especially for George Cukor's direction and Sam Levitt's lighting; also for the man with the scissors who cut it down to one hour fifty minutes without losing any of the best bits.

127

20,000 LEAGUES UNDER THE SEA

1954

A Walt Disney production. *Producer:* Walt Disney. *Director:* Richard Fleischer. *Screenplay:* Earl Felton—*from the novel by* Jules Verne. *Director of Photography:* Franz Planer. *Underwater Photographer:* Till Gabbani. *Music:* Paul Smith. *Art Director:* John Meehan. *Special Effects:* John Hench and Josh Meador. *Editor:* Elmo Williams. CinemaScope. Technicolor. 126 minutes.

CAST

Kirk Douglas . . . . *Ned Land*
James Mason . . . . *Captain Nemo*
Paul Lukas . . . . *Professor Aronnax*
Peter Lorre . . . . *Conseil*
Robert J. Wilke . . . . *Mate on 'Nautilus'*
Carleton Young . . . . *John Howard*
Ted de Corsia . . . . *Captain Farragut*
Percy Helton . . . . *Diver*
Ted Cooper . . . . *Mate on 'Lincoln'*
Edward Marr . . . . *Shipping Agent*
Fred Graham . . . . *Casey Moore*
J. M. Kerrigan . . . . *Billy*

SYNOPSIS

Because the shipping lanes of the Pacific Ocean, in 1868, are suddenly menaced by an awesome monster, the U.S. Government sends a naval frigate to search the area. On board are Ned Land, a harpoonist, Professor Aronnax, a marine biologist, and his assistant, Conseil. The monster sinks the frigate, but picks up Ned, Aronnax and Conseil, who discover it is, in fact, a submarine called the *Nautilus* commanded by a strange and embittered man, Captain Nemo, who means to destroy everything he can because the world has treated him and his crew badly.

While the *Nautilus* takes the prisoner-guests on a voyage around the world beneath the sea, Aronnax and Conseil are content to learn about Nemo's science, but Ned resents his captivity and inserts notes into bottles containing the exact location of Nemo's secret island and tosses them into the sea.

After surviving encounters with a hostile warship and a giant squid, the *Nautilus* reaches the secret island only to discover that the area is full of war-

With Kirk Douglas and Peter Lorre.

ships waiting at the harbour. Nemo manages to get ashore and set a time-bomb. On his way back he is mortally wounded and his last orders are for a straight-down course. Ned, Aronnax and Conseil escape and, from a small boat, watch an enormous explosion obliterate the island, the warships and the *Nautilus*.

REVIEWS

'Lavish and spectacular . . . none of the performances, however, comes up to those of the fish.'—*Daily Express*

'A very good film. . . . James Mason seems just the man for Captain Nemo.'—*Daily Mail*

'A film full of surprises . . . the biggest is that at least 120 of its 126 minutes are tedious.'—*Daily Sketch*

'[Disney's] pictorial conception of this inventive tale is, on the whole, a trifle crude. . . . Mr. Mason does well in the livelier moments.'—*The Times*

'The new Walt Disney is much the best he has done with actors and adventure—which isn't saying much.'—*New Statesman*

'Some fine underwater photography, and the film's big scene in which a giant squid tries to take on the Captain's submarine should scare the wits out of you. . . . As the Captain James Mason is an impressive figure.'—*The New Yorker*

'It's super-duper stupendous hokum . . . a box-office bombshell.'—*Daily Mirror*

James Mason (1974):
The *Daily Express*'s critique, which was clearly intended to deflate the egos of Messrs. Douglas, Lorre, Lucas and Mason, is totally invalid, since the fish we saw were no more than walk-ons and came off no better than the actors. Actually the only performer of real distinction was a seal whose name, if I recall correctly, was Jackie Horner. Here was a forceful personality, supported by a technique that could not be faulted.

FOREVER DARLING

1956

A Zanra production released by M.G.M. *Producer:* Desi Arnaz. *Director:* Alexander Hall. *Original Story and Screenplay:* Helen Deutsch. *Director of Photography:* Harold Lipstein. *Music:* Bronislau Kaper. *Art Directors:* Ralph Berger and Albert Pyke. *Song: 'Forever Darling'—lyrics by Sammy Cahn and sung by* The Ames Brothers. *Editors:* Dann Cahn and Bud Molin. Eastmancolor. 91 minutes

CAST

Lucille Ball . . . . *Susan Vega*
Desi Arnaz . . . . *Lorenzo Xavier Vega*
James Mason . . . . *The Guardian Angel*
Louis Calhern . . . . *Charles Y. Bewell*
John Emery . . . . *Dr. Edward R. Winter*
John Hoyt . . . . *Bill Finlay*
Natalie Schafer . . . . *Millie Opdyke*
Mabel Albertson . . . . . . *Society Reporter*
Ralph Dumke . . . . *Henry Opdyke*
Nancy Kulp . . . . *Amy*
Willis B. Bouchey. . . . . . *Mr. Clinton*
Ruth Brady. . . . . *Laura*

SYNOPSIS

When a pretty socialite, Susan Bewell, and a serious-minded young scientist, Larry Vega, marry, it is, according to their friends, 'A marriage made in Heaven'. However, as a result of a project Larry is working on—a special kind of insecticide—which keeps him working late at the laboratory—as well as Susan's preoccupation with her lightweight friends—their marriage soon begins to suffer.

Then Susan's Guardian Angel appears. She believes she is losing her mind, but her father assures her that guardian angels are part of the family heritage and she should therefore allow herself to be guided by him.

Through the good counsel of the angel, she begins to mature emotionally and realises that, in order to save her marriage, she must help her husband rather than try to equate with him by being independent.

Susan accompanies Larry on a field experiment and nearly wrecks the trip. Eventually, though, her guardian angel intervenes and gives her one more chance to prove a worthy partner for her husband. She accepts his advice and their marriage is saved.

REVIEWS

'I suppose one word for *Forever Darling* is "cute" though it's not precisely the first word that comes to mind.'—*Daily Express*

'For players as distinguished as Mason and Miss Ball, it struck me as a clear case of cruelty.'—*Star*

'A sorry apology for comedy . . . I trust they paid Mr. Mason handsomely for aiding and abetting this disaster, because he is going to be a long time living it down.'—*Daily Sketch*

'Lethally unfunny.'—*News Chronicle*

'I think this must be the saddest farce I ever saw.'—*Evening Standard*

James Mason (1974):

One has to admire the critics. They can always think of something to say. In a case like this words fail me.

With Lucille Ball and Desi Arnaz.

With Lucille Ball in *Forever Darling.*

131

BIGGER THAN LIFE

1956

A 20th Century-Fox production and release. *Producer:* James Mason. *Director:* Nicholas Ray. *Screenplay:* Clifford Odets and Nicholas Ray—*from an original story by* Cyril Hume and Richard Maibaum. *Director of Photography:* Joe MacDonald. *Music:* David Raksin. *Art Directors:* Lyle Wheeler and Jack Martin Smith. *Editor:* Louis Loeffler. CinemaScope. Eastmancolor. 95 minutes.

With Walter Matthau and Barbara Rush.

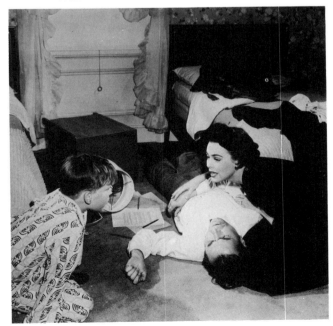

With Barbara Rush.

CAST

James Mason	*Ed Avery*
Barbara Rush	*Lou*
Walter Matthau	*Wally*
Robert Simon	*Dr. Norton*
Christopher Olsen	*Richie Avery*
Roland Winters	*Dr. Ruric*
Rusty Lane	*La Porte*
Rachel Stephens	*Nurse*
Kipp Hamilton	*Pat Wade*
Betty Caulfield	*Mrs. La Porte*
Virginia Carroll	*Mrs. Jones*
Renny McEvoy	*Mr. Jones*
Bill Jones	*Mr. Byron*
Dee Aaker	*Joe*
Jerry Mather	*Freddie*
Portland Mason	*Nancy*
Natalie Masters	*Mrs. Tyndal*
Richard Collier	*Milkman*
Lewis Charles	*Dr. McLennan*
William Shallert	*Pharmacist*
John Monoghan	*Cabby*
Gus Schilling	*Druggist*
Alex Fazer	*Clergyman*
Mary McAdoo	*Mrs. Edwards*
Mary Carver ⎰ Eugenia Paul ⎱	*Salesladies*
Gladys Richards	*Lab Nurse*
David Bedell	*X-ray Doctor*
Ann Spencer	*Nurse*
Nan Dolan	*Dr. Norton's Nurse*

SYNOPSIS

Ed Avery, a schoolteacher, suffers from attacks of pain and is sent to hospital to have the illness diagnosed. The doctors warn him that unless he agrees to take a course of the drug cortisone, he will die within a year. He accepts their diagnosis, which proves successful, but soon becomes addicted to the drug as it makes him feel more intelligent, brighter and bigger. These feelings, however, are also coupled with periods of acute depression.

Ed Avery thinks he is a genius, treats his wife Lou with contempt, and lavishes all his affection on his son Ritchie—while, at the same time, behaving towards him with great severity and almost sadistic cruelty. Ritchie cannot understand this contradiction

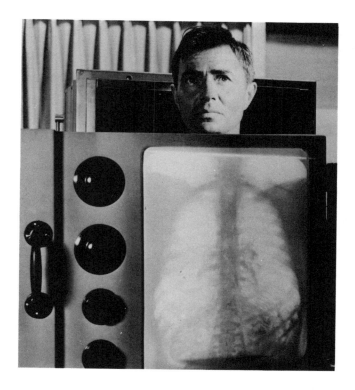

With Barbara Rush.

in his father's nature, and rebels against it. Avery catches Ritchie attempting to destroy the cortisone tablets, and, fearing that his beloved son will grow up to be a criminal, plans to kill his entire family, including himself.

A violent scene breaks out and Avery chases Ritchie through the house. He is overpowered by a friend, Wally Gibbs, and taken to hospital in a coma, where he regains consciousness and undergoes a new cure which will bring him peace of mind and win back the affection of his wife and son.

REVIEWS

'You do not have to have a medical degree to detect a high dosage of questionable hokum and a low pulse-rate of entertainment in Mr. Mason's first essay as a Hollywood producer. . . . Bad medicine, this film.'—*Daily Express*

'*Bigger than Life* is wrecked not by the seeming exaggeration indulged in by Mr. Mason, who takes the cortisone, but by the stupidity shown by his wife (Miss Barbara Rush). . . . Mr. Mason is always an actor, a point in his favour, and he acts away like anything, but it is all wasted because his wife persists in behaving as though the family is living on a desert island instead of in a crowded town. The script, in forcing her to behave like a fool, destroys the effect it is trying to achieve; the mistake is not an unimportant detail, but a fatal flaw. A pity, because *Bigger than Life* is trying to say something

too important to be laughed off and shrugged away.' —*The Times*

'Tense . . . taut and intriguing.'—*Daily Mirror*

'Mason's acting is superbly terrifying in a provocative 'X' certificate picture.'—*News of the World*

'Mason has treated himself to a hunk of cheap, lurid melodrama and audiences to one of his most 'ham' performances.'—*Daily Sketch*

'A ludicrous exercise.'—*Financial Times*

James Mason (1974):

It seems that the film contained some mysterious ingredients which inflamed practically all known critics, with the exception of Messrs. Jean-Luc Godard and Truffaut.

As far as its reception in the U.S. was concerned I was aware of two things that made it unacceptable. One, it was shot in CinemaScope and processed by Eastmancolor, a combination which had hitherto been lavished only on heavily theatrical fare, whereas we were aiming at a quasi-documentary effect. Second unacceptable item was the casting of myself as a run-of-the-mill American school-teacher. The U.S. public could not accept me as such, since they knew that James Mason was an uncooperative import who should be seen only in glum foreign parts. Thus the film was thought well of only in countries where I did not carry this embarrassing identification. I can't explain why they took such a dismal view of it in England.

133

ISLAND IN THE SUN

1956

A 20th Century-Fox production and release. *Producer:* Darryl F. Zanuck. *Director:* Robert Rossen. *Screenplay:* Alfred Hayes—*from the novel by* Alec Waugh. *Director of Photography:* Frederick Young. *Music:* Malcolm Arnold. *Art Director:* William C. Andrews. *Songs:* 'Island in the Sun' and 'Lead Man Holler' *by* Harry Belafonte and Irving (Lord) Burgess. *Editor:* Reginald Beck. Cinema-Scope. Technicolor. 120 minutes.

With Basil Sydney and Joan Collins.

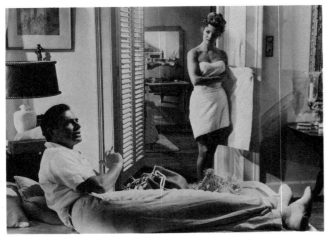

With Patricia Owens.

CAST

James Mason	*Maxwell Fleury*
Joan Fontaine	*Mavis*
Dorothy Dandridge	*Margot Seaton*
Joan Collins	*Jocelyn*
Michael Rennie	*Hilary Carson*
Diana Wynyard	*Mrs. Fleury*
John Williams	*Colonel Whittingham*
Stephen Boyd	*Euan Templeton*
Patricia Owens	*Sylvia*
Basil Sydney	*Julian Fleury*
John Justin	*Denis Archer*
Ronald Squire	*The Governor*
Hartley Power	*Bradshaw*
Harry Belafonte	*David Boyeur*

SYNOPSIS

Maxwell Fleury, eldest son of a wealthy Santa Marta family, announces his intention to oppose David Boyeur, a popular native Union leader, in the forthcoming elections. A journalist digs up stories relating to Fleury's coloured ancestry which Maxwell uses as election propaganda. Boyeur is having an affair with Mavis Norman, a white woman, and Denis Archer, the Governor's aide, is having an affair with Boyeur's ex-girlfriend, Margot Seaton. Maxwell's sister, Jocelyn, fears that adverse publicity will prevent her marrying the Governor's son Euan Templeton and allows herself to become pregnant.

Maxwell accuses Carson, a war hero, of having an affair with his wife Sylvia and, incensed by Carson's scorn for his ancestry, flies into a fit of passion and kills him. Maxwell loses the election and, unable to live with the burden of Carson's death, gives himself up to the Police Inspector, who suspects Maxwell but has no proof. Meanwhile, Jocelyn has discovered she is not Maxwell's daughter, and therefore not coloured, and marries Euan. They leave for England on the same plane as Denis and Margot. Watching the departing couples, Boyeur rejects Mavis's love on the grounds that it will threaten his political career; and the Governor and the Police Inspector discuss what will happen to Maxwell, now awaiting trial, and to the island with its birth pangs of self-government.

With (left to right) Joan Fontaine, Harry Belafonte, Hartley Power, Patricia Owens, and Michael Rennie.

REVIEWS

'The film is so slack, uneven and untidy. . . . Mr. Mason gives of his best.'—*The Times*

'The movie goes no distance at all in solving Santa Mara's colour problem, but the colour photography is beautiful.'—*Time* magazine

'Wonderful to see . . . not so good to hear.'—*Evening News*

'The eye is often charmed, but the mind remains unsatisfied.'—C. A. Lejeune, *Observer*

'*Island in the Sun*, for all the reality of the problems it touches, remains big, handsome, but remote.'—*Daily Telegraph*

'With five separate stories to keep going *Island in the Sun* flounders along from bad to worse . . . expensive, pretentious and dull. . . . James Mason glowers through his part with an accent I can only describe as Caribbean Welsh.'—*Evening Standard*

'It distorts the colour question into the shape of a boudoir keyhole . . . as socially significant as the magazines in a dentist's waiting room.'—*Sunday Express*

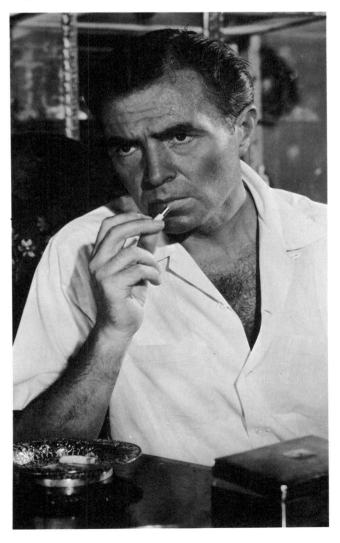

James Mason (1974):

I tried to sit it through when it was appearing on British TV, hoping to derive reminiscent pleasure from the backgrounds. But the carry on in foreground obliged me to switch to another channel.

It was clear that the *Evening Standard* did not like my 'Caribbean Welsh', but I would have hated myself if I had not had a go at it, for it was the way everyone spoke in Grenada, where we shot much of the film. One of the blessings of this island was the almost total absence of pukka English.

CRY TERROR

1958

A Virginia and Andrew Stone production released by M.G.M. *Producers:* Virginia and Andrew Stone. *Directed and Written by:* Andrew Stone. *Director of Photography:* Walter Strenge. *Music:* Howard Jackson. *Editor:* Virginia Stone. 96 minutes.

CAST

James Mason . . . . *Jim Molner*
Rod Steiger. . . . . *Paul Hoplin*
Inger Stevens . . . . *Joan Molner*
Neville Brand . . . . *Steve*
Angie Dickinson . . . . *Kelly*
Kenneth Tobey . . . . *Frank Cole*
Jack Klugman . . . . *Vince*
Jack Kruschen. . . . . *Charles Pope*
Carleton Young . . . . *Robert Adams*
Barney Phillips . . . . *Pringle*
Harlan Warde . . . . *Operative No. 1*
Ed Hinton . . . . *Operative No. 2*
Chet Huntley . . . . *Himself*
Roy Neal . . . . *Himself*
Jonathan Hole . . . . *Executive*
William Schallert . . . . *Henderson*
Portland Mason . . . . *Pat's School Friend*
Mae Marsh. . . . . *Woman in Elevator*
Terry Ann Ross. . . . . *Pat Molner*

SYNOPSIS

Amalgamated Airlines is informed that a bomb has been placed aboard one of their planes. When the particular plane lands, the F.B.I. locate and detonate the bomb. This is watched by a TV repairman, Jim Molner who realises that the bomb was one he had once made for a wartime friend, Paul Hoplin, in the hope of winning a manufacturing contract from the armed services.

Later that day, Hoplin holds up Jim, his wife Joan and daughter Pat, and takes them to his penthouse hideaway. Hoplin's idea is to threaten the airline with another bomb, this time with no warning unless a ransom is paid. The airline company is helpless and is forced to agree to his demands. While Joan is sent to collect the money, Hoplin holds Jim and Pat as hostages. The F.B.I., however, are already on Hoplin's trail, for they have discovered that it was his girlfriend Kelly who had placed the original bomb.

Joan collects the money and returns to the penthouse, discreetly followed by F.B.I. agents. Jim manages to escape, but Joan is forced to kill one of Hoplin's henchmen in her attempt to get away. Hoplin pursues her into the underground while he himself is followed by the F.B.I. agents. Just as he reaches her, Hoplin falls on to the electric rail and finds himself trapped between an oncoming train and the agents. There is no escape for him.

REVIEWS

'A cliff-hanging thriller with a novel idea.'—*Daily Express*

With Jack Klugman.

With Inger Stevens and Terry Ann Ross.

With Rod Steiger.

'The story makes very little sense.'—*Time* magazine
'Neither [Rod] Steiger nor Mason looked as though he enjoyed this film any more than I did.'—*Star*
'A magnificently expert essay in excitement. You won't believe a moment of the tale, but you won't take your eyes off the screen either.'—*Evening News*
'Though not very original, it is all rather exciting and keeps you on the edge of your seat.'—*News Chronicle*
'Like a Hitchcock film of goodish vintage.'—*Manchester Guardian*
'James Mason, Rod Steiger and Inger Stevens appear in it, but not noticeably for their good.'—C. A. Lejeune, *Observer*

James Mason (1974):
Andy Stone, the director of this film, was an extremely expert pioneer in the matter of shooting exclusively on real locations. His films' basic situations were also at this time invariably original, *pace* the *News Chronicle*. The terror in this case was triggered by the placing of a small bomb aboard an aircraft. Had it not been for Andy perhaps no-one would have thought of this trick.

With Inger Stevens.

THE DECKS RAN RED

1958

A Virginia and Andrew Stone production released by M.G.M. *Producers:* Virginia and Andrew Stone. *Directed and written by* Andrew Stone. *Director of Photography:* Meredith M. Nicholson. *Editor:* Virginia Stone. 84 minutes.

CAST

James Mason . . . . *Captain Edwin Rummill*
Dorothy Dandridge . . . . . *Martina*
Broderick Crawford . . . . *Henry Scott*
Stuart Whitman . . . . *Leroy Martin*
Katherine Bard . . . . *Joan Rummill*
David Cross . . . . *Mace*
Joel Fluellen . . . . *Cook*
Jack Kruschen . . . . *First Officer*

SYNOPSIS

Ed Rummill, first mate of a luxury liner, is finally given command of a rusty, broken-down freighter called the S.S. Berwind, whose captain has just died. When he takes over, however, he finds himself in the middle of a tense atmosphere of resentment and unrest, aggravated further by the employment of a Maori cook and the cook's beautiful coloured wife, Martina. Rummill learns that most of the trouble stems from an unscrupulous deck-hand, Henry Scott, and his accomplice, Leroy Martin, who have a plan to murder the captain and crew, scuttle the ship and claim salvage money. Rummill, however, discovers their plan and, after a brutal and bloody fight throughout the ship, manages to kill Scott and thereby break the conspiracy.

REVIEWS

'Some of the dialogue, at moments of crisis, is odd indeed.'—*The Times*

'The plot is supposed to be true, but I cannot accept the dialogue as true of anything, except perhaps *A Child's Garden of Clichés*. Mason is lumbered with speaking his thoughts with lines such as 'Those fatal seconds ticked away, then an idea struck me'. A pity the idea never struck Mr. Mason that he should have abandoned ship immediately he read the script.'—*Evening Standard*

'This is the kind of ill-made, insultingly stupid picture which harms an industry that is genuinely trying to produce films that are well worth paying money to see . . . if this kind of stuff is all Hollywood can give [James Mason], couldn't he be persuaded home?'—*Sunday Express*

'I couldn't believe a word of the banal dialogue and Captain Mason seemed all at sea the whole time.'—*News of the World*

'James Mason [is] hopelessly miscast.'—*Financial Times*

'James Mason, Broderick Crawford and Dorothy Dandridge spend their time looking slightly sea-sick at finding themselves involved in it.'—*Spectator*

James Mason (1974):
Miscast again. Shucks!

With Dorothy Dandridge.

With Jack Kruschen and John Gallaudet.

NORTH BY NORTHWEST

1959

An Alfred Hitchcock/M.G.M. production released by M.G.M. *Producer and Director:* Alfred Hitchcock. *Associate Producer:* Herbert Coleman. *Screenplay:* Ernest Lehman. *Director of Photography:* Robert Burks. *Music:* Bernard Herrmann. *Art Directors:* William A. Horning and Merrill Pye. *Editor:* George Tomasini. *Credit Titles:* Saul Bass. VistaVision. Technicolor. 136 minutes.

CAST

Cary Grant . . . . *Roger Thornhill*
Eva Marie Saint . . . . *Eve Kendall*
James Mason . . . . *Phillip Vandamm*
Jessie Royce Landis . . . . . . *Clara Thornhill*
Leo G. Carroll . . . . *Professor*
Philip Ober . . . . *Lester Townsend*
Josephine Hutchinson. . . . . . *Handsome Woman*
Martin Landau . . . . *Leonard*
Adam Williams. . . . . *Valerian*
Edward Platt . . . . *Victor Larrabee*
Robert Ellenstein . . . . *Licht*
Les Tremayne . . . . *Auctioneer*
Philip Coolidge. . . . . *Dr. Cross*
Patrick McVey . . . . *Chicago Policeman*
Edward Binns . . . . *Captain Junket*
Ken Lynch . . . . *Chicago Policeman*

SYNOPSIS

The Professor, a C.I.A. agent, forces the hand of a foreign espionage organisation by creating a mythical man called 'Mr. Kaplan'. The spy chief, Phillip Vandamm, mistakes advertising executive Roger Thornhill for 'Kaplan', kidnaps him, takes him to the Townsend estate and forces a large quantity of whisky down him. He is arrested on a drunken driving charge, but the police do not believe his improbable story.

Thornhill goes to the U.N. building, where Townsend is addressing a meeting, and finds himself, on film, holding the murder weapon of the real Mr. Townsend who has just been killed. The picture makes headline news and Thornhill, remembering that 'Kaplan' was to have addressed a meeting in Chicago, catches a transcontinental express from the Grand Central Station. The C.I.A. realise their plan has taken an unexpected turn. Having taken great care to validate their creation, they can do nothing to jeopardise their own agent, and cannot help Thornhill even though he might be killed by Vandamm, who still believes him to be 'Kaplan'.

Another interested party is Eve Kendall, who mis-directs the police as Thornhill boards the train. They are attracted to each other, but he is unaware she has exchanged notes with Vandamm, who is following him. Thornhill's fears about Eve, however, are later confirmed when he sees her talking to Vandamm at an auction sale in Chicago. The Professor makes himself known to Thornhill and recruits his aid in catching Vandamm, which culminates in a showdown across the giant Thomas Jefferson statue on Mt. Rushmore.

REVIEWS

'Hitchcock is still the master of suspense, [and] has lost none of his brilliant individualism, none of his power to keep us mesmerically entertained by

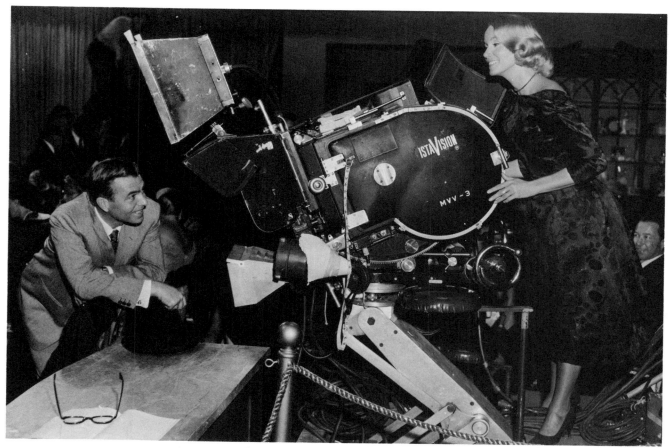

On the set with Eva Marie Saint.

fantasy woven into the fabric of everyday life. . . .
North by Northwest is by no means faultless: it is
too long, and the melodrama of the ending is quite
out of key. Yet most of all Hitchcock impresses on
us his sheer professionalism in making the
implausible almost plausible and twisting the banal
to make the bizarre. James Mason has seldom been
so charmingly sinister.'—*Evening Standard*
'*North by Northwest* is a tense, super thriller by
Hitchcock and one of the best things he has ever
done.'—*Daily Express*
'Mr. Hitchcock, the wizard, has worked the trick
again.'—*News of the World*
'*North by Northwest* persuades me that Hitchcock
in his late middle-age is becoming prolix. He has
recently been too prone to caricature his own idio-
syncrasies and [should] start sharpening his editorial
scissors.'—*News Chronicle*
'James Mason and Leo G. Carroll may not make the
dramatic carpentry look solid, but they give it a fine
high polish.'—*Daily Telegraph*
'Hitchcock is at the top of his form and more
audacious than ever.'—*Daily Herald*
'Only a master conjurer could get away with this.
Alfred the Great does not burn the cakes. He likes
to have them *and* eat them.'—*Daily Mail*

With Cary Grant.

With Cary Grant and Eva Marie Saint.

JOURNEY TO THE CENTRE OF THE EARTH

1959

A 20th Century-Fox production. *Producer:* Charles Brackett. *Director:* Henry Levin. *Screenplay:* Walter Reisch and Charles Brackett—*from the novel by* Jules Verne. *Director of Photography:* Leo Tover. *Music:* Bernard Herrmann. *Songs:* 'My Love Is Like a Red, Red Rose' by Robert Burns; 'Twice as Tall' and 'The Faithful Heart' by Sammy Cahn and James Van Heusen. *Art Directors:* Lyle Wheeler, Franz Bachelin and Herman A. Blumenthal. *Special Effects:* L. B. Abbott, James B. Gordon and Emil Kosa. *Editors:* Stuart Gilmore and Jack W. Holmes. CinemaScope. DeLuxe Color. 130 minutes.

CAST

Pat Boone . . . . *Alec McEwan*
James Mason . . . . . *Professor Oliver Lindenbrook*
Arlene Dahl . . . . . . *Carla*
Diane Baker . . . . . . *Jenny*
Thayer David . . . . . *Count Saknussemm*
Peter Ronson. . . . . . *Hans*
Robert Adler . . . . . . *Groom*
Alan Napier . . . . . . *Dean*
Alex Finlayson . . . . *Professor Bayle*
Ben Wright. . . . . . . *Paisley*
Mary Brady . . . . . . *Kirsty*
Frederick Halliday . . *Chancellor*
Alan Caillou . . . . . . *Rector*

SYNOPSIS

Intrigued by the unusual weight of a gift paperweight, Professor Lindenbrook of Edinburgh University melts it down and finds it contains a message from a dying explorer, Arne Saknussemm, who was known to have attempted a journey to the centre of the earth. Accompanied by his star pupil, Alec McEwan, Lindenbrook sets off for Iceland where he finds a rival expedition planned by his Swedish counterpart, Professor Goetaborg; but that Goetaborg has been murdered by a descendent of Arne, Count Saknussemm, who plans his own expedition. Goetaborg's widow, Carla, joins Lindenbrook's party and, after descending by way of a volcanic crater, they encounter hazards of landslide, prehistoric reptiles and a shipwreck in a subterranean sea. They come face to face with the Count, who has tried to kill Alex, and reluctantly allow him to join their expedition.

The Count, however, is killed by a falling boulder while the party stumble across the lost city of Atlantis as well as the skeleton of the long-lost explorer, Arne Saknussemm. In an attempt to blast their way through a shaft that has blocked their exit, the released updraught projects them at a terrific force to the earth's crust as Atlantis crumbles into dust. Emerging into the Mediterranean, they are picked up by fishermen and taken back to Edinburgh and a civic reception.

REVIEWS

'A super glossy, unintentionally hilarious version of a Jules Verne adventure story which will raise mocking giggles from scientific schoolboys and happy condescending smiles from their papas . . . a very odd film indeed; almost a collector's piece.'— *Sunday Express*

'The story retains its interest almost throughout the two hours and a bit it takes to run. Mr. James Mason manages, at one and the same time, to have his tongue in his cheek and to keep it in its proper place, to parody the rôle, yet to play it straight.'—*The Times*

'This is all gloriously outrageous film fun, with James Mason playing it absolutely right; ham ham all the way, thickly cut with plenty of fat.'—*Daily Express*

With Arlene Dahl.

With Pat Boone, Peter Ronson and Arlene Dahl.

'What glorious nonsense it is, but we will happily believe anything in this most rich and plummy piece of hokum.'—*Evening Standard*

'Hilarious science fiction, full of straight-faced extravagances and marred only by a moment or two of the statutory cruelty to animals (to iguanas this time). I haven't enjoyed nonsense of this sort so much for years.'—Dilys Powell, *Sunday Times*

'Wonderfully done.'—*Star*

'Preposterous, but not quite the way its makers intended . . . studded with unintentional laughs.'—*Daily Herald*

'Laughs of the unrewarding kind . . . you laugh at, but not with the characters . . . a lot of deliberate unintentional fun.'—*Evening News*

James Mason (1974):

Producer Charles Brackett supplied a good script and the technicians could not be faulted, so I guess it must have been actors and director who so let down the English critics. The one sequence I specially liked was that which showed the group of explorers on a raft in the centre of the earth. A type of maelstrom was created by back-projectors,

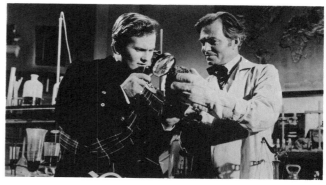

With Pat Boone.

lightning-flashers, water-tossers, wind-blowers and raft-rotators. This was happening to great effect in the week prior to that famous luncheon party at the Twentieth Century-Fox studio in honour of Chairman Khrushchev, for whose entertainment scenes were re-enacted from *Can Can*, another film being made there at the same time. I thought that it would have been a much better idea to re-enact our raft sequence with all those marvellous technicians doing their stuff. The Chairman and his wife, whose one desire was to get to Disneyland, would have had much more fun and their good taste would not have been insulted.

143

A TOUCH OF LARCENY

1959

A Foxwell production released by Paramount. *Producer:* Ivan Foxwell. *Director:* Guy Hamilton. *Screenplay:* Roger Macdougall, Paul Winterton, Ivan Foxwell and Guy Hamilton—*from the novel* The Megstone Plot *by* Andrew Garve. *Director of Photography:* John Wilcox. *Music:* Philip Green. *Art Director:* Elliot Scott. *Editor:* Alan Osbiston. 91 minutes.

With Vera Miles.

With George Sanders.

CAST

James Mason . . . . *Commander Max Easton*
George Sanders. . . . . . *Sir Charles Holland*
Vera Miles. . . . . *Virginia Killain*
William Kendall . . . . . *Husband*
Barbara Hicks . . . . *Miss Price*
Peter Barkworth . . . . . *Sub.-Lt. Brown*
Robert Flemyng . . . . . *Commander Larkin*
Ernest Clark. . . . . *Commander Bates*
Mavis Villiers. . . . . . . *Adele Parrish*
Macdonald Parke. . . . . *Jason Parrish*
Jimmy Lloyd . . . . *Nightclub Singer*
Stanley Zevie . . . . *1st Russian Officer*
André Mikhelson. . . . . *2nd Russian Officer*
Harry Andrews. . . . . . *Captain Graham*
Frederick Piper . . . . . . *Hall Porter*
Percy Herbert. . . . . . . *1st Policeman*
Dickie Owen . . . . *2nd Policeman*
William Mervyn . . . . . *Captain Balfour*
Duncan Lamont . . . . . *1st Special Branch Man*
Gordon Harris . . . . . . *2nd Special Branch Man*
Charles Carson . . . . . . *Robert Holland*
Basil Dignam . . . . *Lt.-Commander P.R.O.*
Rosemary Dorken . . . . *Wren Officer*
John Le Mesurier . . . . . *Admiral*
Rachel Gurney . . . . . . *Clare Holland*
Waveney Lee . . . . *Marcia Holland*
Martin Stephens . . . . . *John Holland*
Alexander Archdale . . . . *Local Doctor*

SYNOPSIS

Commander Max Easton, a highly decorated ex-submarine officer now attached to the Admiralty, meets an old chum, Charles Holland, and falls in love with his fiancée, Virginia. Realising she is marrying him for money and security, Max proposes an ingenious scheme whereby he will weave a trail of red herrings that will, inevitably, lead both the Admiralty and the Press to believe he has defected to the Russians with valuable top-secret documents.

While this is going on, Max's alibi will be that he has been shipwrecked on a lonely Scottish island and unable to return to base. All goes according to plan, except that he finds himself genuinely marooned and without radio assistance. Virginia, who placed a message for help in a bottle to be washed ashore in case of a real emergency, realises something has gone

drastically wrong and informs Charles, who contacts the authorities.

Max is picked up and finds that, instead of suing for defamation of character, he is heading for prison. Virginia is furious with Charles for having betrayed Max and breaks off the engagement, although still refusing to have anything to do with Max. Undeterred, Max parries the accusations by the police, and Virginia, believing he will not attempt anything dishonest to win her favour, decides to forgive his misdemeanours and marry him.

REVIEWS

'James Mason's performance, bland and wryly humorous, pursues its objective with the tenacity of a homing torpedo . . . his portrayal of Commander "Rammer" Easton indicates that we may well see more of Mason sweet as well as Mason sour. The whole is refreshing, light and welcome, and, without recourse either to bedroom or deadpan humour, restores to British screen comedy something that has been missing since Ealing died.'—*Evening Standard*

'A sparkling British picture . . . it not only wipes out those dull Hollywood years giving him [Mason] full stature again. We see Mason with new eyes, as a light comedian in the top rank.'—*Daily Sketch*

'James Mason comes into his own again in the British-made *A Touch of Larceny*, as well-mannered and gay a film as we have seen in months.'—*News of the World*

'A beguilingly polished comedy, reminiscent in its style, urbanity and sheen of the sort of thing Ernst Lubitsch was doing in the 1930s.'—*Daily Mail*

'Watching James Mason, I thought sadly of how long it's been since he's done anything but variations of *The Man in Grey*.'—*Daily Express*

'One of the few all-round professionals to brighten our lives is Mr. James Mason, whose performance is the most distinguished part of *A Touch of Larceny*. Though we have seen him mainly in dramatic rôles of late, he has now been permitted to take wing as a fully-fledged comedian with the most beguiling results . . . the whole thing runs easily and smoothly, with some unusually literate dialogue and some stylish direction. . . . James Mason is a joy to watch, and giving, arguably, his best performance since that other profiteer from secrets, Cicero in *Five Fingers*. He walks effortlessly away with the film.'—*The Times*

'A new star is born—James Mason. Here he is the rogue magnificent. It is an astonishing performance.' —*Star*

'A British film, not for the first time, has done its best to ruin a novel. Paul Winterton's *The Megstone Plot* was a wry thriller of more than average intelligence. As *A Touch of Larceny*, it plays for comedy and becomes itself absurd.'—*New Statesman*

'Everything goes so smoothly that the end would seem to come too soon . . . a compliment I couldn't pay to many pictures.'—C. A. Lejeune, *Observer*

'It shows that the strong, mannered, and unusually melodramatic screen personality of James Mason can be harnessed with an air of happy naturalness, to comedy.'—*Guardian*

THE TRIALS OF OSCAR WILDE

(U.S. title THE MAN WITH THE GREEN CARNATION)

1960

A Warwick Viceroy production released by Eros Film Distributors. *Executive Producers:* Albert Broccoli and Irving Allen. *Producer:* Harold Huth. *Directed and written by* Ken Hughes—*from the books* The Stringed Lute *by* John Fernald *and* The Trials of Oscar Wilde *by* Montgomery Hyde. *Director of Photography:* Ted Moore. *Music:* Ron Goodwin. *Art Directors:* Ken Adam and Bill Constable. *Editor:* Geoffrey Foot. Technirama. Technicolor. 123 minutes.

CAST

Peter Finch	*Oscar Wilde*
John Fraser	*Lord Alfred Douglas*
Yvonne Mitchell	*Constance Wilde*
Lionel Jeffries	*Marquis of Queensberry*
Nigel Patrick	*Sir Edward Clarke*
James Mason	*Sir Edward Carson*
Emrys Jones	*Robbie Ross*
Maxine Audley	*Ada Leverson*
James Booth	*Alfred Wood*
Paul Rogers	*Frank Harris*
Lloyd Lamble	*Charles Humphries*
Sonia Dresdel	*Lady Wilde*
Ian Fleming	*Arthur*
Laurence Naismith	*Prince of Wales*
Naomi Chance	*Lily Langtry*
Michael Goodliffe	*Charles Gill*
Liam Gaffney	*Willie Wilde*
Gladys Henson	*Landlady*
Cecily Paget-Bowman	*Lady Queensberry*
Meredith Edwards	*Auctioneer*

SYNOPSIS

The first night of *Lady Windermere's Fan* is a triumph for the playwright Oscar Wilde, marred only by an embarrassing scene afterwards between the Marquis of Queensberry and his son Lord Alfred Douglas (Bosie). This only serves to intensify the rumours surrounding Wilde and his relationship with Bosie, and leads the Marquis to blame Wilde for his son's proclivities and lack of family feeling. Wilde, however, despite his affection for his wife and children, finds it impossible to resist the fascination Bosie holds for him, even though his home is invaded by blackmailers and his work is constantly interrupted by Bosie's ever-increasing demands.

Because of failing health and impending bankruptcy, Wilde goes to Brighton to work on his new play *The Importance of Being Earnest*. Bosie follows him there, but Wilde sends him away, only to resume the relationship when Bosie's younger brother dies. On the opening night of the play, the Marquis calls Wilde a sodomite, and Wilde takes him to court and sues for libel. Wilde refuses to let Bosie testify against his father and, when Carson, Counsel for the Defence, produces clear evidence of Wilde's homosexual practices, the Marquis is acquitted.

Wilde himself is then taken to court on charges of gross indecency but is released on bail when a locked jury is announced. The second trial ends in a conviction for Wilde, who is sentenced to two years' hard labour. This term of imprisonment nearly kills him. On his release, a broken man, he is advised by his loyal and steadfast friends to leave the country

James as Sir Edward Carson.

in order to avoid further persecution and humiliation. He goes to the railway station with his wife, who has allowed him money to live on, but totally ignores Bosie, the man who had helped bring about his downfall, who is lurking in the background.

REVIEWS

'Not only far and away better than the rival version with Robert Morley; it is a magnificent and memorable British film on the huge scale generally attempted only by Hollywood . . . and of which the British film industry can—and should—be proud.'— *Sunday Express*

'It is photographed with taste and distinction . . . and acted with a delicacy that will touch your heart . . . [but] . . . the film fails, and fails badly only in one sequence, when James Mason tries to match Sir Ralph Richardson's performance in the other film as Carson. Richardson makes him look like an amateur. The film sags here as a result.'—*Daily Express*

'Mr. Wilde himself could *not* have expected his rare personality . . . to have been more sympathetically or affectingly dramatised.'—*New York Times*

'Here is tragedy laid bare to the heart given heroic stature. This will surely be one of the year's most notable films. The supporting cast is flawless. Only James Mason as Carson seems to me inferior to his counterpart in the other film.'—*Evening Standard*

'A loser all the way . . . diffuse . . . sprawling . . . without rising to any specific dramatic climax. James Mason makes much less impact dramatically than [Ralph] Richardson in the same key part.'—*Daily Mail*

'*The Trials of Oscar Wilde* reaches out in colour to catch the atmosphere of the period, and on occasions, such as the Café Royal scenes, it does so admirably. . . . Mr. James Mason assumes an Irish accent, but his performance is not quite equal to that of Sir Ralph Richardson.'—*The Times*

James Mason (1974):
Nolo contendere.

THE MARRIAGE-GO-ROUND

1961

A 20th Century-Fox production and release. *Produced and written by:* Leslie Stevens. *Director:* Walter Lang. *Director of Photography:* Leo Tover. *Music:* Dominic Frontiere. *Song: 'Marriage-go-round'* by Alan Bergman, Marilyn Keith and Lew Spence; *sung by* Tony Bennett. *Art Directors:* Duncan Cramer and Maurice Ransford. *Editor:* Jack W. Holmes. CinemaScope. DeLuxe Color. 98 minutes.

CAST
Susan Hayward . . . . *Content Delville*
James Mason . . . . *Paul Delville*
Julie Newmar . . . . *Katrin*
Robert Paige . . . . *Ross*
June Clayworth . . . . *Flo*
Joe Kirkwood Jr. . . . . *Henry*
Mary Patton . . . . *Mamie*
Trax Colton . . . . *Crew Cut*
Everett Glass . . . . *Professor*
Ben Astar . . . . *Sultan*

SYNOPSIS
Paul and Content Delville have been happily married for sixteen years, and both lecture on 'wedded bliss' at the local university. One evening, while awaiting their Swedish house-guests whom they have not seen for ten years, they open the door to a beautiful curvaceous blonde. It is Katrin, who explains that her father has been delayed and will follow later.

Although Katrin is engaged, she informs Paul she has arrived in America to 'borrow' him for mating purposes, believing that his mind and her body would produce the perfect child. Content declines to take the matter seriously while Paul, at first dumbfounded, slowly begins to weaken to her attractions.

Eventually matters are brought to a head with the arrival of a letter from Katrin's father explaining that he is unable to come. Paul wants to send Katrin back to Sweden, but Content, who is unaware of the letter, accuses Paul of being spineless and unable to cope. She changes her mind, however, when she interrupts them exchanging an innocent kiss. Paul is now certain that Katrin must go and makes peace with his wife.

REVIEWS
'Directed with leering ineptitude, and garnished with some of the unfunniest double-entendres I have ever heard, *The Marriage-Go-round* earns its 'X' certificate for sheer distastefulness. Its approach to sex is hypocritical, sniggering and unfunny. Mr. Mason plays his part in a permanent state of understandable embarrassment.'—*Sunday Express*

'The film is as tedious as it is tasteless, and it is very tasteless. Still, after watching poor Mr. Mason being vamped throughout the film by a six-foot female, I begin to understand his readiness to play the part in *Lolita* of a man who is attracted to little girls.'—*Evening Standard*

'James Mason and Susan Hayward manage to speak their arch dialogue without pain.'—*Daily Herald*

'The indecencies done in *The Marriage-Go-round* to the ideas of wit, comedy and gaiety, not to say marriage, are enough to make one weep.'—*Observer*

'Mr. Mason, clumsily and heavily directed, can only flounder about.'—*Sunday Telegraph*

James Mason (1974):
I take it that everyone agrees that a good critic is one whose opinion coincides with one's own? Then in this case we have a line-up of six good critics.

With Julie Newmar.

With Julie Newmar.

149

ESCAPE FROM ZAHRAIN

1961

A Paramount production and release. *Producer and Director:* Ronald Neame. *Screenplay:* Robin Estridge—*from the novel by* Michael Barrett. *Director of Photography:* Ellsworth Fredericks. *Music:* Lyn Murray. *Art Director:* Eddie Imazu. *Editor:* Eda Warren. Panavision. Technicolor. 89 minutes.

CAST

Yul Brynner . . . . *Sharif*
Sal Mineo . . . . *Ahmed*
Jack Warden . . . . *Huston*
James Mason . . . . *Johnson*
   (uncredited)
Madlyn Rhue . . . . *Laila*
Tony Caruso . . . . *Tahar*
Jay Novello . . . . *Hassan*

SYNOPSIS

In an oil sheikdom, Sharif, a revolutionary leader, is rescued from a police van by a group of university students. He escapes from the city with their leader, Ahmed, and several convicts including Huston, an American who has embezzled money from the Zahrain Oil Co. They capture an ambulance belonging to the Company, along with an Arabian nurse, Laila, and begin a long drive across the desert to freedom.

Their journey is hampered by a police ambush, lack of food and water, damage to the ambulance and the attempted treachery of one of the convicts. The romance between Ahmed and Laila is cut short when he is killed by a strafeing aeroplane near a supposedly friendly oasis. After surviving an attack by the army, Sharif, Laila and Huston eventually cross the border. While Huston looks for a ship, Sharif plans an early return together with Laila, who has now fallen in love with him.

N.B. James Mason plays an uncredited rôle as a garage mechanic.

Yul Brynner.

REVIEWS

'Nice of James (unmentioned in the credit titles) to support his friend Ronald Neame, but Garbo herself could have popped up here without being able to save this uninspired script.'—*Daily Telegraph*

'Certainly occupies an evening without strain.'—Dilys Powell, *Sunday Times*

'Ronald Neame sweeps us up unquestionably in a desert melodrama.'—*Evening Standard*

'Painful dialogue.'—*The Times*

LOLITA

1962

An A.A./Seven Arts/Anya/Transworld production released by M.G.M. *Producer:* James B. Harris. *Director:* Stanley Kubrick. *Screenplay, and the original novel, by* Vladimir Nabokov. *Director of Photography:* Oswald Morris. *Music:* Nelson Riddle; *'Lolita' theme by* Bob Harris. *Art Director:* William Andrews. *Editor:* Anthony Harvey. 153 minutes.

CAST

James Mason . . . . . *Humbert Humbert*
Shelley Winters. . . . *Charlotte Haze*
Peter Sellers. . . . . . *Clare Quilty*
Sue Lyon . . . . *Lolita Haze*
Marianne Stone . . . *Vivian Darkbloom*
Diana Decker . . . . . *Jean Farlow*
Jerry Stovin . . . . . . *John Farlow*
Gary Cockrell . . . . . *Dick (Lolita's Husband)*
Suzanne Gibbs . . . . *Mona Farlow*
Roberta Shore . . . . *Lorna*
Eric Lane . . . . *Roy*
Shirley Douglas . . . *Mrs. Starch*
Roland Brand . . . . . *Bill*
Colin Maitland . . . . *Charlie*
Cec Linder. . . . . . . *Physician*
Irvin Allen. . . . . . . *Hospital Attendant*
Lois Maxwell . . . . . *Nurse Mary Lore*
William Greene. . . . *Swine*
C. Denier Warren . . *Potts*
Isobel Lucas . . . . . *Louise (Maid at Haze House)*
Maxine Holden . . . . *Receptionist at Hospital*
Marion Mathie . . . . *Miss Lebone*
Craig Sams . . . . . . *Rex*
John Harrison . . . . . *Tom*
James Dyrenforth . . *Beale Senior*

SYNOPSIS

Humbert Humbert, a lecturer in the U.S., goes to the country after a breakdown to recuperate. Finding his host's house burned down he is sent to the home of a Mrs. Charlotte Haze, a widow. Charlotte Haze, coy, fluttery and typically small-minded, is the kind of woman Humbert detests. When, however, he is introduced to Charlotte's daughter, Lolita, he changes his mind and decides to stay.

The middle-aged Humbert is irresistibly drawn to the young and unconsciously seductive Lolita. He realises his desires are wrong and attributes them to his early love for a girl called Annabella from whom he was parted as a boy. All through his life—until now—Humbert has sought for, and never found the prototype of his childhood love.

Humbert settles into the Haze household, fending off the advances of Charlotte and trying to keep his relations with the attractive child-woman within bounds. Time passes and Humbert's passion for Lolita grows as the young girl weaves her half-unconscious spells around him.

Charlotte, who has fallen in love with Humbert and resents even her own daughter, decides to send Lolita away to summer camp and later to boarding school. Humbert is placed in an impossible position: either he will lose Lolita altogether or he must marry her mother in order to keep near her. He marries Charlotte and a strange *ménage-à-trois* is set up.

While Lolita is away in camp Charlotte discovers, from her husband's diary, that he loves Lolita. She runs from the house and is killed by a car as she crosses the street. Humbert drives to Lolita's camp,

saying that her mother is ill, and takes the girl away with him. Humbert and his Lolita drive across the country staying in motels as father and daughter after Humbert has broken the news of her mother's death to her.

Lolita is at first flattered and fascinated by Humbert's passion for her and for a few short months they are happy. Then Lolita becomes bored and treats the enslaved Humbert cruelly. She talks of her own home and of having friends her own age. Humbert, making a desperate effort to keep her, takes another post as a lecturer in Beardsley College. He rents a house and tries to make a home for Lolita. The girl, coarsened and spoiled, rebels against Humbert's jealous authority and begins to lie to him and to meet her friends on the sly. They quarrel violently but, temporarily reconciled, set out on another aimless journey together.

This time, though, they are not really alone. For, unknown to Humbert, and to Lolita's delight, following them close behind is Clare Quilty, a degenerate playwright who, ever since she appeared in a play of his at school, has been attracted to Lolita.

Lolita meets him secretly, falls ill, and eventually runs away from the hospital (and Humbert) with him.

Humbert, crazy with love and grief, searches but cannot find her anywhere. He goes back to Beardsley and the house they once shared together.

Three years later, he receives a letter from Lolita saying she is now married, pregnant and in need of money. He hurries to Lolita's home and forces the girl to tell him who it was that stole her away from him. She laughs and replies, 'Clare Quilty.' Humbert begs her to return to him, but she laughs again.

Finally, he gives her the money she wants, and goes away to track down Quilty and to take his revenge.

REVIEWS

'Mason, in a rôle few actors would accept, gives a brilliant portrayal . . . he succeeds in making you feel sorry for, instead of disgusted at, the love-sick Humbert.'—*New York Daily News*

'*Lolita* is the saddest and most important victim of the current reckless adaptation fad.'—*Time* magazine

'It is clear that Nabokov respects the novel. It is equally clear that he does not respect the film—at least, as it is used in America. . . . He has given to films the *Lolita* that, presumably, he thinks the medium deserves.'—*New Republic*

'James Mason's study of his unquenchable obsession is timed and studied to perfection, but never for a moment moving.'—*Daily Express*

'*Lolita* is James Mason's acting triumph . . . in the

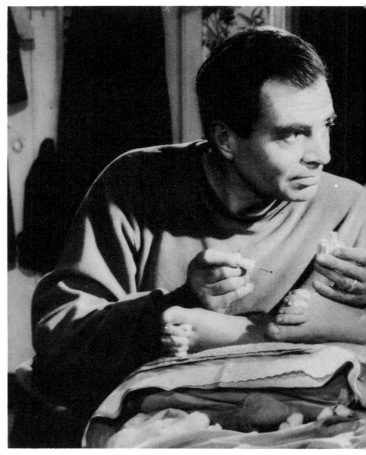

With Sue Lyon.

ironic approach of the early scenes, he is supreme.'—Dilys Powell, *Sunday Times*

'. . . a luscious film . . . James Mason [though] distinctly too young, brilliantly suggests the kind of charming but unprincipled man who would marry a widow out of lust for her daughter.'—*Sunday Telegraph*

'Credit must go to James Mason for his truly brilliant playing—urbane, literary, intelligent, often ridiculous, often pathetic, and always, surprisingly, sincere.'—*Guardian*

James Mason (1974):

From *Time* magazine I further received an unkind cut of a sort of which not everyone can boast of having been at the receiving end. The reviewer did not like my effort and said that the film would have been so much better if Peter Sellers had played the rôle of Humbert. What made this comment memorable to me was that in abbreviated form the review reappeared weekly for an agonisingly long period in the column headed 'Current and Choice' (or whatever they call it).

With Shelley Winters.

HERO'S ISLAND

1962

A Daystar/Portland production released by United Artists. *Producers:* Leslie Stevens and James Mason. *Written and directed by* Leslie Stevens. *Director of Photography:* Ted McCord. *Music:* Dominic Frontiere. *Editor:* Richard Brookway. Panavision. Technicolor. 94 minutes.

CAST
James Mason . . . . *Jacob Webber*
Kate Manx . . . . *Devon Mainwaring*
Neville Brand . . . . *Kingstree*
Rip Torn. . . . . *Nicholas*
Warren Oates. . . . . *Wayte*
Brendan Dillon . . . . *Thomas Mainwaring*
Robert Sampson . . . . *Enoch*
Dean Stanton . . . . *Dixey*
Morgan Mason . . . . *Callen*
Darby Hinton. . . . . *Jafar*
Robert Johnson. . . . . *Pound*
Bill Hart . . . . *Meggett*
John Hudkins. . . . . *Bullock*

SYNOPSIS
In 1718 Thomas and Devon Mainwaring, together with their three children and a family friend, Wayte, settle on Bull Island, off the coast of Carolina. Formerly bonded, they are now free and have the island bequeathed to them. Three fishermen, Enoch, Nicholas and Dixey, who claim the island is theirs, attack the family and kill Thomas—ordering the others to leave. A mystery man, Jacob Webber, is washed ashore lashed to a raft. He offers to help Devon but, because she is sternly religious, is reluctant to resort to violence, though he does so when the fishermen return from the mainland with Kingstree, a brutal overseer, and his two stewards. Jacob now reveals himself as the pirate Blackbeard, Major Stede Bonnett, and attacks the well-armed opposition. He kills Kingstree and the stewards, and is saved from being killed himself when Devon shoots Enoch. Jacob leaves the island and Devon is now free to bring up her children without hinderance.

The mystery man who reveals himself as Blackbeard.

With Kate Manx, Morgan Mason, Rip Torn and Warren Oates.

REVIEWS

'A strange but interesting little film . . . very well acted by James Mason.'—*The Times*

'Not even the decidedly gory action sequences that stud the picture can quite eliminate the sense of earnest textbook-like recreation rather than excited creativity.'—*Saturday Review*

'An unoriginal and carelessly plotted melodrama, none of which is credible. . . . James Mason gives a professional performance.'—*Films in Review*

'This film is sufficiently strange to be almost a curiosity . . . an odd mixture, but worth seeing for the best moments.'—*Monthly Film Bulletin*

James Mason (1974):

This 'Nice little film' was made in seventeen days on the island of Catalina. On completion it enjoyed the same sort of momentary success as *Caught*. It was made much of by the executives of United Artists and applauded on the 'Bel Air circuit'; but, when offered to the paying public, the response was nil.

TIARA TAHITI

1962

A Rank Organisation production and release. *Producer:* Ivan Foxwell. *Director:* William T. Kotcheff. *Screenplay:* Geoffrey Cotterell and Ivan Foxwell—*from the novel by* Geoffrey Cotterrell. *Director of Photography:* Otto Heller. *Music:* Philip Green. *Song:* 'Tiara Tahiti' *by* Norman Newell, *sung by* Danny Street. *Art Director:* Alex Vetchinsky. *Editor:* Antony Gibbs. Eastmancolor. 100 minutes.

CAST

James Mason . . . . *Capt. Brett Aimsley*
John Mills . . . . *Lt.-Col. Clifford Southey*
Claude Dauphin . . . . . . *Henri Farengue*
Herbert Lom . . . . *Chong Sing*
Rosenda Monteros. . . . . *Belle Annie*
Jacques Marin . . . . *Desmoulins*
Libby Morris . . . . *Adele Franklin*
Madge Ryan. . . . . *Millie Brooks*
Gary Cockrell. . . . . . . *Joey*
Peter Barkworth . . . . . *Lt. David Harper*
Roy Kinnear . . . . *Capt. Tom Enderby*

SYNOPSIS

When Lt.-Col. Clifford Southey, the pompous and self-esteemed commander of a British garrison in Germany during the Second World War discovers that Capt. Brett Aimsley has been unexpectedly attached to his regiment, he tries to conceal the fact from the rest of the unit that he was once employed as a clerk by Brett's firm in peacetime. Southey soon finds his discipline and authority undermined by the popular Brett but, discovering that Brett is attempting to smuggle black-market goods, manages to exact his revenge by having him captured, court-martialled and cashiered. Undaunted, Brett sails for Australia unaware that Southey has caused his downfall. On the way, however, Brett discovers his spiritual home is Tahiti and settles down, finding an idyllic relationship with a beautiful girl, Belle Annie. When the war ends, Southey goes into business and becomes a wealthy tycoon. He arrives in Tahiti, hoping to build a tourist hotel, and sees his old rival standing on the quay. Southey accepts an invitation to Brett's house where, after a few drinks, he confesses to him that he was responsible for tipping off the customs. The two men fight and Southey leaves Brett lying unconscious. A thug, employed by a crafty shopkeeper Chong, who wants Belle Annie, seizes his chance and attempts to strangle Brett. When Brett is discovered and taken to hospital, Southey is arrested on an attempted murder charge. Brett, however, questions Chong, guesses the truth of the matter and decides to get his revenge on Southey by not informing the authorities. Southey is thrown out of Tahiti, leaving Brett to continue his happy life with Belle Annie.

REVIEWS

'The plot is contrived but Mason and Mills, together for the first time, play it strictly for laughs. And get them.'—*Daily Express*

'Mills and Mason are in tip-top form . . . it is a refreshing piece of escapism.'—*Evening Standard*

'A mismanaged tale of social conflict.'—*New Statesman*

'James Mason's easy caddishness does not weary with the years and passing fashions . . . the scenario is clear and taut.'—*Financial Times*

'A very civilised, light, ironic comedy. . . . Mr. James Mason plays the disreputable drifter so impeccably, that his teasing charm cannot be long resisted.'—*The Times*

'Mason and Mills, a splendid new partnership in character comedy . . . Mason reminds us what a master of droll mockery the screen has neglected all these years.'—*Daily Mail*

'An odd film . . . at once cruel and crude.'—*Spectator*

'The direction is at fault . . . too slow . . . but I certainly won't blame the acting of the two principals . . . [Mason and Mills] are an entertainment in themselves.'—Dilys Powell, *Sunday Times*

James Mason (1974):

My old father unaccountably read the novel on which this film was based, though he was no great book reader. He said that he could not see how we were to make a film of it. He showed better judgement than Ivan Foxwell or I—if one is to believe the evidence of the box office.

James as Capt. Brett Aimsley.

With Claude Dauphin.

TORPEDO BAY

(FINCHE DURA LA TEMPESTA. Alternative Italian title BETA SOM)

1964

A Galatea/Panorama production released by B.L.C./British Lion/Albion. *Producer:* Bruno Vailati. *Director:* Charles Frend. *Screenplay:* Pino Belli, Augusto Frassineti, Alberto Ca'zorzi, Charles Frend, Bruno Vailati and Jack Whittingham. *Director of Photography:* Gabor Pogany. *Art Director:* Georgio Giovanini. *Editor:* Giancarlo Cappelli. 78 minutes.

CAST

James Mason . . . . *Blayne*
Lilli Palmer. . . . . *Lygia da Silva*
Gabriele Ferzetti . . . . *Leonardi*
Alberto Lupo. . . . . *Magri*
Valeria Fabrizi. . . . . *Susanne*
Geoffrey Keen . . . . *Hodges*
Andrea Checchi . . . . *Michelizzi*
Renato de Carmine. . . . . *Ghedini*
Andrew Keir. . . . . *O'Brien*
Danielle Vargas . . . . *Brauzzi*

SYNOPSIS

When Commander Leonardi tries to force his Italian submarine through the Gibraltar Straits, the British Admiralty mobilises several anti-submarine craft led by Commander Blayne to hunt and destroy it. Badly shaken and damaged, Leonardi surfaces to find himself in international waters near Tangiers, where he is given permission to stay in port for two weeks, providing, at the end of this period, he either scuttles his ship or puts out to sea. Blayne also puts into port to keep surveillance, and a fragile truce is observed by both crews.

Leonardi meets and falls in love with Lygia, a doctor, who is tormented by doubts concerning his plans. While the two commanders are drawn together by a mutual respect for each other's courage and fairness, Hodges, the head of British Intelligence in Tangiers, is determined that the Italian sub-marine should remain neutral, or be destroyed. Through Lygia, Hodges tries to persuade Leonardi to accept internment, but Leonardi unfairly suspects her of being a spy and puts out to sea. Blayne follows and tries to sink the submarine, but Leonardi cleverly manages to turn the odds against him and inflict a fatal blow.

REVIEWS

'It is bad enough when a British film poses the last war as a kind of sporting contest and ignores the fact that the enemy's driving force was fascism. But when the Italians do it, it is intolerable. I was shocked to see this travesty of war-time struggles on the screen.'—*Daily Worker*

'Full of naive messages about international brother-hood, this rather dated film survives mainly through its cast.'—*Monthly Film Bulletin*

'Lacking any particular distinction, and only occasionally exciting, this war picture cannot have more than a limited appeal. James Mason plays with a stiff upper lip and a terrific suppression of emotion.'—*Kine Weekly*

'Moderately gripping. James Mason plays the captain as if to the manner born.'—*Daily Cinema*

James Mason (1974):

This, too, was a good film since it introduced me to Syracuse and Rome. Unfortunately scant attention was paid to screenwriting and valuable footage was wasted on a romantic side issue. But the Italian submarine commander's daring escape from the attentions of the British Navy through the straits of Gibraltar at the time of Italy's collapse in World War II was no unworthy subject for an Italian film pro-duction. I am shocked that the *Daily Worker*'s representative was shocked.

With Gabriele Ferzetti.

THE FALL OF THE ROMAN EMPIRE

1964

A Samuel Bronston production released by Rank. *Producer:* Samuel Bronston. *Director:* Anthony Mann. *Screenplay:* Ben Barzman, Basilio Franchina and Philip Yordan. *Director of Photography:* Robert Krasker. *Music:* Dmitri Tiomkin. *Art Directors:* Venierio Colasanti and John Moore. *Special Effects:* Alex Weldon. *Editor:* Robert Lawrence. Panavision. Technicolor. 165 minutes.

CAST

Sophia Loren . . . . *Lucilla*
Stephen Boyd . . . . *Livius*
Alec Guinness . . . . *Marcus Aurelius*
James Mason . . . . *Timonides*
Christopher Plummer . . . . *Commodus*
Anthony Quayle . . . . *Verulus*
John Ireland . . . . *Ballomar*
Mel Ferrer . . . . *Cleander*
Omar Sharif . . . . *Sohamus*
Eric Porter . . . . *Julianus*
Douglas Wilmer . . . . *Niger*
Peter Damon . . . . *Claudius*
Andrew Keir . . . . *Polybius*
George Murcell . . . . *Victorinus*
Lena von Martens . . . . *Helva*
Gabriella Licudi . . . . *Tauna*
Rafael Luis Calvo . . . . *Lentulus*
Norman Wooland . . . . *Virgilianus*
Virgilio Texera . . . . *Marcellus*
Michael Gwynn . . . . *Cornelius*
Guy Rolfe . . . . *Marius*
Finlay Currie . . . . *Caecina*

With John Ireland.

SYNOPSIS

At the height of the Roman Empire, Emperor Marcus Aurelius informs his adopted son Livius that he wishes him to be his successor. Cleander, a blind court prophet, overhears this and plots to kill Caesar before the announcement. In a forest skirmish with the Barbarians, Livius saves Caesar's son, Commodus, and punishes the cowardly gladiators. Commodus challenges him to a chariot contest, but Livius again saves his life.

Livius and the Emperor's daughter, Lucilla, are in love; but when he dies, uttering 'Livius', and Commodus proclaims himself Caesar, she marries the Armenian King, Sohamus, to prove solidarity with the Eastern frontier. Livius pledges support and Commodus appoints him Commander of the Army. Timonides, a Greek philosopher, attempts to win over the Barbarians after Livius has captured their leader. Lucilla returns to Rome, warning of unrest over new taxes, but Commodus sends her home and banishes Livius for pleading their cause. However, when the Eastern army sides with the rebels, Commodus begs Livius to help repel them. In spite of Lucilla's pleas to unite their forces, Livius wages battle and Sohamus is killed. Livius takes Lucilla in his arms and heads for Rome, and Commodus offers to share the throne. Livius refuses, wanting a new Rome, and Commodus orders the destruction of a Barbarian village promised safety by Livius.

Timonides is killed while trying to stop the attack, and when Lucilla and Livius arrive they find the village destroyed. At the gates of Rome, Livius leaves Lucilla and his army outside while he effects the surrender of Commodus. However, the Senate supports Commodus as Emperor and he sends wagons of gold to the gates to buy off the army. Lucilla is saved by some loyal soldiers and rushes to the palace to kill Commodus. She meets Verulus and learns that he is the true father of Commodus who, overhearing this, slays the unarmed ageing gladiator.

Commodus orders the Barbarians and Livius to be burned at the stake and Lucilla, rushing to his aid,

is tied beside him. About to ignite the pyre, Commodus remembers his debt to Livius and offers to fight with javelins, inviting the gods to settle the dispute. In a brutal contest, Livius wins and, as

With Alec Guinness.

161

James with Friedrich von Ledebur, Master of the Horse.

Commodus is dying, frees Lucilla and renounces the throne. While the Senators are bidding their wealth for the empty throne, Lucilla and Livius slip away knowing that, although some may die, the Brotherhood of Man will live for ever.

REVIEWS

'An epic to make one cheer rather than cringe; a credit to the art of the spectacle film.'—*Daily Express*

'This is one of the best all-round epics I have ever seen . . . The film has magnificent sets . . . spectacular action and even has more than a modicum of visible and audible scholarship. James Mason excels as the soul of wisdom playing a Greek philosopher.' —*Evening Standard*

'*The Fall* has intellectual pretensions and not much action, and what action there is . . . is very clumsily handled. Mason is good [as Timonides]. Sophia Loren plays Marcus Aurelius's daughter. And does she look bored! What sensitive girl wouldn't?'—*Guardian*

'James Mason . . . fighting steel with logic, has one of the film's best scenes . . . excellent performance.' —*Sunday Express*

'One reverts to the deliciously sordid details of actual history because they are so much more interesting than anything that takes place in this movie . . . a dreary, ponderous affair.'—*Newsweek*

'After a while one is beaten down and exhausted by the noise, the talk, the massive pictures, and all for the sake of a paragraph of uncertain ancient history . . . even actors like Alec Guinness, Christopher Plummer and James Mason must be content to work with their broadest brushes.'—*Financial Times*

James Mason (1974):

Friedrich von Ledebur was the Master of the Horse, and we had ample time for riding with him in the mountains. So it was not such a bad film.

THE PUMPKIN EATER

1964

A Romulus/Jack Clayton production released by Columbia/B.L.C. *Producer:* James Woolf. *Director:* Jack Clayton. *Screenplay:* Harold Pinter—*from the novel by* Penelope Mortimer. *Director of Photography:* Oswald Morris. *Music:* Georges Delerue. *Art Director:* Edward Marshall. *Editor:* James Clark. 118 minutes.

CAST

Anne Bancroft . . . . *Jo Armitage*
Peter Finch . . . . *Jake Armitage*
James Mason . . . . *Bob Conway*
Cedric Hardwicke . . . . . *Mr. James*
Richard Johnson . . . . . . *Giles*
Janine Gray . . . . *Beth Conway*
Maggie Smith . . . . *Philpot*
Eric Porter . . . . *Dr. Ingrams*
Rosalind Atkinson . . . . . *Mrs. James*
Harold Scott . . . . *Mr. Armitage*
Faith Kent . . . . *Nanny*
Yootha Joyce . . . . *Woman in Hairdresser's*
Frank Singuineau . . . . . . *The Jamaican*

SYNOPSIS

Jo Armitage, an attractive and extraordinarily fertile woman, lives with her fourth husband, Jake, a successful film writer, in a fashionable house surrounded by all the trappings of wealth. She had been introduced to Jake by her third husband, Giles, and, after the birth of her sixth child, left Giles and married Jake. Now, despite the strong emotional and physical ties between Jo and Jake, she is unable to adapt to his life in show business and wants him to settle down to a permanent and domestic existence. With the marriage slowly breaking up, Jo survives Jake's affair with a gushing and feckless girl, Philpot, but by now her family has increased by the arrival of yet another child.

After suffering a breakdown in Harrod's, and an encounter with an unbalanced woman in a hairdresser's salon, Jo consults a psychologist, but without much success. Then, after the funeral of her father, and the confirmation of yet another pregnancy, Jo and Jake decide she should undergo sterilisation. When she returns home, Jo is crisp, decisive and her old self again. Bob Conway, a guest who once made an unreciprocated pass at her at a studio party thrown for Jake, re-enters her new life with the revelation that Jake has been having an affair with his wife Beth, the leading lady of Jake's new film, and that she is going to have Jake's child. Completely demoralized, Jo fights with Jake, leaves him and goes straight to Giles' bed. The following morning Jake phones Giles to tell him that his father

With Anne Bancroft.

With Peter Finch.

has died. At the funeral Jake refuses to notice Jo and she falls in the mud chasing after him. She goes to their new, unfinished house in the country and spends the night alone but is awakened by the sound of children's voices. Jo sees Jake leading her family up the hill and goes down to meet them, resigned to accepting her life with him and the fact that there are no practical alternatives.

REVIEWS

'There never was a film so rawly memorable as this . . . Harold Pinter's brilliant script captures the complexity of life itself . . . James Mason's sand-paper voiced other husband gives the film a lot of its sardonic humour. . . . *The Pumpkin Eater* is a magnificent film . . . one of the best films made anywhere.' —*Evening Standard*

'*The Pumpkin Eater* is rich, warm and painfully alive. . . . Harold Pinter wrote the screenplay which is acute as you'd expect and funnier than you might suppose . . . a singularly truthful film. James Mason walks the wire of tragi-comedy with some courage and to his resounding credit.'—*Sunday Telegraph*

'James Mason persistently extends his range . . . his portrait here of the vindictive acquaintance is an extraordinary explosion of vicious fury.'—Dilys Powell, *Sunday Times*

'The film of the year.'—*Evening News*

'One can positively feel the strain as everyone concerned resolved that, come what may, it is going to be the film that will set us all back on our heels. Well, it is not; not by a long way. It is solid, serious, intelligent, stylish. . . . It is also, for the most part, quite dead. A sad disappointment.'—*The Times*

James Mason (1974):

The Times was unfair, I think, in suggesting that this was a pretentious film. One must look elsewhere for its failure to grip. For all his enormous talent, I choose to look in Pinter's direction.

LORD JIM

1965

A Columbia/Keep production released by Columbia/B.L.C. *Produced, directed and written by* Richard Brooks—*from the novel by* Joseph Conrad. *Director of Photography:* Frederick Young. *Music:* Bronislau Kaper. *Art Directors:* Bill Hutchinson and Ernest Archer. *Special Effects:* Cliff Richardson. *Editor:* Alan Osbiston. Super Panavision. Technicolor. 154 minutes.

CAST

Peter O'Toole . . . . . . *Lord Jim*
James Mason . . . . . . *Gentleman Brown*
Curt Jurgens . . . . . . *Cornelius*
Eli Wallach . . . . *The General*
Jack Hawkins . . . . . . *Marlow*
Paul Lukas . . . . *Stein*
Akim Tamiroff . . . . . *Schomberg*
Daliah Lavi . . . . *The Girl*
Ichizo Itami . . . . *Waris*
Tatsuo Saito . . . . . . *Chief Du-Ramin*
Eric Young . . . . *Malay*
Andrew Keir . . . . *Brierly*
Jack MacGowran . . . . *Robinson*
Walter Gotell . . . . . . *Captain of the S.S. 'Patna'*
Noel Purcell . . . . *Captain Chester*
Serge Reggiani . . . . . *French Lieutenant*
Rafik Anwar . . . . *Moslem Leader*

SYNOPSIS

After serving his apprenticeship under the paternal eye of Capt. Marlow, Jim, an incurable romantic and idealist, becomes a first officer in the Mercantile Marine. He dreams of the day when his mettle will be tested but, when that day comes, Jim, signing up with a broken-down pilgrim ship—the S.S. Patna—foolishly commits an act of cowardice which results in an official discharge and the cancellation of his sailing papers.

Hoping for a second chance to redeem himself, Jim agrees to take some explosives to the natives of Patusan—a journey deep into the unmapped jungles of the East where a feudal war-lord is terrorising the population. He is caught by the self-styled General and tortured, before finally being helped to escape by a native girl. While Jim is trying to organise the natives to resist, the General's partner, Cornelius, hires the help of a notorious river pirate, Gentleman Brown. Eventually Jim and Gentleman Brown meet and agree to a truce, but the pirate doubles back to the village in the hope of stealing the temple treasures. Jim, who is aware of this, keeps guard and, when the raiders approach, kills them by firing a cannon loaded with precious stones. His friend, Waris, is killed in the skirmish and Jim, in order to appease his father, ceremoniously sacrifices his own life.

REVIEWS

'Richard Brooks has taken Conrad's great novel and made it into a film of stature and substance . . . the film is a succession of fine performances. The bearded James Mason . . . is outstanding.'—*Daily Express*

'Brooks's obvious approach . . . is inhibiting and stifling . . . a cold monument to literature. James Mason, Curt Jurgens and Akim Tamiroff comport themselves with honor.'—*Newsweek*

'The first half hour or so is extraordinarily heavy-handed. Thereafter, things speed up a trifle and some of the action scenes are not too badly managed, but the whole thing is horribly lifeless, eminently respectable and well-meaning, but somehow embalmed. Mr. James Mason is as splendid as ever in a pretty insignificant rôle.'—*The Times*

'*Lord Jim* is a vast, teeming, colourful and spectacular experience. . . . James Mason indulges in some wicked scene-stealing . . . big and alive and exciting. . . . It is cinema.'—*The Sun*

'A tedious, tortuous, wordy voyage . . . a highly obscure saga, visually superb, verbally supine.'—*Daily Mirror*

'Unlucky Jim . . . far worse than a comic strip, it is a Reader's Digest version of Conrad's novel.'—*Guardian*

'The real acting comes from the strong supporting cast—and right at the head marches James Mason.' —*Evening Standard*

James Mason (1974):
This was a good film in the sense that we all got to visit the Far East in a style consistent with the demands of our guilds and our agents.

On the other hand most of the critics and moviegoers seem to have found it a bit of a bore. And it was long enough to need an intermission. Consequently those who chose to go home at this point missed the bearded James Mason comporting himself with honour, since his rôle featured only in the second half.

166

GENGHIS KHAN

1965

An Irving Allen/C.C.C. (Berlin)/Avavla (Belgrade) production released by Columbia, B.L.C. *Producer:* Irving Allen. *Director:* Henry Levin. *Screenplay:* Clarke Reynolds and Beverley Cross—*from the novel by* Berkely Mather. *Director of Photography:* Geoffrey Unsworth. *Special Effects:* Bill Warrington and David Warrington. *Music:* Dusan Radic. *Art Directors:* Heino Weidemann and Mile Nickolic. *Editor:* Geoffrey Foot. Panavision. Technicolor. 126 minutes.

CAST

Stephen Boyd	*Jamuga*
Omar Sharif	*Temujin-Genghis Khan*
James Mason	*Kam Ling*
Eli Wallach	*The Shah of Khwarezm*
Françoise Dorleac	*Bortei*
Telly Savalas	*Shan*
Robert Morley	*The Emperor of China*
Michael Hordern	*Geen*
Yvonne Mitchell	*Katke*
Woody Strode	*Sengal*
Kenneth Cope	*Subodai*
Roger Croucher	*Kassar*
Don Borisenko	*Jebai*
Patrick Holt	*Kuehluk*
Suzanne Hsaio	*Chin Yu*
George Savalas	*Toktoa*
Carlo Cura	*Temujin as a child*
Gustavo Rojo	*Altan*
Dusan Vujsic	*Ho Mun Tim*
Jovan Tesic	*Fut Su*
Andreja Marcic	*Chagedai*
Thomas Margulies	*Jochi*
Yamata Pauli Linda Loncar	*Indian Girls*
Branislav Radovic	*1st Slave Dealer*
Zvonko Jovcic	*2nd Slave Dealer*

SYNOPSIS

The young son of a slaughtered Mongol chieftain, Prince Temujin is brought up as a slave in the camp of Jamuga, the evil leader of the Merkit tribe. Growing to manhood, he escapes to the mountains

accompanied by a negro mute, Sengal, and a holy man, Geen, and begins to build a tribe around him consisting mainly of Mongol prisoners rescued from the Merkits. He also abducts the Princess Bortei, who is betrothed to Jamuga, and marries her. She becomes his devoted wife and bears him a son.

Bortei is recaptured by Jamuga before Temujin rescues her and leads his band eastwards towards China. He gains the favour of the Court and the Emperor by repelling the Merkits who have attacked the Great Wall, and by capturing Jamuga. The Emperor bestows upon Temujin the title of 'Genghis Khan' but, when Temujin decides to leave China, he fears he will return with an invading army, and arranges for Jamuga to assassinate him. Genghis Khan is forewarned of the plot and escapes with his army before setting out on his march of conquest. He manages to defeat the Merkits, and slays Jamuga in single combat. But, with the defeated tribe offering their allegiance, Genghis Khan is himself dying from wounds and is forced to hand over to his son, who has seen the realisation of his father's dream of a united land.

REVIEWS

'If this is magnificence, give me the Ambersons. James Mason, equipped with an upper set of false rabbit teeth, brings off a genuine feat of impersonation as an effetely beaming Oriental diplomat.'— Kenneth Tynan, *Observer*

'In the rôle of a 12th century Chinese, James Mason turns in probably the worst character performance of the year . . . certainly the most absurd of his career.' —*Evening News*

'A lively historical adventure . . . the sense of fun is communicated through the performances—notably of James Mason and Robert Morley and Michael Hordern.'—*Financial Times*

'James Mason with a pig-tail, gummed up eyes, the kind of false teeth you find in a toy shop, and sing-song falsetto voice is an outrage on a good actor.' —*Evening Standard*

'James Mason wraps himself so completely in the rôle as to achieve the best character performance of the whole picture.'—*Daily Mail*

'Best of all [is] James Mason parodying the falsetto voice and sing-song intonations with which the Chinese speak English. Velly funny.'—*Daily Telegraph*

'More entertaining than the usual run of spectaculars . . . James Mason manages to be extremely funny without sending the film up, as well as convincing.' —*Guardian*

James Mason (1974):

Speaking of outrages, as the *Evening Standard* insists on doing, the only substantial one in my case was the wearing of a pigtail by a Chinese Foreign Minister (or whatever I was supposed to be) in the 12th century. Ask your Chinese friends about this.

LES PIANOS MÉCANIQUES

(U.S. title THE UNINHIBITED)

1965

C.I.C.C. Films Borderie/Precitel/Francos Film/ Standard Film/Tera Explorer Film/Cesaro Gonzales released by Prodis. *Director:* Juan Antonio Bardem. *Screenplay and original novel by* Henri-François Rey. *Director of Photography:* Jabor Pogany. *Music:* George Delerue. *Art Director:* Enrique Alonçon. *Editor:* Juan Antonio Bardem. Eastmancolor. 95 minutes.

CAST

Melina Mercouri . . . . *Jenny*
Hardy Kruger . . . . *Vincent*
James Mason . . . . *Regnier*
Didier Haudepin . . . . *Daniel*
Jose Maria Monpin. . . . . *Tom*
Luis Inouni . . . . *Bryant*
Renaud Verley. . . . . *Serge*
Martine Ziguel. . . . . *Nadine*
Maurice Teynac. . . . . *Reginald*
Keiko Kishi . . . . *Nora*
Karine Mossberg . . . . *Orange*

SYNOPSIS

In order to recuperate after a nervous breakdown, Vincent, an unhappy young man, arrives in a small town on the Costa Brava, Caldeya, where he immediately finds himself involved in the private lives of the inhabitants. The social centre of the town is a nightclub-bar run by an attractive middle-aged woman, Jenny, with whom Vincent has a brief, intense affair. She leaves him, however, for an alcoholic novelist, Regnier, who is desperately trying to recapture lost inspiration. At the same time, Regnier's precocious son, Daniel, is emotionally upset by the death of a close friend. The lives of these people become interwoven as they attempt to solve their various problems.

REVIEW

'James Mason, Melina Mercouri and Hardy Kruger cannot do much with this surface melodrama . . . gradiloquent . . . cliché ridden. James Mason floats through his rôle.'—*Variety*

With Hardy Kruger.

With Melina Mercouri.

James Mason (1974):
Being based on the book by Henri François Rey
and directed by Juan Bardem there was inevitably
much that was good in the film. However, there were
laughs in the wrong places. Anyone who sees the film
will know why. But the epithets thrown at it by the
gent from *Variety* miss the mark.

THE BLUE MAX

1966

A 20th Century-Fox production and release. *Producer:* Christian Ferry. *Director:* John Guillermin. *Screenplay:* David Pursall, Jack Seddon and Gerald Hanley—*from the novel by* Jack D. Hunter. *Director of Photography:* Douglas Slocombe. *Music:* Jerry Goldsmith. *Art Director:* Fred Carter. *Special Effects:* Karl Baumgartner, Maurice Ayres and Ron Ballinger. *Aerial Photography:* Skeets Kelly. *Editor:* Max Benedict. CinemaScope. DeLuxe Color. 155 minutes.

CAST

George Peppard . . . . *Bruno Stachel*
James Mason . . . . . *Count von Klugermann*
Ursula Andress . . . . *Countess Kaeti*
Jeremy Kemp . . . . . *Willi von Klugermann*
Karl Michael Vogler . *Heidemann*
Loni von Friedl . . . . *Elfi Heidemann*
Anton Diffring . . . . . *Holbach*
Peter Woodthorpe . . *Rupp*
Harry Towb . . . . . . *Kettering*
Derek Newark . . . . . *Ziegel*
Derren Nesbitt . . . . *Fabian*
Friedrich Ledebur . . *Field Marshall von Lenndorf*
Roger Ostime . . . . . *Crown Prince*
Hugo Schuster . . . . *Hans*
Tim Parkes . . . . *1st Pilot*
Ian Kingsley . . . . . . *2nd Pilot*
Ray Browne . . . . . . *3rd Pilot*
Carl Schell . . . . *Baron von Richtofen*

SYNOPSIS

To win the 'Blue Max', a highly coveted medal awarded to outstanding German fighter pilots, is the single-minded ambition of a young and attractive pilot, Bruno Stachel. For this reason he is unpopular with the other pilots and, when on a mission with fellow pilot Willi von Klugermann, his 'kill' is unconfirmed, but Willi's tally makes him eligible for the medal, Stachel becomes even more obsessed and resolves to let nothing stand in his way. He captures and shoots down a British plane above his airfield—a cold-blooded act which makes him even more unpopular with his colleagues but which catches the attention of Count von Klugermann, Willi's uncle, who has arrived with his beautiful wife, Kaeti, to present the Blue Max to Willi. Kaeti, who is having an affair with Willi, is also impressed with Stachel's exploits and they, too, become lovers.

As the weeks go by, Stachel's tally begins to rise until he is within one 'kill' of getting the medal. While returning from a mission with Willi, they both try to out-fly each other and Willi is killed when his plane crashes. Stachel uses the opportunity to claim Willi's last 'kill' and win the medal. The station commander, Heidemann, suspects the truth, but the Count overrides this and plans to award Stachel the medal at the launching of a new plane he (Stachel) is testing. When Kaeti is unable to persuade Stachel to run away with her to Switzerland, she informs the Count that Heidemann's suspicions were true. The Count also learns that the plane has developed a fault and should not be flown. He does not, however, tell Stachel, who innocently climbs into the pilot's seat and takes off —to his death.

REVIEWS

'James Mason's Prussian aristocrat exuding rarefied courtesy and control is easily the finest thing in the film.'—*Sunday Express*

'James Mason, as the over-bearing count, is splendid.'—*Daily Express*

'*The Blue Max* is one of the best ever made about the air battle in World War One. . . . Undeniably the

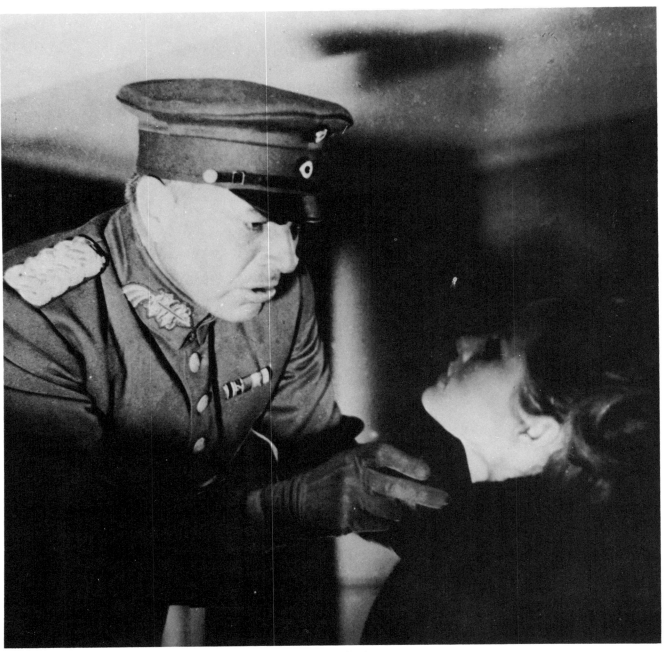

With Ursula Andress.

film bogs down occasionally in the cliché treatment of character and plot—but the intelligence of the players, especially James Mason, keeps our attention on it until it can spread its wings again.'—*Evening Standard*

'A Sunday supplement picture of a war, but not the war itself . . . the film never gets a bite on its period.'—*Observer*

'John Guillermin has directed a film which certainly has an authentic flavour, but it is enfeebled by having no attitude, no sense of purpose. Begins to get interesting 25 minutes before it ends.'—*Financial Times*

'An often spectacular, if oddly indeterminate epic . . . The aerial sequences are excellent, but on the ground the film does not seem at all sure what it really wants to say, or where it really wants to go.'—*Sun*

'Diffuse and emotionally flat despite its expert airborne excitement . . . synthetic melodrama.'—*Time* magazine

'The most thrilling parts of the film are the scenes in the air.'—*Guardian*

James Mason (1974):
It was not only the airplanes who scored, but also Douglas Slocombe who photographed them.

GEORGY GIRL

1966

An Everglades production released by Columbia Pictures. *Producers:* Otto Plaschkes and Robert A. Goldston. *Director:* Silvio Narizzano. *Screenplay:* Margaret Forster and Peter Nichols—*from the novel by* Margaret Forster. *Director of Photography:* Ken Higgins. *Music:* Alexander Faris. *Songs:* *'I'm Gonna Leave Her'* by The Mirage; *'Georgy Girl', music* by Tom Springfield, *lyrics by* Jim Dale, *sung by* The Seekers. *Art Director:* Tony Woollard. *Editor:* John Bloom. 99 minutes.

CAST

James Mason	*James Leamington*
Alan Bates	*Jos*
Lynn Redgrave	*Georgy*
Charlotte Rampling	*Meredith*
Bill Owen	*Ted*
Clare Kelly	*Doris*
Rachel Kempson	*Ellen*
Denise Coffey	*Peg*
Dorothy Alison	*Health Visitor*
Peggy Thorpe-Bates	*Hospital Sister*
Dandy Nichols	*Hospital Nurse*
Terence Soall	*Salesman*
Jolyan Booth	*Registry Office Clerk*

SYNOPSIS

At 22, and still a virgin, Georgy, believing herself to be unattractive to the opposite sex, suffers from an over-sized self-rejection complex. Her parents, Ted and Doris, are employed by James Leamington, a wealthy man, who, although married, is childless. He has always looked upon Georgy as a daughter, but now, not quite 50, his feelings are beginning to change and he asks her to become his mistress. Georgy is able to postpone giving him a straight answer to his unsolicited proposition when she discovers that her flat-mate, Meredith, a violinist, is pregnant, and that she intends to marry her latest lover, a charming but fickle young man, Jos.

While James, the persevering benefactor, waits for an answer, Meredith's brazen egotism becomes obvious even to the selfish Jos, who realises he is falling in love with Georgy, just as much as she is

With Lynn Redgrave.

falling in love with him. Finally they become lovers, only to discover that Meredith has been taken to hospital in labour. When the baby arrives, Jos and Meredith want the child to be adopted, but Georgy, horrified at their callousness, decides to become the 'de facto' mother. While Meredith leaves the hospital looking for new conquests, Georgy is torn between her passion for Jos, her mother-love for the baby and James's love for her. Fully realising the unsatisfactory state of her life, Georgy decides that her ultimate happiness will lie in marrying James, who will provide love and security for both herself and the child.

REVIEWS

'Silvio Narizzano's direction makes the film dance over the moral implications like a bubble in a breeze. . . . The whole film is a delight.'—*Daily Express*
'*Georgy Girl* is enjoyable, though at times it tends to be swamped in an avalanche of gimmicks. James Mason is excellent.'—*Sunday Express*
'In *Georgy Girl* one feels that its makers have looked at rather too many English movies.'—*Saturday Review*

'Lynn Redgrave makes a fairly unsavoury and unlikely tale seem savoury and likely. . . . James Mason responds splendidly to Silvio Narizzano's lively direction.'—*Daily Mail*
'A delightful comedy.'—*Evening News*
'Miss Redgrave's tom-boy, ugly duckling charm is simply exploited for an hour and a half with constantly diminishing returns.'—*Guardian*
'Too many clichés, and the serious bits weigh decidedly heavy.'—*The Times*
'The script is one long knowing retort, spoken very fast and hard. James Mason walks through in a trite part as a farcical Northern sugar daddy. He is far too good to waste like this.'—*Observer*
'Acted with zeal and skill and directed with restless vim . . . beautifully played by James Mason.'—*Evening Standard*

James Mason (1974):

A delightful adventure directed resourcefully by a Narizzano unimpeded by executive know-how. The right people in the right jobs, from Lynn Redgrave to the Seekers. Not since *The Seventh Veil* had I been connected with such a palpable hit.

With Lynn Redgrave in *Georgy Girl.*

THE DEADLY AFFAIR

1966

A Sidney Lumet production released by Columbia Pictures. *Producer and Director:* Sidney Lumet. *Screenplay:* Paul Dehn—*from the novel* Call for the Dead *by* John Le Carré. *Director of Photography:* Frederick Young. *Music:* Quincy Jones. *Art Director:* John Howell. *Editor:* Thelma Connell. Technicolor. 107 minutes.

CAST

James Mason . . . . *Charles Dobbs*
Simone Signoret . . . . *Elsa Fennan*
Maximilian Schell . . . . *Dieter Frey*
Harriet Andersson . . . . *Anna Dobbs*
Harry Andrews . . . . *Inspector Mendel*
Kenneth Haigh . . . . *Bill Appleby*
Roy Kinnear . . . . *Adam Scarr*
Max Adrian . . . . *Adviser*
Lynn Redgrave . . . . *Virgin*
Robert Flemyng . . . . *Samuel Fennan*
Corin Redgrave . . . . *Director*
Les White . . . . *Harek*
June Murphy . . . . *1st Witch*
Frank Williams . . . . *2nd Witch*
Rosemary Lord . . . . *3rd Witch*
Kenneth Ivew . . . . *Stagehand*
John Dimech . . . . *Waiter*
Julian Sherrier . . . . *Head Waiter*
Petra Markham . . . . *Daughter at Theatre*
Denis Shaw . . . . *Landlord*
Maria Charles . . . . *Blonde*
Amanda Walker . . . . *Brunette*
Sheraton Blount . . . . *Eunice Scarr*
Janet Hargreaves . . . . *Ticket Clerk*
Michael Brennan . . . . *Barman*
Richard Steele ⎱ . . . . *Businessmen*
Gertan Klauber ⎰
Margaret Lacey . . . . *Mrs. Bird*
Judy Keirn . . . . *Stewardess*
And members of the Royal Shakespeare Company performing *Edward II*.

SYNOPSIS

Charles Dobbs, 'Control' agent, makes a security check interview on Samuel Fennan, a top Foreign Office official, and is surprised to learn, later, of the man's apparent suicide. He is sent to interview the dead man's wife, Elsa, a German Jewess who has experienced much suffering in the Nazi concentration camps during the War, and comes away suspecting that the suicide is not as simple as it looks. His adviser, strangely, wants the whole affair left alone and Dobbs angrily resigns, only to follow up the case on his own. He enlists the aid of Mendel, an ex-police inspector and the department's unofficial liaison on the case, and Appleby, a young colleague in his office.

Dobbs finds himself trailed by a car and, when he and Mendel track the car down, a murderous attack is made on them. Meanwhile, his private life is also

With Robert Flemyng in *The Deadly Affair.*

With Harriet Andersson.

worrying him because his wife Anna, who has never concealed her affairs from him, decides to go away to Zurich with Dieter Frey, a German friend of Dobbs's, whom he had controlled as an agent in Austria during the War. Released from hospital, Dobbs decides he must break Elsa and force her to tell him the truth regarding her husband. In doing so, however, he is forced to reject personal values for the dubious morality of his profession—the spy game.

REVIEWS
'The climax is as gaspingly exciting as the best of the thrillers Alfred Hitchcock used to make.'—*Evening Standard*
'A thriller which is realistic and often witty . . . superbly played by James Mason.'—*Daily Express*
'The Lumet direction keeps the screen vividly alive in all scenes . . . James Mason is entirely convincing.' —*Herald Tribune*
'*The Deadly Affair* is a lively thriller. I have seldom seen James Mason as good.'—*Sunday Express*
'The Le Carré world of conscious-striken intelligence

agents retains its engrossing melancholy.'—*Spectator*
'A most ingenious sub-thriller.'—*New Statesman*
'The violence is never pointless and the whole film is a most skilful organisation of action, motive and character. James Mason is at his best.'—Dilys Powell, *Sunday Times*
'Lumet has turned out an almost totally satisfying bit of entertainment. It is not great art, but it's a very absorbing hundred minutes . . . of all the cast it is only Mason who occasionally overdoes it.'—*Guardian*
'James Mason, giving one of his best performances, makes a sympathetic and recognisable whole of the character of the agent.'—*Sun*

James Mason (1974):
John Le Carré is the best of all spy storytellers, and his agents are consequently far from glamorous and equally far from becoming box-office attractions. One hopes that one of these days a director will find a formula for making a hit picture from one of his stories without sacrificing Le Carré's truthfulness.

180

STRANGER IN THE HOUSE

1967

A de Grunwald production released by Rank. *Producer:* Dimitri de Grunwald. *Directed and written by:* Pierre Rouve—*from the novel* Les Inconnus dans la Maison *by* Georges Simenon. *Director of Photography:* Ken Higgins. *Music:* Patrick John Scott. *Song: 'Ain't That So?' by* Eric Burdon and The Animals. *Art Director:* Tony Woollard. *Editor:* Ernest Walter. Eastmancolor. 104 minutes.

With Geraldine Chaplin.

CAST

James Mason . . . . *John Sawyer*
Geraldine Chaplin . . . . . *Angela Sawyer*
Bobby Darin . . . . *Barney Teale*
Paul Bertoya . . . . *Jo Christophorides*
Ian Ogilvy . . . . *Desmond Flower*
Bryan Stanyon . . . . *Peter Hawkins*
Pippa Steel . . . . *Sue Phillips*
Clive Morton . . . . *Col. Flower*
James Hayter . . . . *Harley Hawkins*
Megs Jenkins . . . . *Mrs. Christophorides*
Lisa Daniely . . . . *Diana*
Moira Lister . . . . *Mrs. Flower*
Yootha Joyce . . . . *Girl at Shooting Range*
John Menderson . . . . . . *Old Clerk*
Rita Webb. . . . . *Mrs. Plaskett*
Danvers Walker . . . . . . *Chetham*
Julian Orchard . . . . *Policeman*
Ivor Dean . . . . *Inspector Colder*
Marjie Lawrence. . . . . . *Brenda*
Lindy Aaron. . . . . *Angela as a child*
Lucy Griffiths. . . . . *Library Cleaner*
Charlotte Selwyn. . . . . . *Salesgirl*
Melinda May . . . . *Librarian*
Tom Kempinski . . . . . . *Shop Assistant*
Sheila White . . . . *Hazel*
Toni Palmer. . . . . *Doorwoman*
Michael Standing . . . . . *Fashion Photographer*
Anne Hart . . . . *Barmaid*

SYNOPSIS

John Sawyer, a former eminent barrister, has become a recluse since his wife left him 15 years ago. His only contact with the outside world is his young and pretty daughter, Angela, who lives with him and has a close circle of friends who have nothing in common with his own generation. While she visits cafés and discotheques, John finds some solace by drinking whisky and playing old gramophone records.

On the fringe of Angela's group is Jo Christophorides,

With Dimitri de Grunwald.

With Geraldine Chaplin.

a Cypriot, who is tolerated rather than accepted only because Angela loves him. When a new member of the clan, Barney Teale, a licentious ship's steward, is found murdered in John's house, Jo is the prime suspect. John decides to defend the boy, although the case looks hopeless, and he treats the opening proceedings with the contempt he feels they deserve. He has, however, one trick up his sleeve which he plays at a 21st birthday party given for Desmond, another friend of Angela's, by his father, the town's chief constable. Because Barney had discovered that Desmond was impotent, Desmond had murdered him and pointed the blame at Jo. This experience leads John to a greater understanding of the younger generation and a reconciliation with life itself.

REVIEWS

'As a drama, this story, taken from a Simenon novel, is fraught with improbability and loaded with overdrawn characters. Nevertheless, it is well worth seeing for James Mason's brilliant performance.'—*Daily Express*

'Mason contributes another fine performance. But there are gaping incongruities in the story, and the main characters are, for the most part, unbelievable.' *Sunday Express*

'Curse the day James Mason, a fine actor on happier occasions, was induced to play the part of a once famous barrister who's taken to drink after losing a client's life and his own wife's affections.'—*Evening Standard*

'A succession of set-pieces in a weird assortment of styles . . . a ragbag, but it is never dull.'—*The Times*

'Bad writing and poor direction . . . there are moments when James Mason brings the picture to flickering life.'—*Observer*

'*Stranger in the House* is so bad except when that incorruptible pro James Mason is on camera . . . the dialogue has that peculiarly hallucinatory quality of translation.'—*New Statesman*

'A patchwork of fragments which might well have come from different films . . . practically all the scenes with James Mason are witty, expert, professional in every respect.'—*Financial Times*

'James Mason gives a great big performance, and one which he obviously enjoyed as much as we do.' —*Guardian*

James Mason (1974):

I'd had the feeling it wouldn't work. After its bad reception in England I was further mortified when an executive of the company that was to distribute it in the U.S. told me, with the air of one who has solved an abstruse conundrum, that he had thought of the perfect title for transatlantic use: COP OUT. And he was not kidding.

With Ian Ogilvy.

THE LONDON NOBODY KNOWS

1967

A Norcon production released by British Lion. *Producer and Director:* Norman Cohen. *Screenplay and Original Book:* Geoffrey Fletcher. *Additional Material:* Brian Comport. *Director of Photography:* Terry Maher. *Music:* Wilfred Burns—*featuring music-hall songs sung by* Francis Barlow and John Rutland. *Editor:* David Gilbert. *Narrator:* James Mason. Eastmancolor. 48 minutes.

SYNOPSIS

Acting as narrator and guide, James Mason pays homage to the unfashionable parts of London—the emphasis being on the relics of a former age (mostly Victorian) that have survived the modern bulldozers in pursuit of progress. He visits the old Bedford Theatre, the 'catacombs' beneath the Camden Freight Terminal, the Chapel Street Market and a Salvation Army hostel.

REVIEWS

'A documentary that scarcely stands up to its all-sweeping title. James Mason is bland, amiable, but often seeming a shade bored. His tone and expression is that of a man who clearly wishes to be home with his hands thankfully clutching a dry martini.'— *Daily Sketch*

'A colourful documentary.'—*Daily Mail*

James Mason (1974):

There were passages in this film which hinted that the director had a talent for comedy. This hint encouraged the Boulting Brothers to hire Norman Cohen to direct the film versions of *Till Death Us Do Part* and *Dad's Army*. The film took me on some interesting strolls in parts of London with which I was not familiar. Various groups made some money from the film's distribution. So everyone was happy, even probably the man from the *Daily Sketch*, who, quite rightly, pointed out the discrepancy between title and content. I assumed that we were stuck with the title because Cohen was using Geoffrey Fletcher's book of that name as his point of departure.

James on location for *The London Nobody Knows* (bottom right with Norman Cohen).

DUFFY

1968

A Martin Manulis/Columbia (British) production released by Columbia. *Producer:* Martin Manulis. *Director:* Robert Parrish. *Screenplay:* Donald Cammell and Harry Joe Brown Jr.—*from an original story by* Donald Cammell, Harry Joe Brown Jr. and Pierre de la Salle. *Director of Photography:* Otto Heller. *Music:* Ernie Freeman. *Song: 'I'm Satisfied' by* Cynthia Weil, Barry Mann and Ernie Freeman, *sung by* Lou Rawls. *Art Director:* Phillip Harrison. *Editor:* William Kemplen. Technicolor. 101 minutes.

CAST

James Coburn	*Duffy*
James Mason	*Charles Calvert*
James Fox	*Stefane Calvert*
Susannah York	*Segolene*
John Alderton	*Antony Calvert*
Guy Deghy	*Captain Schoeller*
Carl Duering	*Bonivet*
Tutte Lemkow	*Spaniard*
Marne Maitland	*Abdul*
André Maranne	*Inspector Garain*
Julie Mendez	*Belly Dancer*
Barry Shawzin	*Bakirgian*

SYNOPSIS

Charles Calvert, a British banker and shipping tycoon, is cunning and ruthless. He has two sons by different mothers: Stefane, a wealthy idler, and Antony, a downtrodden clerk who works for his father. Both sons hate their father and plan to rob him of the several million dollars he is transferring from Tangiers to Marseille by ship. Together with Stefane's mistress, the beautiful Segolene, they

With James Fox in *Duffy.*

With James Fox in *Duffy*.

enlist the help of an exiled American criminal living in Tangiers—Duffy.

After the clever and successful coup, Duffy and Segolene, who has become his mistress, lay low while Stefane looks for a buyer. Duffy, however, receives conflicting cables and smells a trick. He discovers that Segolene is also Calvert's mistress and that they have double-crossed them all from the beginning. By a neat act of table-turning, Duffy hands the money to the police and claims the 50-thousand dollar reward.

REVIEWS

'In spite of the hip jargon, the laconic presence of James Coburn, the sensuous charm of Susannah York, the result is as invigorating as a glass of warm milk at bedtime. Like man, I don't really dig it too much. It just isn't my scene.'—*Daily Express*
'An abysmal "swinging" comedy.'—*Evening Standard*
'Too much of the film is ragged and casual, with improvisatory dialogue full of fluffs, giggles and last year's with-it chat. . . . Only the indestructible James Mason, surveying the whole proceedings with calm contempt, conveys real authority.'—*The Times*
'A brittle, silly, pretty, frivolous spoof . . . not a film for the serious student of cinema. I loved it . . . superb James Mason.'—*Observer*
'A shabby, spurious, hippy-obsessed yarn . . . fails miserably.'—*Sunday Express*
'I didn't dig, man.'—*Sun*
'Makes one squirm with embarrassment.'—*Evening News*
'There's only extreme tedium in this complicated story.'—*Daily Telegraph*
'Entertaining, but moderately mindless.'—*Guardian*
'Unmitigated tosh.'—*New Statesman*

James Mason (1974):

Tosh perhaps, but surely not unmitigated. For instance the basic plot was better than your average heist story, I thought. It must have been that hippy stuff which so upset the English critics.

190

MAYERLING

1968

A Corona/Winchester production released by Warner-Pathé. *Producer:* Marcel Hellman. *Director:* Terence Young. *Screenplay:* Terence Young—*from the books* Mayerling *by* Claude Anet *and* The Archduke *by* Michael Arnold. *Director of Photography:* Henri Alekan. *Art Director:* Maurice Colasson. *Music:* Francis Lai. Panavision. Eastmancolor. 141 minutes.

CAST

Omar Sharif.	*Crown Prince Rudolf*
Catherine Deneuve. . . .	*Maria Vetsera*
James Mason	*Emperor Franz Josef*
Ava Gardner	*Empress Elizabeth*
James Robertson Justice	*Edward, Prince of Wales*
Genevieve Page.	*Countess Larisch*
Andrea Parisy.	*Crown Princess Stephanie*
Ivan Desny	*Count Josef Hoyos*
Charles Millot.	*Count Taafe*
Maurice Teynac	*Moritz Szeps*
Roger Pigaut	*Count Karolyi*
Fabienne Dali.	*Mizzi Kaspar*
Bernard Lajarrige	*Loschek*
Moustache.	*Bratfisch*
Mony Dalmes.	*Baroness Helen Vetsera*
Lyne Chardonnet.	*Hannah Vetsera*
Alain Saury	*Baltazzi*
Irene von Meyendorff. .	*Countess Stockau*
Veronique Vendell	*Lisl Stockau*
Jean-Claude Bercq	*Duke Michael of Braganza*
Jacques Berthier	*Prince John Salvator*
Howard Vernon	*Prince Montenuevo*
Jean-Michel Rouziere . .	*Police Superintendent*
Roger Lumont	*Inspector Losch*
Jacqueline Lavielle. . . .	*Marinka*
Jacques Dorfmann. . . .	*Rioting Student*
Anthony Stuart.	*Head Gardener*
Pierre Verneti.	*Court Tailor*

SYNOPSIS

Prince Rudolf, heir to the throne of the Austrian Empire, is against the autocratic rule of his father, the Emperor Franz Josef, and openly sympathises with rebel elements who urge for a more democratic status for the people, and the secession and independence of Hungary. Also, he is weary of his

With Omar Sharif.

spiteful wife, the Princess Stephanie, and receives only partial consolation from his affair with an actress, Mizzi.

Rudolf meets and falls in love with a delightful young girl, Maria Vetsera. His attentions are diverted briefly by the return of his adored and adoring mother, the Empress Elizabeth, and the state visit of Edward, the Prince of Wales. His romance with Maria develops into a 'Grand Passion' which disquiets the Emperor, and he arranges for Maria to be sent to Venice. Rudolf, however, fetches her back to Vienna and flouts etiquette by presenting her at Court.

When Rudolf's implication in the unsuccessful Hungarian uprising becomes known, he is forced to take Maria, on his mother's advice, to the royal hunting lodge at Mayerling. There, the lovers make a suicide pact, pledging eternal love. Rudolf shoots Maria as she lies sleeping, and then turns the gun upon himself.

With Genevieve Page.

With Omar Sharif.

REVIEWS

'The script is basically dull, with just the occasional descent into absurdity . . . the film is ponderous without being weighty. Considering it is meant to be the love story of a towering love affair, it also seems curiously and antiseptically passionless. As so often, the best performance comes from James Mason.'—*The Times*

'Terence Young's film *Mayerling* tries to solve one mystery that's baffled historians: how did Rudolf, Crown Prince and heir to the Austro-Hungarian Empire, come to be found shot dead with his teenage mistress in a hunting lodge in 1889? But it only succeeds in setting up another mystery: how did so many usually excellent actors and actresses come to make such a dull film? James Mason, predictably, comes off best as the Emperor Franz Josef.'—*Evening Standard*

'The film refuses to deviate from all that is staid, trite and unoriginal. James Mason as the emperor does nothing we have not seen him do before—and better. . . . So insipid, so inartistic and so stupefyingly boring an epic, is *Mayerling*.'—*Sunday Express*

'The impression is less of the first swallow heralding that returning summer of high movie romanticism we are all supposed to be pining for, than of a vaguely uneasy cuckoo.'—*Spectator*

'A luscious film. It dazzles the eye, but it does not touch the senses, and it offends the truth. Worst of all, it is just a bit dull . . . best of all, James Mason.' —*Evening News*

'The film does not really deserve or make the most of its distinguished cast . . . James Mason gives the monstrous Franz Josef a certain humanity and sympathy.'—*Financial Times*

'A very tedious Royal scandal. It almost goes without saying that James Mason and, perhaps, Genevieve Page are the only ones with an authentic feeling for character.'—*Sunday Telegraph*

James Mason (1974):

I am sorry that the *Sunday Telegraph* lacked conviction about Geneviéve Page. Why the 'perhaps'? But I like the 'It goes without saying'. I seem to remember that in some magazines, which the present editor happily missed, I scored another 'MISCAST'.

AGE OF CONSENT

1969

A Nautilus production released by Columbia. *Producers:* James Mason and Michael Powell. *Director:* Michael Powell. *Screenplay:* Peter Yeldham—*from the novel by* Norman Lindsay. *Director of Photography:* Hannes Staudinger. *Music:* Stanley Meyers. *Art Director:* Dennis Gentle. *Editor:* Anthony Buckley. Panavision. Technicolor. 98 minutes.

CAST

James Mason . . . . *Bradley Morahan*
Helen Mirren. . . . . *Cora*
Jack MacGowran . . . . *Nat Kelly*
Neva Carr-Glyn . . . . *Ma Ryan*
Antonia Katsaros . . . . *Isabel Marley*
Michael Boddy. . . . . *Hendricks*
Harold Hopkins . . . . *Ted Farrell*
Slim Da Grey . . . . *Cooley*
Max Moldrun . . . . *TV Interviewer*
Frank Thring . . . . *Godfrey*
Dora Hing . . . . *Receptionist*
Clarissa Kaye . . . . *Meg*
Judy McGrath . . . . *Grace*
Lenore Katon . . . . *Edna*
Diane Strachan . . . . *Susie*
Roberta Grant . . . . *Ivy*
Prince Nial . . . . *Jaspar*

SYNOPSIS

Brad Morahan, a famous Australian painter, is disenchanted with life in New York and returns home, to an island on the Great Barrier Reef, hoping to recover his lost enthusiasm and original vitality. Among the inhabitants of the island are: Miss Isabel Marley, a plump spinster of independent means; a gin-soaked harridan named Ma Ryan and her sexy granddaughter, Cora. Brad sees Cora swimming underwater and asks her to model for him. She enjoys the attention he shows, and saves the money towards her ambition of becoming a hairdresser.

A drifter, Nat Kelly, arrives on the island, and strikes up a friendship with Miss Marley, who is flattered by his manner. Nat, although a former friend of Brad's, steals 300 dollars of his money, takes a boat and leaves the island. Ma Ryan, while disapproving

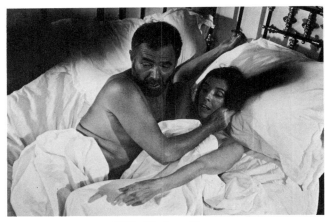

With Clarissa Kaye.

of Cora's friendship with Brad, is frightened they will discover she has stolen Cora's money cache. Inevitably, Cora finds out, and Ma Ryan, in a cliff-top struggle, accidentally falls to her death. With Nat arrested by Trooper Hendricks, Brad and Cora are relieved that they too have not been charged with Ma Ryan's death and are now free to start a new relationship between themselves.

REVIEWS

'Mr. Mason is relaxed and amiable, Mr. MacGowran is mildly funny, and Miss Mirren is attractive to watch, but some of the minor rôles are played very unconvincingly indeed. There is, however, a dog called Godfrey who turns in a good performance as a likeable dog.'—*Daily Express*

'Not particularly entertaining, and not particularly well made.'—*Sunday Express*

'I wish James Mason had not involved himself with this unlikely outback story. For it is a bore.'—*Sun*

'A rambling, dawdling affair, but the scenery looks good.'—*Daily Mail*

'The film succeeds by its charm and its conviction.' —*Financial Times*

'An amiable film which all concerned seem to have enjoyed, and not without reason.'—*Daily Telegraph*

'A temporary aberration . . . a lapse of judgement . . . best forgiven and forgotten.'—*Observer*

With Helen Mirren in *Age of Consent.*

With Helen Mirren.

James Mason (1974):

I had become deeply involved in the making of this film and I was pleased with the result. Therefore it was some disappointment that the film was not better received. In spite of the selection printed here, the reviews were generally not bad enough to discourage audiences.

I rationalised that it was especially difficult to sell a film which offered nudity without lubricity. And actually Columbia made no serious effort to solve the problem. It is not unfair to say that our case set a new low in salesmanship. Michael Powell and I were persuaded to cut certain passages from the film in order not to be burdened with the difficult and (in this case) unsuitable 'X' certificate, and to hit the family audience with an 'R'. Not being overly long it was predictable that it would be released in tandem with another film of similar length and, one assumed, one carrying a similar 'R' certificate. No sir, the companion piece selected by the salesmen of Columbia and the Rank circuit flaunted an 'X', believe it or not.

I am not insisting that our film deserved to be a hit elsewhere than in Australia, where it made heaps of money. But I had nursed a secret hope that we might succeed in breaking through the known reluctance in British and U.S. markets to accept films made in Australia. That break-through was not to be achieved until Barry Mackenzie came along with the magic new ingredient, 'chundering'.

If for no other reason *Age of Consent* should be seen because in it that wonderful actor Jackie McGowran made one of his last screen performances.

THE SEA GULL

1969

A Warner Bros. production released by Warner-Pathé. *Producer and Director:* Sidney Lumet. *Translated and adapted by* Moura Budberg *from the play by* Anton Chekhov. *Director of Photography:* Gerry Fisher. *Production Design and Costumes:* Tony Walton. Editor: Alan Heim. Technicolor. 141 minutes.

CAST

James Mason . . . . *Trigorin*
Venessa Redgrave . . . . *Nina*
Simone Signoret. . . . . *Arkadina*
David Warner . . . . *Konstantin*
Harry Andrews . . . . *Sorin*
Denholm Elliot . . . . *Dorn*
Eileen Herlie. . . . . *Polina*
Alfred Lynch. . . . . *Medvedenko*
Ronald Radd. . . . . *Shamraev*
Kathleen Widdoes . . . . *Masha*

SYNOPSIS

Late in nineteenth-century Russia, Konstantin, a sensitive young man who wants to become a writer, lives on the estate of his invalid uncle, Sorin. Konstantin's life is beset with the dull ache of frustration, for he is deeply in love with a girl from the neighbouring estate, Nina, who tolerates him but does not love him. His mother, the brilliant and successful actress Arkadina, is too preoccupied with herself to give him more than random interest and does not care to be reminded that she has a son in his twenties. Masha, daughter of Sorin's manager, is hopelessly in love with Konstantin, while she, in turn, is wooed by the local schoolmaster, Medvedenko, whom she utterly despises.

Foreground (left to right): Simone Signoret, James Mason, David Warner, Vanessa Redgrave and Harry Andrews.

One day, Konstantin lays a dead sea gull at Nina's feet with the dark warning that some day he, too, will be dead. Nina regards this with indifference and, instead, coquettishly flirts with a house guest and admirer of Arkadina, Trigorin, a famous novelist. She tells him that she intends to go to Moscow and become an actress, and Trigorin, pleasurably excited by her attentions, advises her to contact him there. In the following two years Nina becomes Trigorin's mistress. She bears him a son, but the child dies and Trigorin deserts her. Still without any encouragement, Konstantin follows her about hoping to win her regard.

Once again, the same people are assembled at Sorin's estate. Masha has married Medvedenko, although their union is not a happy one, while Nina still proclaims her love for the selfish Trigorin and still rejects Konstantin's love. As the weekend draws to a close, a spiritual darkness settles over the house and Konstantin, realising finally the hopelessness of his feelings, walks out to the lake and shoots himself.

REVIEWS

'Regretfully, one has to admit that Sidney Lumet's version of *The Sea Gull*, though extremely well acted, is often painfully slow and cumbersome. . . . James' Mason's Trigorin, so diffident that he can't even look Nina in the eye when first introduced, is a fine study of a weak-willed, unworldly man who is only truly happy when writing or fishing.'—*The Times*

'Playing straight with Chekhov pays off—but only up to the point where the cinema's possibilities do not remind you of the stage's limitations. Up to that point, Sidney Lumet has made a skilful, smooth, impeccably acted theatrical version of *The Sea Gull.'*
—*Evening Standard*

'The actors perform as if they were all on the edge of a nervous breakdown . . . Chekhov called *The Sea Gull* a comedy, but any traces of wit have been pretty well destroyed by Lumet's lumbering technique.'—*Time* magazine

'I would not rate this adaptation highly. There are too many distractions.'—*The Listener*

'The two outstanding performances come from James Mason and Simone Signoret.'—*Daily Mirror*

'Surely there's more to Trigorin than James Mason's surprisingly dull impression of the second-rate literary lion?'—*Sunday Telegraph*

'Comes over with agonising pathos.'—*Evening News*

SPRING AND PORT WINE

1970

An E.M.I.-Anglo presentation of a Memorial film released by Warner-Pathé. *Producer:* Michael Medwin. *Director:* Peter Hammond. *Screenplay and Original Play:* Bill Naughton. *Director of Photography:* Norman Warwick. *Art Director:* Reece Pemberton. *Editor:* Fergus McDonell. Technicolor. 101 minutes.

CAST

James Mason	*Rafe Crompton*
Susan George	*Hilda Crompton*
Diana Coupland	*Daisy Crompton*
Rodney Bewes	*Harold Crompton*
Hannah Gordon	*Florence Crompton*
Len Jones	*Wilfred Crompton*
Keith Buckley	*Arthur Gasket*
Adrienne Posta	*Betty Duckworth*
Avril Elgar	*Betsy Jane Duckworth*
Frank Windsor	*Ned Duckworth*
Ken Parry	*Pawnbroker*
Bernard Bresslaw	*Lorry Driver*
Arthur Lowe	*Mr. Aspinall*
Marjorie Rhodes	*Mrs. Gasket*
Joe Greig	*Allan (TV Man)*
Christopher Timothy	*Joe (TV Man)*
Eddie Robertson Sandra Downes	*Pay Clerks*
Maria Mantella George Nutkins Reg Green Jack Howarth	*Weavers*
Brian Mosley Bryan Pringle John Sharp	*Bowlers*

SYNOPSIS

The Crompton family live in a terraced house in Bolton, Lancashire. Rafe, a self-educated perfectionist and disciplinarian, works at the local mill with his teenage daughter, Hilda, and youngest son, Wilfred. His two elder children, Florence and Harold have jobs unconnected with mill life, leaving the home to be run by his good-natured wife, Daisy, whose only failing is an inability to balance the household accounts.

One Sunday, Hilda becomes the catalyst of trouble

With Susan George in *Spring and Port Wine*.

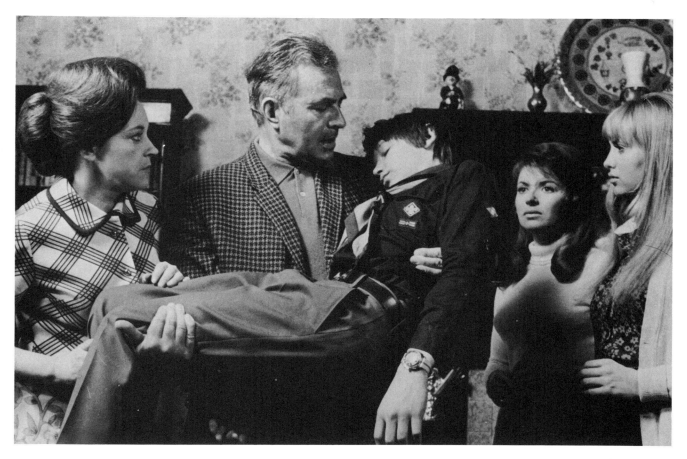

With (left to right) Diana Coupland, Len Jones, Hannah Gordon and Susan George.

when she refuses to eat a fried herring served for high tea. Rafe commands that it shall be served at all meals until eaten. Throughout the week, Hilda adamantly refuses the fish and finally, with Florence now staying at her fiancé's house, to avoid the arguments, she spends the night with the Cromptons' neighbours, the Duckworths. Wilfred, hoping to relieve the tension, gives the stale fish to the cat, but, when forced to swear to his father that he is not responsible for the missing dish, is overcome by the pressure and faints.

Hilda, who suspects she is pregnant, returns home to borrow money from her mother to go and live in London. Daisy decides to pawn Rafe's new overcoat, but in the meantime Hilda has managed to persuade Florence to help her. Daisy realises that Rafe will discover the missing coat before she can return it and, rather than face his wrath, rushes from the house after leaving a note hinting of suicide. Rafe reads the note and runs to the canal. He finds Daisy and begs forgiveness, promising that in future he will be more tolerant of the younger generation and less dominating to his family.

REVIEWS

'A grizzled and grave James Mason plays dad, and it's a performance that surely draws a tap-root strength from the star's own Huddersfield background. . . . Peter Hammond's unobtrusive direction amply serves the abundant good acting.'—*Evening Standard*

'It has a warmth and a humanity that is universal. Beautiful performances by all concerned.'—*Daily Express*

'As perceptive and warm-hearted a picture as I have seen for many a day.'—*Daily Mail*

'The film certainly succeeds. It's a real bit of allright.'—*People*

'As an example of contemporary British cinema, it is, I'm sad to say, shameful.'—*Observer*

'A thoroughly ingratiating film . . . The enormous psychological upheaval needed to soften the dictatorial father into an understanding dad is hardly conveyed at all in Mason's too attractive character study.'—*Sunday Telegraph*

'An amiable film, but even James Mason (and you can't do much better than James Mason) can't rescue a film which collapses into the totally implausible.'—Dilys Powell, *Sunday Times*

'The film is not dislikeable: just superficial and aggressively cosy.'—*New Statesman*

207

With Len Jones.

COLD SWEAT

(Italian title L'UOMO DALLE DUE OMBRE)

1971

A Robert Dorfman, Les Films Corona and Fair-Film co-production released by M.G.M.–E.M.I. *Producer:* Robert Dorfman. *Director:* Terence Young. *Screenplay:* Shimon Wincelberg and Albert Simonin—*from the novel* Ride the Nightmare *by* Richard Matheson. *Director of Photography:* Jean Rabier. *Music:* Michel Magne. *Art Director:* Tony Roman. *Editor:* Johnny Dwyre. Eastmancolor. 94 minutes.

CAST

Charles Bronson . . . . *Joe Martin*
Liv Ullmann. . . . . *Fabienne*
James Mason . . . . *Ross*
Jill Ireland . . . . *Moira*
Michel Constantin . . . . *Whitey*
Jean Topart . . . . *Katanga*
Yannick Delulle. . . . . *Michele*
Luigi Pistilli. . . . . *Fausto*

SYNOPSIS

Joe Martin, an American living in Villefranche with his wife Fabienne and her daughter Michele, owns a small fishing boat which he hires out to customers. Fabienne knows nothing of Joe's past, especially an incident in which he had gone free while another man, Ross, had been sent to prison. Joe is forced to confide this secret, however, when he argues and kills Whitney who, on the instructions of Ross, had wanted him to undertake a mysterious expedition in his boat. Having disposed of the body, Fabienne and Joe return to their apartment where they find Ross and his two henchmen, Fausto and Katanga, now even more insistent that Joe takes them to the Lerin islands where a Turkish boat carrying drugs is waiting for them. Ross's plan consists of Fausto and Joe meeting his mistress, Moira, who is bringing the money for the trip, at the airport, while holding Fabienne and Michele as hostages.

With Charles Bronson, Jean Topart and Luigi Pistilli.

With Luigi Pistilli.

Fausto is knocked unconscious by Joe who, pretending to be one of the accomplices, meets Moira, takes her to a lonely hut and locks her in. When they all get to the hut, Joe quickly realises that Ross has no intention of exchanging Fabienne and Michele for Moira. He attacks Ross, who is wounded in the fight by a shot from Katanga. Joe convinces Ross that he must have medical attention and takes Moira to Grasse to look for a doctor, knowing if Ross dies Katanga will kill his wife and daughter. Ross is seriously wounded and, despite Fabienne's efforts to save him, dies. Fabienne and Michele escape but, when Joe, Moira and the doctor arrive, they all fall into Katanga's hands. On the way to the island, Katanga shows an interest in Michele, and Joe, taking advantage of this distraction, gets hold of a rocket-gun and kills him. The nightmare over, they get back to the port where the crowds are happily celebrating the 14th of July.

REVIEWS

'Perhaps it is a better film in French, but the Common-market frying pan has reduced three individual actors down into tastelessness. James Mason [is] disastrously miscast.'—*Monthly Film Bulletin*

'Passable action fare without that needed fillip of character delineation . . . a tale oft seen from Hollywood.'—*Variety*

'An unconvincing story that does nothing for any of the cast—'who, admittedly, don't do much for it. James Mason wears a funny hat and a Southern accent, and dies gallantly.'—*CinemaTV Today*

James Mason (1974):

I can't agree with the man from the *Monthly Film Bulletin* who insisted that I was miscast. I was in fact cast into it by circumstances which I had no wish to control since it is always a pleasure to work with Terence Young. So I was to be an American who had been in prison with Charles Bronson. English critics who had come around to thinking of me exclusively as Mason the Bible reader may have been surprised, but the Bronson public proliferates in Italy, Japan, South America and, above all, in France where, the year in which we shot the film, he was voted the world's most attractive human male; and in all such countries I am sure they had no difficulty in accepting me as a man from Tennessee.

With Liv Ullmann in *Cold Sweat*.

BAD MAN'S RIVER

1972

A Scotia International production released by Scotia-Barber Distributors. *Producer:* Bernard Gordon. *Director:* Gene Martin. *Screenplay:* Philip Yordan and Gene Martin. *Director of Photography:* Alexander Ulloa. *Music:* Waldo de los Rios. *Song:* 'Bad Man's River' written by Richard Morris, *composed and sung by* Jade Warrior. *Art Director:* Julio Molino. *Editor:* Antonio Ramirez de Loayra. Eastmancolor. 90 minutes.

CAST
Lee Van Cleef . . . . *King*
James Mason . . . . *Montero*
Gina Lollobrigida . . . . *Alicia*
Simon Andreu . . . . *Angel*
Diana Lorys . . . . *Dolores*
John Garko . . . . *Pace*
Aldo Sanbrell . . . . *Canales*
Jess Hahn . . . . *Odie*
Daniel Martin . . . . *False Montero*
Luis Rivera . . . . *Orozco*
Lone Ferk . . . . *Conchita*
Eduardo Fajardo . . . . *Duarte*
Sergio Fantoni . . . . *Fierro*
Per Barclay . . . . *Reverend*

SYNOPSIS
The King Gang—boss Roy King, Ed, Angel and Tom—are four of the most wanted men in Texas. After robbing a bank at Bodie's Landing, for the second time, they catch a fast Eastbound train and split the proceeds. One by one the gang leaves the train until only Roy is left. He sees a beautiful blonde, Alicia, who, in the course of the journey, seduces him into marriage, has him committed to a State asylum and runs off with his money. A few months later, King escapes from jail and meets up with his gang at Bodie's Landing, where they catch a paddle steamer going down the Rio Grande. On board they accept an offer from a man claiming to be the Mexican revolutionary Montero (and married to Alicia who is now a brunette) to blow up a Mexican arsenal. After the job, however, they are cheated of payment by Montero who, Alicia claims,

With Lee Van Cleef and Gina Lollobrigida.

214

With Gina Lollobrigida in *Bad Man's River.*

is a government agent who has tricked the Mexican authorities into giving him a million dollars to replace the lost amunition. The Gang set off after Montero but find themselves ambushed by another gang, also after the cheque. When Montero is killed in the crossfire, a search reveals nothing, but Dolores, a revolutionary sympathiser, tells them that Montero is, in fact, alive, and that Alicia has the cheque.

They find the real Montero hiding in a cabin in Alicia's suite and learn that the money has been banked and can only be claimed by him. On the way there, however, they are captured by revolutionaries and taken as prisoners to a Mexican fort under Col. Fierro. The Mexican Army, led by Governor Duarte, surrounds the fort and opens fire. The Gang and Montero effect a daring escape by driving a reinforced old car through Duarte's ranks, and set off for Laredo where the money is banked. Montero claims the money but, as it is being handed over, Alicia, with her new friend, Billy the Kid, relieves them of it. The King Gang set off in pursuit . . .

REVIEWS
'A waste of talent.'—*Sun*
'A light-hearted Western.'—*Sunday Express*
'An agreeable if over-stretched lark . . . unlikely to prove a milestone in James Mason's career.'—*Daily Mail*
'*Bad Man's River* goes under wasting the talents of Gina Lollobrigida and James Mason.'—*Guardian*
'A film that tries much too hard to be a riot of fun and succeeds only in being a shambles.'—*Cinema TV Today*

James Mason (1974):
I learned a lesson. When shooting a Western in Spain one should not say to oneself: 'Never mind, no-one is going to see it,' because that will be just the film which the Rank Organisation will choose to release in England.

With Lee Van Cleef and Gina Lollobrigida.

KILL!

(U.S. title KILL! KILL! KILL!)

1972

A Procinex/Alexandre Salkind/Mexo (Madrid) Cocinor production. *Producer:* Alexandre Salkind. *Written and directed by* Romain Gary. *Director of Photography:* Edmond Rechad. *Music:* Berto Pisano and Jacques Charmont. *Editor:* Robert Dwyre. Eastmancolor. 102 minutes.

CAST

Jean Seberg. . . . . *Emily*
James Mason . . . . *Alan*
Stephen Boyd . . . . *Killian*
Curt Jurgens. . . . . *Chief*
Daniel Emilfork . . . . *Inspector*
Henri Cacin . . . . *Lawyer*

SYNOPSIS

Alan, an American Interpol agent, is sent to Italy to investigate the activities of an international heroin smuggling organisation. His wife, Emily, who longs for romantic excitement, travels there before him and meets another agent, Killian, an embittered man who has set himself up as a vigilante executioner of the world's top drug smugglers. Although Alan hopes to break the ring by orthodox methods, Killian believes that only ruthless ploys will be successful. Emily and Killian fall in love, and she also becomes involved when she finds a few dead bodies in her car. After following up various clues, Emily and Killian, together with a slightly corrupted Alan, manage to assassinate the heroin dealers.

REVIEWS

'An exceptionally violent and lurid melodrama . . . early Hitchcock belatedly revived.'—*International Herald Tribune*
'Visually harsh and needlessly brutal . . . pretentiously written . . . indulgently directed. [Stephen] Boyd and Mason are both effective and perform with discipline . . . dialogue clichés tumble from the characters' mouths . . .'—*Hollywood Reporter*
'The film has a sense of humour that keeps it from falling into coyness and viciousness for its own sake . . . an out and out melodrama . . . even camp.'—*Variety*

James Mason (1974):

This film was a French-Spanish-German-Italian co-production. The language was English. It had the misfortune to emerge in Paris the same week as *The French Connection*, to which the critics compared it unfavourably. The only review which I saw was a little pearl that appeared in the *Gazette de Lausanne* which contained the following objectionable reference to the actors: 'Il réunit des vedettes un peu bedonnantes dans leur popularité, mais . . .' (My dictionary says that the verb bedonner means 'to grow paunchy or pot-bellied'.)

CHILD'S PLAY

1973

A David Merrick production for Paramount released by C.I.C. *Producer:* David Merrick. *Director:* Sidney Lumet. *Screenplay:* Leon Prochnik—*from the play by* Robert Marasco. *Director of Photography:* Gerald Hirschfeld. *Music:* Michael Small. *Art Director:* Philip Rosenberg. *Editors:* Edward Warschilka and Joanne Burke. Movielab colour. 100 minutes.

CAST

James Mason	*Jerome Malley*
Robert Preston	*Joseph Dobbs*
Beau Bridges	*Paul Reis*
Ronald Weyand	*Father Mozian*
Charles White	*Father Griffin*
David Rounds	*Father Penny*
Kate Harrington	*Mrs. Carter*
Jamie Alexander	*Sheppard*
Brian Chapin	*O'Donnell*
Bryant Fraser	*Jennings*
Mark Hall Haefeli	*Wilson*
Tom Leopold	*Shea*
Julius Lo Iacono	*McArdle*
Christopher Man	*Travis*
Paul O'Keefe	*Banks*
Robert D. Randall	*Medley*
Robbie Reed	*Class President*
Paul Alessi Anthony Barletta Kevin Coupe Christopher Hoag Stephen McLaughlin	*Students*

SYNOPSIS

When Paul Reis returns as sports instructor to St. Charles, a Catholic school for boys, he is enthusiastically welcomed by the English master, Joseph Dobbs. Reis soon senses a mysterious and sinister atmosphere apparently stemming from the unpopularity of the Latin master, Jerome Malley—known as Lash—who was due for retirement the previous term but has decided to stay on. Malley believes that Dobbs, who would have taken over the senior class had he retired, is responsible for the strange telephone call and pornographic literature

he has been bombarded with, and inciting the students to force him to retire.

Reis discovers a boy being brutally beaten by the other students and learns there have been other outbreaks of violence. None of the victims, though, is prepared to talk. The headmaster, Father Mozian, who is aware that Malley is suffering from a persecution complex and is also worried about his dying mother, urges him to be less strict with the boys. But the violence continues and a boy nearly loses his eyesight. Finally Malley is not longer able to cope with the situation and, having been ordered by Father Mozian not to take any more classes, commits suicide by jumping off the school roof. Reis discovers that Dobbs has been responsible for the persecution and confronts him with the truth. The students, who have been listening to this conversation, begin to close in on Dobbs. As Reis leaves the room, the students, imbued with the violence that Dobbs has preached, raise their hands to attack the man responsible for all the trouble—Dobbs.

REVIEWS

'Though necessarily limited in emotional range, James Mason's performance is felt from the inside. . . . but this is a director's and writer's picture and that's the problem.'—*Village Voice*

'Throughout the film, one can hear the theatrical boards creaking and although James Mason gives his usual reliable performance, even he cannot cope

with a dying mum, girlie magazines, unfeeling pupils *and* the Devil.'—*Monthly Film Bulletin*

'Mason delivers a solid performance as a man whose hate of his fellow professor is exceeded, he says, only by Preston's hate of him. Role is deeply dramatic, and Preston, in a different type of characterisation, lends equal potency.'—*Variety*

'James Mason is marvellous, a standout as an aging language teacher, a dedicated but hard taskmaster who claims to be the victim of obscenities scrawled in lavatories, malicious phone calls and pornographic mail. The emphasis he places in class on a Latin proverb, "Trust, like the soul, never returns once it is gone", may convey the author's meaning in the play.'—*Daily News*

'This is not, however, a movie in which the ending doesn't live up to the quality of the melodrama itself. With the exception of the performance of Mr. Mason, who is fine as the mad, exhausted Latin teacher, everything in *Child's Play* seems to be rather cheaply tricky . . .'—*New York Times*

'Mason is riveting as the sad, frumpy, old-maidish Latin professor whose mother is dying and whose mind seems to be going.'—*Los Angeles Herald-Examiner*

'James Mason is superb as a kind of misanthropic Mr. Chips. As written, the port is little more than a cartoon. Mason turns it into a full portrait of a frightened man in the process of being destroyed.'—*Time*

'. . . and includes one very good performance by

With Robert Preston in *Child's Play*.

With Ronald Weyand.

With Robert Preston.

Robert Preston as Dobbs and one magnificent performance by James Mason as Malley. . . . And Mason creates one of the finest monster-victims since Peter Lorre's "M". In a somewhat barren movie year, one is grateful for even such a modest, mixed success as this one.'—*Newsweek*.

James Mason (1974):
I never got to see the film since its release was only the thinnest of trickles. Consequently I never learned why Paramount had so little faith in it. Some of the reviews in America were quite good.

THE LAST OF SHEILA

1973

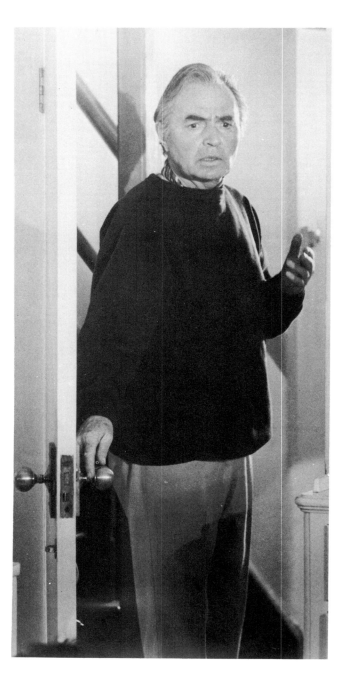

Released by Columbia-Warner. *Producer and Director:* Herbert Ross. *Original Screenplay:* Anthony Perkins and Stephen Sondheim. *Director of Photography:* Gerry Turpin. *Music:* Bill Goldenberg. *Song:* 'Friends' *sung by* Bette Midler. *Art Director:* Ken Adam. *Editor:* Edward Warschika. Technicolor. 119 minutes.

CAST

Richard Benjamin . . . . *Tom*
Dyan Cannon. . . . . *Christine*
James Coburn. . . . . *Clinton*
Joan Hackett . . . . *Lee*
James Mason . . . . *Philip*
Ian McShane . . . . *Anthony*
Raquel Welch. . . . . *Alice*
Yvonne Romaine. . . . . *Sheila*
Pierro Rosso . . . . *Vittorio*
Serge Citon . . . . *Guido*
Robert Rossi . . . . *Captain*
Elaine Geisinger ⎫
Elliot Geisinger ⎭ . . . . *American Couple*
Jack Pugeat . . . . *Silver Salesman*
Martial . . . . *Locksmith*
Maurice Crosnier. . . . . *Concierge*

SYNOPSIS

Exactly one year after Sheila Green ran out of a Hollywood party and was killed in a car accident by an unidentified hit-and-run driver her husband, the film producer Clinton Greene, invites six personalities, all of whom attended the party, to board his yacht in the Mediterranean for a week's holiday. His idea is to involve them all in a 'murder game' psychologically designed to strip their innermost secrets and expose each to the other. Two couples are married: Tom, a frustrated screenwriter, and his wealthy, eccentric wife Lee, and Alice, a glamour queen, with her ambitious manager Anthony. The other guests are a jaded movie director, Philip, and a Hollywood agent, Christine.

On the set of *The Last of Sheila* with visitor Michael Caine.

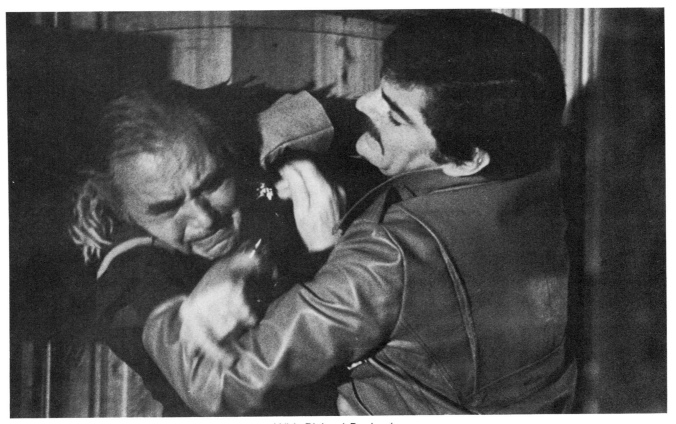

With Richard Benjamin.

With Richard Benjamin.

With Morgan Mason, Associate Director.

Each person is assigned a guilty secret, and given clues to discover who hides the secret. Then, when an attempt is made to murder Christine, after which Clinton is found dead, Lee hysterically admits she was the driver of the car and has killed Clinton. Matters become complicated, however, when Lee herself is found dead, apparently having committed suicide. Philip goes over the evidence and decides that Tom, knowing his wife to be guilty of Sheila's death, twisted the game to his own ends by killing Clinton and making it appear, even to her, that Lee was responsible. Prevented from disposing of Philip by the fortunate arrival of Christine, Tom has to concede defeat—and agrees to finance a film, *The Last of Sheila*, with his new-found wealth.

REVIEWS

'The film is completely improbable, and ridiculously contrived.'—*Daily Express*

'Anthony Perkins and Stephen Sondheim have outsmarted themselves in crafting their script. Their plot is so fiendishly difficult that their characters spend most of their time bogged down in endless explanatory scenes. Only canny James Mason and Joan Hackett suggest lives independent of their existence as counters on the Sondheim-Perkins board.'—*Time* magazine

'Films like this make one wonder how movies ever caught on. Or if they will continue to do so. James Mason saunters through admirably, with nasal contempt.'—*Daily Mail*

'The plot is so tricky, it defeats itself.'—*Sunday Telegraph*

'The formula is in the time-honoured tradition, but

231

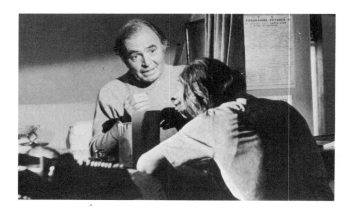

the setting and style make it outstanding.'—*Evening News*

'Too smart by half.'—Dilys Powell, *Sunday Times*

'The film is so busy trying to impress, it often lets the thread of the plot get lost amid the finery.'—*Sunday Mirror*

'It should be fun, but it isn't.'—*Observer*

James Mason (1974):

I really could not understand why the British critics wrote of this film with such disdain. I was completely on the side of Perkins, Sondheim and Herb Ross, a director of enormous talent and unflagging patience, in thinking that it was intriguing and funny and deserving of an audience's attention. Granted it called for a great deal of attention, more than the critics were evidently prepared to lend. The *Sunday Mirror*, for example, lost the plot through inattention, not on account of its 'finery'.

One concession I have to make: in the cinema in which I saw it (The Columbia) some of the dialogue got lost, especially some of the jokey passages spoken by James Coburn and Dyan Cannon.

(Left to right) James Mason, Raquel Welch, James Coburn, Joan Hackett, Ian McShane, Dyan Cannon and Richard Benjamin.

THE MACKINTOSH MAN

1973

A Newman/John Foreman/John Huston production released by Columbia-Warner. *Producer:* John Foreman. *Associate Producer:* Bill Hill. *Director:* John Huston. *Screenplay:* Walter Hill—*from the novel* The Freedom Trap *by* Desmond Bagley. *Director of Photography:* Ossie Morris. *Art Director:* Alan Tompkins. *Editor:* Russell Lloyd. Eastmancolor. 99 minutes.

With Harry Andrews.

CAST

Paul Newman	*Rearden*
Dominique Sanda	*Mrs. Smith*
James Mason	*Wheeler*
Harry Andrews	*Mackintosh*
Ian Bannen	*Slade*
Nigel Patrick	*Soames-Trevelyan*
Peter Vaughan	*Brunskill*
Donald Webster	*Jervis*
Hugh Manning	*Prosecutor*
Roland Culver	*Judge*
Leo Genn	*Rollins*
Michael Poole	*Mr. Boyd*
Eric Mason	*Postman*
Percy Herbert	*Taffe*
Jenny Runacre	*Gerda*
John Bindon	*Buster*
Ronald Clarke	*Attendant*
Antony Viccars	*Salesman*
Dinny Powell	*Young*
Douglas Robinson	*Danahoe*
Jack Cooper	*1st Motor-cyclist*
Marc Boyle	*2nd Motor-cyclist*
Michael Hordern	*Brown*
Keith Bell	*Palmer*

SYNOPSIS

Furnished with a false identity as a thief by the mysterious Angus Mackintosh and his 'secretary', Mrs. Smith, Joseph Rearden carries out a daring diamond robbery in Hatton Garden. After an anonymous tip-off, Rearden is arrested, charged and sentenced to 20 years' imprisonment, and finds himself in a top-security jail with a convicted Russian spy, Slade. Soames-Trevelyan, another convict, offers to include Rearden, at a price, in an escape bid organised by a gang called Scarperers. Both Slade and Rearden are lifted over the wall, taken to Ireland under an armed guard and sedated.

The escape had, in fact, been planned by Mackintosh and his daughter, Mrs. Smith, in the hope that Rearden would be able to break the Scarperer's organisation and expose its leader, the eminent politician, Sir Geoffrey Wheeler. When Rearden's rescuers learn that a government agent was involved in the escape they turn sour on their 'prisoners' whereupon Rearden manages to escape and contact Mrs. Smith, who flies to Ireland bringing news that her father has been seriously injured in a car accident.

Believing Slade to be aboard Wheeler's yacht,

James as politician Sir Geoffrey Wheeler.

Rearden and Mrs. Smith pursue the boat to Malta and join a party being given by Wheeler. Smith sees Slade in a cabin and manages to warn Rearden, but is drugged and caught by Wheeler. Rearden persuades the local police to search the boat, but Wheeler manages to bluff his way out of suspicion and Rearden is forced to escape. He returns, however, and compels one of the crew to take him to Wheeler and Mrs. Smith, who have now left the boat. In a nearby church, Rearden is confronted by Wheeler holding Slade and Mrs. Smith at gunpoint. Wheeler suggest they all go their various ways, to which Rearden agrees. But, as Slade and Wheeler prepare to leave, Mrs. Smith draws a gun and shoots them down, leaving Rearden shocked and bewildered as she walks away.

REVIEWS

'I doubt whether there will be any complaints from spy-thriller addicts and those seeking an undemanding night's entertainment.'—*Daily Express*
'Though a solid enough job it is, for Huston, a surprisingly pedestrian one. James Mason is excellent as a wealthy right-wing MP.'—*Observer*
'Who on earth directed this enigmatic series of bashings and chases? Good heavens—was it really John Huston?'—Dilys Powell, *Sunday Times*
'An enjoyable convoluted thriller.'—*Sunday Telegraph*
'How pleasant after so many cops and robbers pieces to have something lively and clever.'—*Daily Telegraph*
'A far-fetched and fairly derivative spy story.'—*Financial Times*
'The trouble with John Huston's *The Mackintosh Man* is that, give or take a sequence or two, it could have been made by almost anybody.'—*Guardian*
'The more it went on, the less I believed it. But to blazes with belief! I still enjoyed its penny-dreadful melodramatics.'—*Daily Mail*

James Mason (1974):

They say that the novel on which this was based, *The Freedom Trap* by Desmond Bagley, was not half bad.

FRANKENSTEIN: THE TRUE STORY

1974

A Universal Picture distributed by C.I.C. *Producer:* Hunt Stromberg Jr. *Director:* Jack Smight. *Screenplay:* Christopher Isherwood and Don Bachardy—*from the novel by* Mary W. Shelley. *Director of Photography:* Arthur Ibbetson. *Music:* Gil Melle. *Editor:* Richard Marden. 123 minutes.

CAST

James Mason . . . . *Dr. Polidori*
Leonard Whiting . . . . *Victor Frankenstein*
David McCallum . . . . *Henry Clerval*
Jane Seymour . . . . *Agatha/Prima*
Nicola Pagett . . . . *Elizabeth Fanshawe*
Michael Sarrazin . . . . *The Creature*
Michael Wilding . . . . *Sir Richard Fanshawe*
Clarissa Kaye . . . . *Lady Fanshawe*
Agnes Moorehead . . . . . *Mrs. Blair*
Margaret Leighton . . . . . *Foreign Lady*
Ralph Richardson . . . . . . *Lacey*
John Gielgud . . . . *Chief Constable*
Tom Baker . . . . *Sea Captain*
Dallas Adams . . . . *Felix*
Julian Barnes . . . . *Young Man*
Arnold Diamond . . . . *Passenger in Coach*

SYNOPSIS

In 19th-century England, Dr. Victor Frankenstein, his fiancée Elizabeth, and her parents Lord and Lady Fanshawe are attending the funeral of Victor's brother William, who was accidentally drowned.
Young Victor, a recent medical-school graduate, is bitter over his brother's fate and voices aloud his wish that men could have power over life and death.

With Clarissa Kaye in *Frankenstein: The True Story.*

With Clarissa Kaye.

Later, on his way to Edinburgh by stagecoach, Victor witnesses the aftermath of an accident involving a ploughboy. He accompanies the youth to a hospital where the latter's arm is amputated by a surgeon, Henry Clerval.

Victor sees Clerval deposit the arm in a black leather bag, and later the surgeon tells him that a new era in science is emerging that will enable men to have power over death.

Victor's reaction is mixed, but eventually he joins Clerval in his research (much to the anger and disappointment of his fiancée) and later learns that the ploughboy's arm has been preserved, and imbued with a life of its own.

When a number of local men are killed in a quarry accident, Frankenstein and Clerval appear on the scene, ostensibly to aid the injured, but in reality to choose parts of bodies for their next major experiment—the creation of a living creature. The experiment is duly carried out—and results, at first, in a perfect specimen of man. But as the days pass, the 'creature' slowly begins to deteriorate in looks. Clerval, meantime, has died of some unnamed illness, and his place is taken by Dr. Polidori, who is determined to succeed where Clerval and Frankenstein have failed. The result of Polidori's labours is Prima —a beautiful, flawless young woman—who, unlike the 'creature', does not disintegrate. But, having created his decomposing 'creature', Frankenstein is stuck with him. It is only at the climax of the film— true to Mary Shelley's original ending—that both

Frankenstein and his creator perish in an avalanche in the Arctic.

REVIEWS
'All you need to know about *Frankenstein: The True Story* is that it has a better class of bit player than any horror movie addict could ask.'—*Guardian*
'Words nearly—but not quite—fail me to convey the cheapening effect such a production has on the list of distinguished names involved. James Mason as Dr. Polidori adopts an attitude of inscrutable villainy more suitable for *The Mikado*. How can artists' agents involve their clients in such a mess?'
—*Evening Standard*
'At your peril visit *Frankenstein: The True Story*. You'll be frightened out of your life, not by the horrors but at the piling up of inanities which involve Leonard Whiting . . . and James Mason. Ralph Richardson (as a blind yokel) is lucky to be unable to see what is going on—and John Gielgud is the most unlikely chief constable in police history.'—*Evening News*
'The first few minutes look like bad Hammer, but with the arrival of the monster . . . the film begins to get a grip on itself, injecting some new life into the laboratory scenes. . . . The result is fascinating enough to make it a must for Frankenstein fans.'—*Observer*
'The film bears all the scars of lack of harmony behind the scenes . . . an impish performance by James Mason.'—*Sunday Times*

With Nicola Pagett and Leonard Whiting.

With Leonard Whiting and Michael Sarrazin.

With Clarissa Kaye.

With Leonard Whiting.

11 HARROWHOUSE

1974

A 20th Century-Fox/Elliot Kastner production released by 20th Century-Fox. *Producer:* Elliott Kastner. *Director:* Aram Avakian. *Screenplay:* Jeffrey Bloom—*from the novel by* Gerald A. Browne. *Director of Photography:* Arthur Ibbetson. *Art Director:* Peter Mullins. *Editor:* Anne Coates. Panavision. Eastmancolor. 95 minutes.

CAST

Charles Grodin . . . . *Chesser*
Candice Bergen . . . . *Maren*
John Gielgud. . . . . *Meecham*
Trevor Howard . . . . *Clyde Massey*
James Mason . . . . *Watts*
Peter Vaughan. . . . . *Coglin*
Peter Forbes Robertson. . . . . . . *Hotel Manager*
Joe Powell . . . . *Hickey*

SYNOPSIS

The largest and most powerful diamond cartel in the world is the Consolidated Selling System which is controlled by a group of men who, between them, are able either to generate demand or throttle the market at will. The System's statistics are as stupendous as its ethics are dubious. The security arrangements are second to none, and the men in charge of security are ruthless and brutal. For example, one group of foolhardy criminals who refused to be intimidated by the System's security precautions blew themselves to smithereens after a 'successful' heist when, *en route* from Heathrow Airport to London, they stopped along the hard shoulder of the motorway to take a peek at their haul. The loot was in the bottom of a doctor's bag, and no sooner was the bag opened than a tremble detonator was

triggered off, sending the gang, their swag and the getaway car sky high. . . .

The London headquarters of the Consolidated Selling System are situated in a discreet building in Central London—11 Harrowhouse. It is run like a machine by a man called Meecham whose simple credo is: Nobody beats the System. In the basement, Meecham has a permanent in-house inventory of 20 million carats—more than 4 tons of top-quality stones, roughly estimated at 12 billion dollars. And all that separates the stones from the outside world are Security Chief Coglin, his small army of human guard dogs, and a few 'simple' mechanical aids.

Although 'Nobody beats the System', a young American diamond dealer called Chesser is deter-

mined, with a little help from his friends, such as a wealthy young widow, an oil tycoon and an Englishman, to try.

All prepare to pull off the perfect crime—a textbook exercise during which the raiding party never actually enter 11 Harrowhouse, yet manage to steal four tons of diamonds, literally untouched by human hand.

REVIEWS

'Ineffective caper comedy, outlook thin. Trevor Howard and James Mason appear close to embarrassed in their roles, but John Gielgud at least has the cover of a stoneface prude to hide his inner emotions.'—*Variety*

'. . . the caper proves to be as stimulating as the sight of a housewife vacuum-cleaning the living room carpet . . .'—*Daily Express*

'Very ingenious . . . extremely amusing . . . you must not miss James Mason's performance as an elderly employee dying of cancer . . . a masterly portrayal of a sick, grey and suffering man.'—*Evening News*

'An innocently engaging film . . . but the satellite stars outshine them. John Gielgud, superbly glacially managerial . . . James Mason as a clerk demonstrating, with infinite delicacy, the revenge of humility . . . Trevor Howard as the master crook displaying splendid gifts of insolence and irony—performances like these aren't produced without years of devotion to the difficult business of acting.'—Dilys Powell, *Sunday Times*

'. . . James Mason is beautifully sorrowful as the company servant doomed to death.'—*The Times*

THE MARSEILLE CONTRACT

1974

A Kettledrum production released by Warner-Pathé. *Produced and written by* Judd Bernard. *Director:* Robert Parrish. *Director of Photography:* Douglas Slocombe. *Art Director:* Willy Holt. *Editor:* Willy Kemplen. Eastmancolor. 90 minutes.

CAST

Michael Caine . . . . *Deray*
Anthony Quinn . . . . *Steve Ventura*
James Mason . . . . *Brizard*
Maureen Kerwin . . . . *Lucianne*
Marcel Bozzufi. . . . . *Calmet*
Catherin Rouvel. . . . . *Brizard's Mistress*
Maurice Ronet. . . . . *Briac*
Georges Lycan . . . . *Henri*
Jerry Brouer . . . . *Kurt*
Van Doude. . . . . *Marsac*
Georges Beller. . . . . *Minieri*
Pierre Koulak . . . . *Wilson*
Al Mancini . . . . *Jo Kovakian*
Jonathan Brooks Poole . . . . . . *Kevin*
Gib Grossac . . . . *Fournier*

With Michael Caine and Maureen Kerwin.

SYNOPSIS

A 'tough, hard-hitting gutsy adventure-thriller', *The Marseille Contract* is set in present-day France with the action constantly switching between Paris and the Mediterranean coast. Michael Caine's rôle is that of a hired killer who is paid 50,000 dollars by Anthony Quinn, an American Embassy official in Paris, to liquidate a wealthy and dangerous racketeer played by James Mason.

REVIEWS

'. . . a thriller that throws most of the current clichés . . . into one uneasy story and comes up with not very much . . . Michael Caine and James Mason cannot walk away from the story shambles with any credit.'—*Sunday Telegraph*

'. . . a conventional but tolerable thriller about drug traffic.'—Dilys Powell, *Sunday Times*

'. . . a mindless potpourri of car chases, drug trafficking and assassination.'—*Financial Times*

'. . . the highly charged action sustains the interest . . .'—*Daily Mail*

With Michael Caine.

GREAT EXPECTATIONS

1975

A Transcontinental Film Productions (London) presentation. *Producer:* Robert Fryer. *Director:* Joseph Hardy. *Screenplay:* Sherman Yellen—*from the novel by* Charles Dickens. *Music and Lyrics:* Norman Sachs and Mel Mondel. *Director of Photography:* Freddie Young. *Art Director:* Alan Tomkins. *Music composed and conducted by* Maurice Jarre, *played by* New Philharmonia Orchestra of London. *Editor:* Bill Butler. Panavision. Eastmancolor. 124 minutes.

CAST

Michael York . . . . *Pip*
Sarah Miles . . . . *Estella*
Margaret Leighton . . . . *Miss Havisham*
James Mason . . . . *Magwich*
Robert Morley . . . . *Pumblechook*
Anthony Quayle . . . . *Jaggers*
Heather Sears . . . . *Biddy*
Joss Ackland . . . . *Joe Gargery*
Andrew Ray . . . . *Herbert Pocket*
James Faulkner . . . . *Drummle*
Rachel Roberts . . . . *Mrs. Joe Gargery*
Simon Gipps-Kent . . . . *Boy Pip*
Maria Charles . . . . *Sarah Pocket*
Elaine Garreau . . . . *Cousin Camilla*
Richard Beaumont . . . . *Boy Pocket*
Eric Chitty . . . . *Old Man*

SYNOPSIS

Pip is a rough labouring lad, orphaned and living with his sister and her village blacksmith husband, Joe Gargery. He goes to the help of an escaped convict named Magwich.

His life, he thinks, is destined to be a humble one, but things change dramatically when his Uncle Pumblechook announces that he has been instructed by the rich and eccentric Miss Havisham, who lives in the big Satis House, to find a boy who will visit her and play there.

Pip is chosen, and it is at Satis House that he meets Estella for the first time. She has been brought up by Miss Havisham and from the outset she doesn't hide the fact that she regards Pip as common and below her. From then onwards, he is determined to prove that he is not. The one thing he wants to become, more than anything else, is a gentleman. He wants, very badly, to be able to learn.

Later, fortune smiles on him. Help comes from a benefactor who insists on his (or her) identity being kept secret. Pip goes to London and a young man named Herbert Pocket, with whom he lodges, sets about the task of helping Pip become a gentleman. He is reunited with Estella, too, who is put in his charge at Miss Havisham's request. He is very much in love with her, but she persistently rejects him.

Naturally, he believes Miss Havisham to be his benefactor and from Pocket he learns that the reason for Miss Havisham's strangeness is that the man she was to have married deserted her. She virtually cut herself off from the world. But the benefactor turns out to be Magwich, the convict he once helped, who has escaped to Australia and made good. He is not only repaying Pip's kindness but regards him as a son, believing that his only daughter is dead.

But Magwich is still a wanted man in England. He has risked his life to return to see Pip, who decides that he must get out of the country as soon as possible. Pip intends to go with him and later send for Estella to marry him.

To his profound shock, Pip learns that Estella is going to marry a bearded, attractive rake named Drummle, saying she is weary of her life and is willing to change it, blaming Miss Havisham for making her the hard, disillusioned woman she is. When Pip learns soon afterwards that she is, in fact, Magwich's daughter, he manages to tell his bene-

factor this just before he dies after an accident while trying to leave England.

Pip goes to India and returns as a successful man, now able to help those who helped him in the past.

He again meets Estella. Her husband has treated her brutally, but he is now dead. Rather unwillingly, she reveals to Pip why she rejected him and why she married Drummle. The future can now be theirs.

With Sam Kydd.

With Simon Gipps-Kent.

With Michael York.

MANDINGO

1975

A Dino De Laurentiis Corporation production released by Paramount. *Producer:* Dino De Laurentiis. *Director:* Richard Fleischer. *Screenplay:* Norman Wexler—*based on the novel by* Kyle Onstott, *and upon the play based thereon by* Jack Kirkland. *Director of Photography:* Richard H. Kline. *Music:* Maurice Jarre. *Song 'Born in this Time' sung by* Muddy Waters. *Editor:* Frank Bracht. Technicolor.

CAST

James Mason . . . . *Maxwell*
Susan George . . . . *Blanche*
Perry King . . . . *Hammond*
Richard Ward . . . . *Agamemnon*
Brenda Sykes . . . . *Ellen*
Ken Norton . . . . *Mede*
Lillian Hayman . . . . *Lucrezia Borgia*
Roy Poole . . . . *Doc Redfield*
Ji-Tu Cumbuka . . . . *Cicero*
Paul Benedict . . . . *Brownlee*
Ben Masters . . . . *Charles*
Ray Spruell . . . . *Wallace*
Louis Turenne . . . . *De Veve*
Duane Allen . . . . *Topaz*
Earl Maynard . . . . *Babouin*
Beatrice Winde . . . . *Lucy*
Debbie Morgan . . . . *Dite*
Irene Tedrow . . . . *Mrs. Redfield*

SYNOPSIS

The time of the film is 1840. The place is Falconhurst, a notorious slave-breeding plantation in the turbulent years before the American Civil War. Maxwell is a slave owner who unquestioningly accepts the system. His son Hammond goes along with it because he has known nothing better, yet senses in his feelings for his favourite fighting slave, Mede, and through his sexual affair with another slave, Ellen, that there are alternative relationships than master–slave. Because Falconhurst must have a male heir, he marries Blanche, the daughter of a neighbouring plantation owner. It is the revelation of her perverse sexual nature and her awareness that her husband is sexually involved with a slave girl that brings the story to its violent, tragic conclusion.

With Perry King.

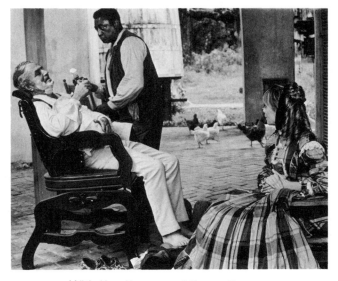

With Ken Norton and Susan George.

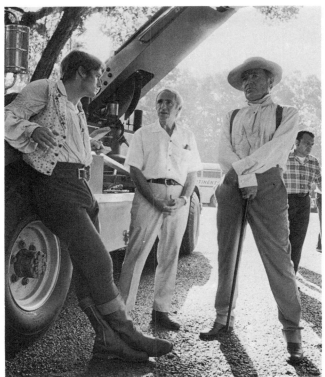

With Perry King and Richard Fleischer.

With Dino De Laurentiis, Ralph Serpe and Richard Fleischer on the set of *Mandingo.*